G000037170

THE BORDERLANDS

Essays on the history of the Ulster–Leinster Border

Carlingford, 1840, by H. Gastineau from Mr and Mrs S. C. Hall, Ireland, *(London, 1842) vol II, p. 423.*

THE BORDERLANDS

Essays on the history of the Ulster–Leinster border

edited by

Raymond Gillespie
and
Harold O'Sullivan

THE INSTITUTE OF IRISH STUDIES
THE QUEEN'S UNIVERSITY OF BELFAST

Published 1989
The Institute of Irish Studies
The Queen's University of Belfast,
Belfast

ISBN 0 85389 333 0

Printed by W. & G. Baird Ltd. Antrim.

Cover design by Rodney Miller Associates.

Contents

List of Illustrations

Notes on Contributors

Victor Buckley is an archaeologist with the Office of Public Works. He is responsible for the *Archaeological inventory of County Louth* (Dublin, 1986) and has written widely on the archaeology of early Christian Ireland.

Margaret Crawford has edited *Famine: the Irish experience 900–1900. Subsistence crises and famine in Ireland* (Edinburgh, 1989) and is currently preparing (with L. A. Clarkson) a history of diet in Ireland.

W. H. Crawford is keeper of material culture in the Ulster Folk and Transport Museum and is an authority on eighteenth century Ulster and on the linen industry.

P. J. Duffy lectures in historical geography in St. Patrick's College, Maynooth and was a senior fellow at the Institute of Irish Studies, Queen's University Belfast in 1988–9. He has written extensively on the historical geography of south Ulster from the seventeenth to the nineteenth centuries.

Raymond Gillespie is the author of a number of books and articles on early modern Ireland including *Colonial Ulster: the settlement of east Ulster 1600–41* (Cork, 1985) and *Settlement and Survival on an Ulster estate* (Belfast, 1987).

Gerard Moran has contributed significantly to the regional history of politics in nineteenth century Ireland including *The Mayo evictions of 1860* (Westport, 1986) and had edited (with Raymond Gillespie) and contributed to *'A various country': essays in Mayo History, 1500–1900* (Westport, 1987).

Harold O'Sullivan is an expert on the history of County Louth. His publications include *Dundalk: a military history* (Dundalk, 1987) (with Joseph Gavin) and articles in the Louth Archaeological Journal and elsewhere.

Brendan Smith is currently completing a doctoral thesis in Trinity College, Dublin on the medieval history of County Louth.

Preface

Most of the essays which make up this volume were given as papers at the first Cuchulainn Country Summer School held in Carlingford between 10 and 12 June 1988. The aim of the School was to examine the 'debatable lands' – south Down, north Louth, south Armagh and south east Monaghan. From the time of the Táin, this has been a complex area of fluctuating political, social and economic fortunes for various groups. These essays are not an attempt to justify any particular political arrangements but seek to explore a new approach to the study and writing of local history in Ireland. Most local history has been written using the county as the area of study. There are good reasons for this given that much of the raw material which historians use was collected on a county basis. This volume offers a different perspective; using a common historical experience of being on a borderland to understand the past. We have examined only one part of the Ulster-Leinster border by way of a case study; looking at its effect on regional society through a series of different perspectives from pre-history to the creation of a modern political border in 1920. We hope that this volume will make a contribution to the understanding of the historical context of areas more usually considered as separate units on either side of a political boundary.

We are grateful to C. J. Lynn and B. G. Scott for providing the maps of the linear earthworks in the south Ulster area and the Dorsey and to the *Ulster Journal of Archaeology* for the distribution map of souterrains.

The production of this volume has been possible because of the enthusiasm of the contributors and the Institute of Irish Studies, Queen's University Belfast. However, this enthusiasm would have been in vain without generous financial support from The Carroll Tobacco Company of Dundalk and it is appropriate that it should be published during the Dundalk heritage year.

R. G.
H. O'S.

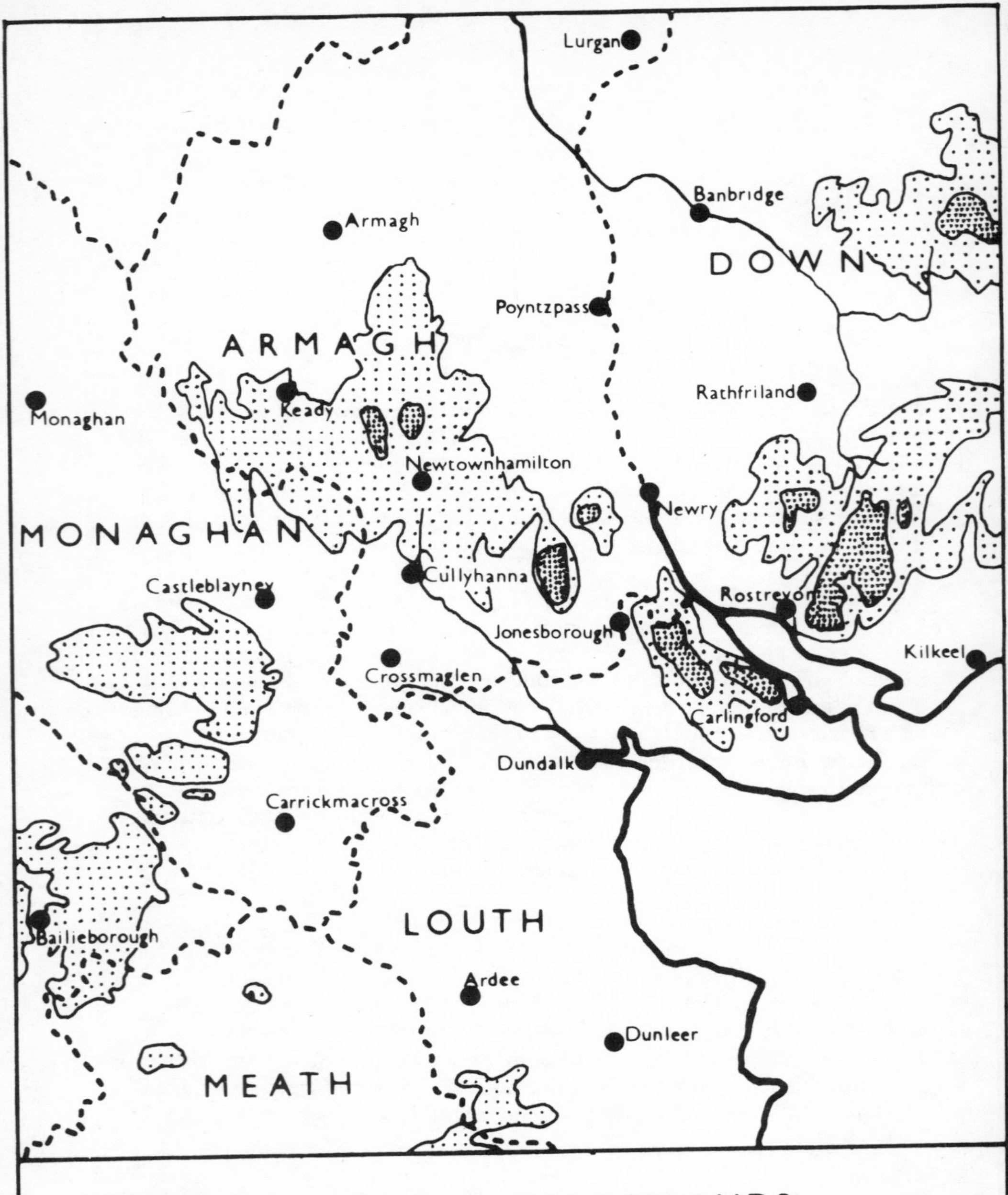

TOPOGRAPHY OF THE BORDERLANDS

County boundary

0 20
km

1 Introduction

RAYMOND GILLESPIE
HAROLD O'SULLIVAN

Historians have expended considerable effort in describing and explaining the political, economic and, to a lesser extent, social consequences of the political partition of Ireland following the Anglo-Irish treaty of December 1920 which marked out a physical boundary on the map of Ireland. Much less effort has been spent in exploring an equally important aspect of the development of partition hinted at by the historian J. C. Beckett. Commenting on the situation in Northern Ireland in 1973, Beckett observed that 'the conviction was gaining ground that the line of division could not be removed from the map until it had first been removed from the minds of men'.[1] Such borders in men's mental map of Ireland are of much greater antiquity than that drawn in 1920. The political organisation of early medieval Ireland was a patchwork of individual lordships each with its own set of political and legal structures and fluctuating boundaries. The boundary areas of these lordships, according to some scholars, were the preserve of certain social groups, and certain kinds of activities were confined to those areas.[2] The Anglo-Norman conquest did little to change this situation as it failed to impose a central authority over the whole island. The resulting patchwork of lordships was well set-out in an account in 1515 of the state of Ireland which described 'more than sixty countries, called regions, in Ireland' in each of which 'the said captains maketh war and peace for himself, and holdeth by the sword, and hath imperial jurisdiction within his room and obeyeth to no other person . . . except only to such persons as may subdue him by the sword'. Many of these lordships were bonded together in wider alliances under more powerful lords, such as the O'Neills in Ulster, and so a hierarchy of political, social and economic boundaries developed in the Irish landscape.[3] Many of these were used by the central government in the sixteenth and seventeenth centuries to define the territorial units which formed the administrative framework for local government in Ireland – the province, county and barony. Some boundaries were more persistent in men's minds than others and most persistent, though often unstable, were those such as the Pale which were determined by a combination of political, economic, social and cultural factors.[4]

It might be expected that such boundaries would disappear with the extension of the rule of the Dublin administration over the whole country after 1603 but yet the seventeenth century historian Geoffrey Keating recognised a wide variety of different social, economic and cultural groups within the island and attempted to explain these and drew boundaries between them by relating them to successive pre-Norman invasions of the country. The division between the north and south of the country, for example representing the division between Eibhear and Eireamhon, two of the Clanna Mileadh, were recorded as being marked by Esker Riadha running from Dublin to Galway. The five provinces were portrayed as the divisions between the five sons of Deala, one of the Firbolg, with a common point at Uisneach, or the hill of Usna in County Westmeath.[5]

This mythological account was an attempt to explain the origins of the internal divisions which were still realities in Keating's day although not necessarily for the quasi-historical reasons which he suggested for their existence. A tract written on the Continent in the 1620s noted that 'Ireland is divided into two parts' and indicated that the northern part was native Irish and Catholic while the southern part was influenced to a greater extent by the English.[6] This division was reflected in differing attitudes and native Irish Ulstermen were by no means comfortable in seventeenth century Munster, George Storey, an officer in the Williamite army, noted in 1691 that after the war the Ulstermen who had fled to Kerry and Clare during the war began to return home 'which was a little odd to see' since it was a long journey, they had no assurance of regaining their farms in Ulster and there was a real risk of retaliation from the settlers. In contrast, land in Munster was cheap and available 'but', Storey noted, 'the reason of this is plain, for there is so great an antipathy between the Ulster Irish and those in other parts of the kingdom, as nothing can be more, and the feuds amongst them greater than between either and their injured protestant neighbours'.[7] Such feelings were mutual and in the 1640s when the papal nuncio, Cardinal Rinuccini, argued with a Munsterman who was 'a very good Catholic' that it was better to have Catholic Ulster soldiers in Munster than heretics he was informed that this was not necessarily the case.[8] This division between the inhabitants of northern and southern Ireland was not a product of the seventeenth century. Distribution maps of archaeological monuments repeatedly show contrasting patterns between the northern and southern parts of the island. Again in the nineteenth century the Ulster-Leinster divide also marked a mental boundary for Ulster unionists in political terms. In the 1820s, for example, the attempt by the Catholic Association to become established in Ulster was described as an invasion.[9]

In some ways this strong division between Ulster and the rest of the island was illusory. Regional cultures and political structures has always existed in Ireland. The real significance of the Ulster border is not so much in its current political and administrative reality but rather that a variety of forms of boundary there persisted for so long in men's minds. This apparent continuity should not disguise the fact that the reasons for the existence and persistence of a border changed dramatically over time. In the medieval period the ethnic difference between the Anglo-Normans of the Pale and the native Irish of Ulster separated Ulster and Leinster. In the seventeenth century the colonisation of Ulster by English and Scots introduced a different type of ethnic factor. The seventeenth century saw Ulster further distinguished from the Pale by its poor economic performance yet by the nineteenth century the tide had turned and it was Ulster's wealth as an industrialised region which marked it off as different. Explaining the reasons for these distinctions is complex. Geographical factors certainly played an important part by physically limiting access to Ulster from the rest of the country to a few passes. Human factors in terms of colonisation and the social changes which resulted were also significant.

An explanation of the reasons for Ulster's difference is beyond the scope of this introduction but the reality of an Ulster-Leinster divide in men's minds even before partition, which itself split the integrity of the province of Ulster, is apparent. The changing nature of the border region between Ulster and the rest of the island, and hence the nature of the border itself, is the subject of the essays in this volume. Not all the modern day political border is examined, only the eastern part of it touching south Down, north Louth, south Armagh and south east Monaghan. This region has a certain cohesiveness as a unit of local study, but yet is a subject which has not attracted the attention of historians who have normally confined their investigations to the somewhat artificial administrative unit of the county. The county approach is, in the main, a matter of convenience since the county was the standard unit for local government from the seventeenth century and for the collection of data by nineteenth century statisticians.[10] Other types of social unit may well be more appropriate for study in some parts of the country.

The Ulster-Leinster borderlands form a unit which maintained its integrity and distinctiveness from before the Norman invasion to the present. Such a regional society has many features which deserve fuller investigation than has hitherto been done. L. M. Cullen, for example, has noted that the violence which characterised County Armagh society in the eighteenth century may well be the result of that county being part of a significant borderland between Ulster and Leinster.[11] This volume is an attempt to define other features which may be characteristic of that borderland and how those features have changed over time according as the nature of the border changed with the growing power of the Dublin administration, the spread of a national market network into the region and changing patterns of national politics. These essays can only begin to delimit some of the features of the Ulster-Leinster border and to provide a framework for further study so that a full political, economic, social and cultural framework for the understanding of the border in 'the minds of men' can be developed.

2 Geographical Perspectives on the Borderlands

P. J. DUFFY

One of the common features of the history of states and of political geography is that before the emergence of modern, centralised states from the seventeenth century, territorial control by administrations was seldom uniform or complete. It was always strongest at the centre and weakest at the edges. Any overview of a large region, such as western Europe over the last 1,000 years, would reveal a series of embryonic cores with intervening borderlands. There were simple reasons of distance and communications for this state of affairs: transport and communications were often under-developed and untenable beyond the centre; military control was difficult to maintain there and tax collection was difficult to implement. Invariably other elements overlay this and bolstered the incomplete control of the marginal territories. The centres were normally located in the richest, most densely populated and urbanised areas, and the marginally controlled zones were often economically marginal also, differentiated economically by their very remoteness from the centre as well as by their poor agricultural, often mountainous, land which was invariably thinly populated.

Control over the marchlands between emerging states was sporadic, fluctuating between one state and another depending on their changing relative strengths. For most of the time these regions evolved a separate existence, a negotiated territorial ad-hocism as a buffer between two or more power blocks. But such existence had an inherent instability and uncertain endurance. As a result of their poverty and lack of administrative cohesion borderlands were condemned to comparative underdevelopment adopting a scavenging form of economy between two power blocks; though in some cases this very position on the edges helped them to develop a mediating economic role as a marketing zone between the two bigger regions. Inevitably such borderlands were bound for incorporation into neighbouring expanding states; only in exceptional situations did border regions emerge as separate states. The process of late incorporation, later settlement and later economic development itself became a mark of distinction in the borderlands and part of its collective folk history which often continues to distinguish it from the older political entities around it.

In many respects Ireland's experience (though on a much smaller scale than Europe's) conforms to this model. Gaelic Ireland before the Anglo-Normans consisted of a multiplicity of small states only very tentatively beginning to unite under a high king. The Anglo-Norman conquest and colonisation was incomplete and the island was left with a range of polities and, inevitably, a number of frontiers and borderlands – most notably between the Pale and the gaelic world, but also to various extents between gaelic and gaelicised territories. The English colony, under growing pressure from the fourteenth century, was constantly aware of its borders and developed elaborate definitional devices – 'marches', 'land of war', 'fasaghe' – as well as a series of legislative and defensive responses, such as the Statutes of Kilkenny and 'black rents', to protect its borders from economic and cultural attrition. Throughout the middle ages, marchlands or borderlands represented a notable feature in landscape and politics, and strategic belts of castles and tower houses are today reminders of the importance of such zones. The subsequent total incorporation of the island of Ireland in the expanding British state in the seventeenth century, using plantation and confiscation as a leading instrument, ultimately eliminated many of the marchlands.

The borderlands focussed on north Louth-south Armagh are not therefore unique in a regional typology. But they have a pedigree and an endurance which sets them apart among Ireland's borderlands. The 'Gap of the North' (as the archetypal 'pass' through the frontier zone), Cúchulainn and the Táin Bó Cuailnge epitomise and celebrate the distinctiveness of this regional interface between Ulster and Leinster 2,000 years ago. More recently A. T. Q. Stewart points to the frequency of 'confrontation and incidents' in border villages like Forkhill 'long before there was any border'.[1] Like many borderland regions this one eludes precise definition. It is best left as a vague entity relatively easily identified in the landscape: from the north of Dundalk it is distinguished by a mountain wall towering over the plain of Louth extending right across Dundalk Bay.[2] From the heights above Ardee the drumlin 'swarm' curving around south Monaghan and Cavan is clearly visible as a different and difficult region. A feature of most borderlands is their lack of internal cohesion, reflected in their historic impenetrability, late settlement and difficulties in internal communications. Cooley, Sliabh Gullion, the Fews, Farney, and districts within, represent landscapes and communities more or less separated from each other where Irish as a spoken language survived among significant proportions of the population up until the end of the nineteenth century.[3] This internal isolation is a feature in many peripheralised and borderland regions and helps to explain their frequent cultural backwardness and underdevelopment.[4]

The south Ulster borderlands have had a distinctive history for at least a 1,000 years. They found themselves on the edge of the most successfully anglicised and feudalised colony in the island in the twelfth century, separating it from the most intractably Gaelic region of mid-Ulster. Throughout the middle ages the south Ulster borderlands were under pressure from these two power blocks – initially from the Anglo-Normans who established a ring of castles in the region and increasingly from the fourteenth century under the overlordship of the O'Neills who had annexed the Fews as their septland. Magennis, O'Hanlon, MacMahon, O'Reilly were the minor lords in this comparatively impoverished and fragmented belt of lordships separating the O'Neills from the English or gaelicised midlands. A recent study refers to the emergence in the thirteenth century of a separate territorial entity in the marches, 'a border area which had its own borders, one with the land of war and one with the land of peace', where mixtures of Irish and English law prevailed and military defence was paramount.[5]

Undoubtedly the economic and cultural landscape of south Ulster reflected its borderland role. The physical juxtaposition of lowlands, hills and mountains provides an important key to understanding the nature of the region. Some of the classic conditions for border zones are present here – the meeting of contrasting physiographic regions which in turn represent the meeting of different agricultural and economic regimes. Many of the prerequisites of trade and commerce ('exchange') were met along frontier divides such as this. The location of Dundalk in the northern extremity of Leinster and the Pale, with outliers at Ardee and Carlingford guarding the lowlands from hostile incursions and with their markets presiding over economic interaction across the frontier, symbolised the role played by borderland communities in this region six and seven hundred years ago.

Though much of the south Ulster region was incorporated in the Ulster plantation scheme of the early seventeenth century, the physical conditions which underlay its earlier borderland role continued to exert an influence defying the successful implementation of the plantation. The greatest density of settlement by the newcomers was in east Ulster, adjacent to the source of the majority of the immigrants in Scotland and the north of England. South Ulster remained remote and continued frontier-like and unattractive. South Armagh, south Monaghan and south-east Cavan – hilly, hostile and harbouring dissidents, such as woodkerne, and dispossessed – was unattractive to settlers and dispersed parts of it were only successfully planted later in the eighteenth century. County Armagh developed as a particularly strong frontier region with cultural and social tensions emerging from the seventeenth century between English, Scots and Irish.[6] South Ulster's role as a borderland between Dublin and the midlands on the one hand and the new colonial 'pale' centred on Belfast and east Ulster on the other deepened as the eighteenth century progressed. The industrial and economic pre-eminence of Belfast in the nineteenth century further emphasised the regional significance of south Ulster. The markets and trading hinterlands of Belfast and the northern manufacturing towns often met with the hinterlands of Dublin and Drogheda on the edge of south Ulster.

The frontier characteristics of this borderland region, therefore, might be seen in retrospect to have had not only an early genesis but, because of its social and economic renewal especially in the eighteenth century when other borderlands were well settled, the south Ulster area is the most enduring frontier region in Ireland. Perhaps ultimately, it is this continuity, supported by the presence of the political border there today, which continues to add immediacy to this enduring borderland region.

The main thrust of the following discussion will be to show how circumstances in the past, influenced by the location of the borderlands *viz-a-viz* broad processes of economic and political change as well as by the inherent topographical characteristics of the region, led to distinctive patterns of population and settlement emerging: how the people in the past contributed to the evolution of a distinctive border landscape by the beginning of the twentieth century. A number of broad themes will be examined to illustrate this process.

I

Placenames represent one of the most enduring indicators of the settlement and cultural history of any area and much valuable work is being undertaken in explaining the meaning of our placenames, especially those derived from Irish language words. Jones Hughes's contribution has been to understand the significance of broad placename elements (such as the suffix -town or prefix drum-) in throwing light on the distinctive geographies of regions in Ireland.[7] In the borderland region under study here, is found one of the more striking territorial contrasts in placename occurrences as shown on map 1. 'English' names, defined very broadly to include those of Anglo-Norman vintage (principally though not always names with the suffix -town) as well as those of more recent origin (such as Deerpark or Mount Hamilton) have been shaded in. By shading each *townland*, a rough reflection of the territorial significance of the placename regimes is obtained. As the map dramatically illustrates, there is an abrupt northern edge to the 'English' placename zone, reflecting the fairly intensively settled English Pale stretching up to and around Dundalk and out along the perimeter lowlands of Cooley, giving way at the drumlin borders to a region of Gaelic names stretching interminably northwards and westwards.

Insofar as a limited analysis of townland names makes it possible to say, Louth is characterised by high intensities of English placenames along the

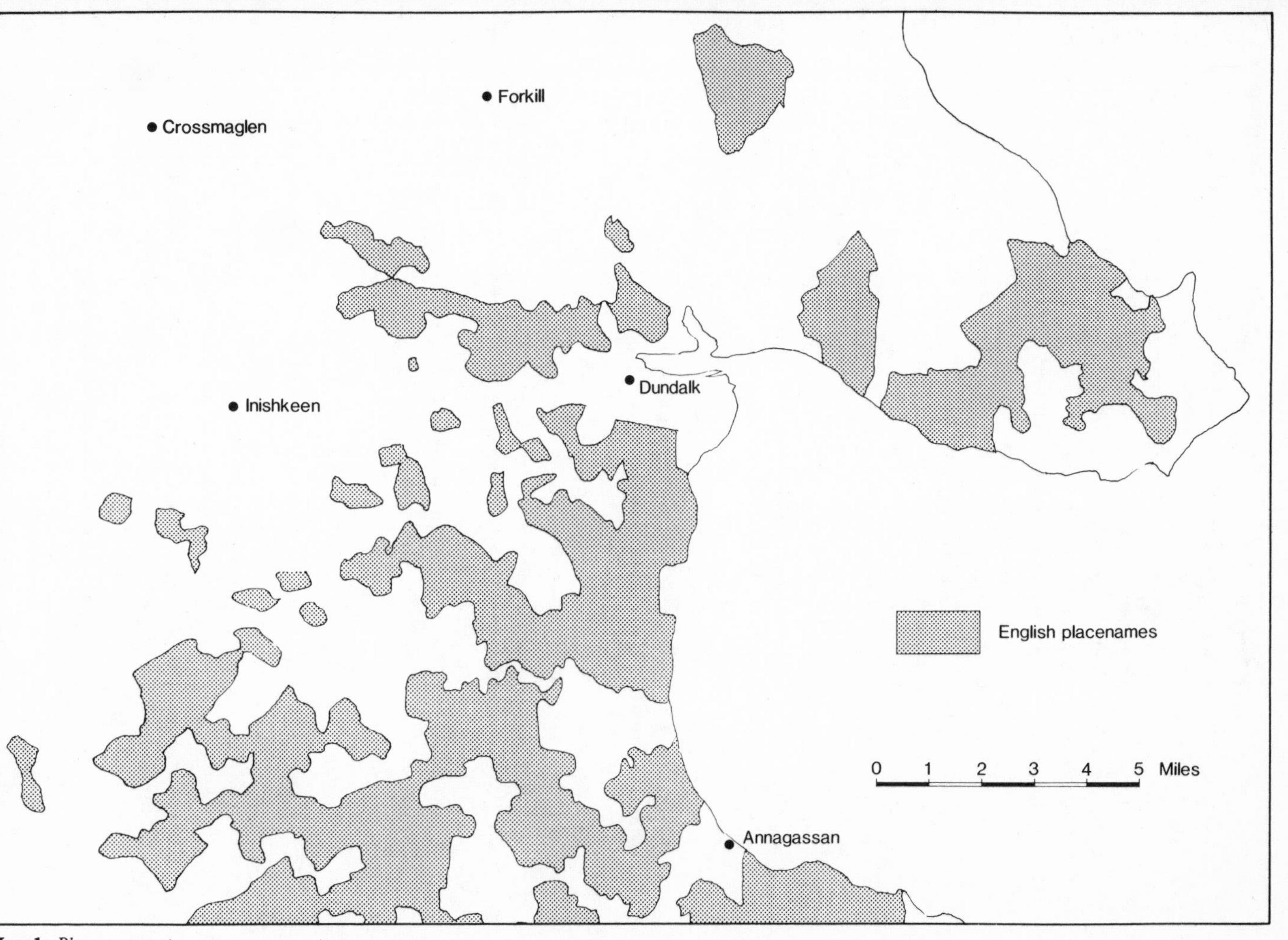

Map 1: *Placenames map.*

well drained valleys of the Dee, Glyde and Fane rivers. The Castletown river marks the most northerly extension of these names with places such as Barronstown, Phillipstown, Newtown(balregan), Castletown. Clearly intensive English colonisation stopped at the transition to poorer, wilder and more hostile environments to the west and north. Though the early Anglo-Norman colony briefly incorporated part of modern south Monaghan (reflected in the mottes in Iniskeen and Donaghmoyne), this short lived expansion has left no lasting placename legacy. Here, and in south Armagh, is the world of Drum-, Cor-, Carrick-, Tully-. Only occasionally in this 'gaelic' landscape are there instances where eighteenth century landlordism succeeded in obliterating the older name, such as at Ravensdale, belonging to Lord Clermont (Fortescue). Occasional attempts by landlords to 'civilise' the names, reflected for example in the fanciful English translation of townland names in Shirley's Farney estate as late as 1788,[8] never succeeded in replacing the deeply-rooted native Irish names that have been celebrated in the twentieth century in much of Patrick Kavanagh's writing.

Obviously analysis of townland names alone is inadequate; a great many sub townland names, once more widespread but mostly now defunct, must also be significant indicators of territorial transition in the cultural landscape. Equally it should be noted that a map of townland names today can only be a shadowy reflection of the waxing and waning of cultural change which would have been especially pronounced in a frontier zone such as this. MacIomhair drew attention to this process in 1301 with references, for example, to Ballyasobeny (MacSuibhne), Ballycandry and Ballykellath which ultimately became Swinestown, Ganderstown and Callystown (in Co. Louth) respectively.[9] There must be no doubt also that the fourteenth and fifteenth centuries witnessed the re-gaelicisation of many placenames in the north and west of Louth, as occurred along other margins of the Pale.

II

Boundaries and territorial limits are an integral part of any borderlandscape. Lines of division will inevitably attain considerable significance in such regions, demarcating as they do the limits of power or influence of one side or another. The actual location, as well as the geometry, of these boundaries will reflect geopolitical processes at local level. In all societies at all times the logic of the territorial imperative has meant that borderlands are particularly sensitive to demarcation lines and so 'marches' were a dominant feature of medieval Europe and lines of castles and fortified houses were landscape markers of boundary transitions. In Gaelic and Celtic societies many ruses were adopted to bolster the symbolic importance of borders by locating burial grounds, monasteries, and crosses on their boundaries. In County Louth large standing stones were used in mainly historic times as boundary markers.[10] Historical geographers have been especially interested in the hierarchy of territorial divisions in Ireland epitomised for example in townland, parish, barony and county.[11] Although much remains to be established about the early significance of many of the smaller territorial units (many of which were defunct by the nineteenth century) as a general rule the essential explanation of the various territorial structures probably lies in Rev William Reeves' view expressed a century and a half ago that they reflect the 'civil peculiarities of the districts while in the possession of the original inhabitants'[12] or the patterns of landownership and politics in the medieval period and earlier. It might be possible to suggest, for example, that different ethnic groups, responding to varying economic and demographic opportunities offered by the environment, went about the territorial organisation of their landscape differently. In what ways, therefore, do the territorial divisions reflect the borderland nature of south Ulster and north Leinster since provincial, county and parish boundaries which in different ways reflect the economic, cultural and political contrasts, found a meeting place here.

The overriding historical and geographical reality in this borderland has been its importance as the meeting place of Ulster and Leinster and while Cooley may have had more associations with Ulster in pre-Norman times, the edge of the drumlin belt and the mountains of south Armagh represented the permanent divide between two of the five historic provinces, or cuige, of Ireland. Though some minor adjustment took place in the early modern period, the county boundaries which were the shired Gaelic lordships of the sixteenth century – Monaghan, Cavan and Armagh – reflect very closely the borders as they had been for many centuries. Physically, apart from instances like the Shannon, where borders coincide with clearly distinctive elements like great rivers, there are few examples where boundaries so finely reflect a borderland as the Monaghan-Armagh-Louth county boundaries coinciding with the southern edge of the most extensive drumlin belt in western Europe. The diocese of Clogher also reflects the territorial experience of the borderland region. Clogher Head in County Louth represents the easternmost extent of Clogher at a time when the kingdom of Oirghialla had temporarily expanded into the plain of Louth just prior to the Anglo-Norman colonisation. Subsequently, Oirghialla retreated to the line of the river Lagan and the Louth part of the Clogher boundary incorporating the parishes of Iniskeen and Killanny is a truer reflection of the frontier geography than is the county boundary. The archdiocese of Armagh, however, extending as it does from the Boyne to Lough Neagh clearly reflects the much older political hegemony of the Ui Neill and straddles the borderlands. It is therefore more of an administrative region, which never accommodated the frontier divide in pre-Norman or post-Norman times and was more symbolic than real in reflecting the ecclesiastical power of Armagh.[13]

In many respects, the baronies reflect the real geography of the borderland and bring out its significant constituent parts. The baronies of Fews, Orior and Farney represent essentially a Gaelic sub-territorialisation of the borderland, facing the lowland baronial territories of Louth, Dundalk and Ardee. MacIomhair's analysis of the townlands of Louth in 1301 has pointed to the crucial role of the baronies in managing borderland power struggles which fluctuated in a north-south direction. They represent the handful of sub areas making up the borderlands belonging to MacMahons, O'Hanlons, Flemings and Dowdalls whose boundaries stopped in the borderlands as a result of the marchland dynamics and military exigencies of centuries prior to the 1600s.

But it is probably the parishes which most clearly reflect the internal contrasts in the territorial geography of the borderlandscape. As smaller units and as more accurate reflections of the changing circumstances at local level, the parishes are extremely interesting structures. The civil parishes, mapped by the Ordnance Survey in the early nineteenth century, represent with some exceptions the medieval legacy of ecclesiastical administrative structures. Additionally, however, because of the links between the church and secular society in the medieval period, the civil parishes also reflect the nature of civil administration at local level. Thus, for example, among the manorial communities of Louth, many of the manors established under the original English settlers in the twelfth century were also constituted into parishes. In the Monaghan area also, the parishes which emerge coincided with sept lands in the Gaelic lordships.[14] It is only when one takes an overview of the whole borderland region (incorporating in this case roughly south Armagh, south Monaghan, north Louth and parts of east Cavan and north Meath) that one sees significant contrasts in the region in terms of territorial structures reflecting by extension, contrasts in economic and land management strategies.

The most immediate contrast is in terms of parish size. The parishes of Louth (with the notable exceptions of the monastic lands of Louth, Ballymascanlon and Carlingford parishes) are uniformly small in size. For example, the average size of a parish in Ardee, Louth and Dundalk Upper baronies is 2,900, 5,800 and 2,400 acres respectively. Parishes in Ardee barony range in size from Cappoge's 1,283 to Ardee's 4,884 acres. In fact, the old parish of Kilpatrick to the south of Ardee was even smaller than Cappoge but had disappeared by the nineteenth century. Were it not for Louth parish's 18,000 acres, the mean parish in Louth barony would be 2,300 acres. In Dundalk Upper, the parishes ranged from Kane's 749 acres to the town of Dundalk's parish of 6,332 acres.

These small, and typical manorial, parishes with all their implications for population, economy and society in the Normanised lowlands of Louth stand in marked contrast with the parish structures to the north and west. In the two Armagh baronies abutting onto Louth (Upper Fews and Upper

Orior) parish sizes averaged 17,000 and 20,400 acres respectively. In the baronies of Farney and Cremourne in Monaghan, parishes were 19,000 and 21,000 acres respectively and in the easternmost baronies of Cavan they averaged 13,500 and 12,000 acres. The difference is extreme. Creggan parish, which spilled over into County Louth measured more than 20,000 acres in its Armagh section. Before 1773 (when Manorhamilton parish was carved out of the northern part of Creggan) it was enormous. Donaghmoyne and Magheross parishes in Monaghan were 25,000 and 17,000 acres respectively. Annaghmullan parish to the north of Magheross in Monaghan was 30,700 acres. In Cavan the parish structures give the appearance of some plantation equalisation with fewer extremes in size, but almost all of them exceed 10,000 acres.

While clearly representing contrasts in the economic capacity of land on both sides of the frontier with poorer areas being more extensive than more productive districts, the parishes also imply differences in land use and economy across the frontier subsequent to the twelfth century settlement, as well as contrasting territorial approaches to ecclesiastical authority. Apart from their small size, the Louth parishes (as in most other manorial regions) also exhibit a considerable amount of fragmentation, obviously reflecting the economic significance of quite small parcels of property in feudal times. The record is full of examples of meticulous manorial administration of property. The Dowdall estates, in Louth and Meath, in the thirteenth century were preoccupied with quantity and quality of each rood of ground 'metes and devises . . . measured and perambulated'.[15] Many Louth parishes (for example Shanlis, Ballymascanlon, Castletown) have small outlying portions isolated from the main parish territory. Even a cursory regional assessment of the parishes in Louth indicates that their boundaries were quite finely delineated implying a significant degree of land-use differentiation, possibly even with well established enclosures. In contrast, the Cavan/Monaghan/Armagh parishes represent a more broad ranging and loose network of territories, with much less attention to the minutiae of small divisions or fine boundary lines. Many of the contrasts also reflect fundamental cultural differences which were epitomised in the way the archdiocese of Armagh was divided *inter hibernicos* and *inter anglicos*. Traditionally the Gaelic church favoured a monastic form of organisation, with more emphasis on monasteries as focal points for the rural population and less on the territorial definition of the parish. In contrast, the feudal colony reflected a more mainland European and reformist emphasis on the secular clergy and the parish as the basic territorial and taxation unit. The contrasts were exacerbated through the middle ages by the opening of Gaelic regions to new regular orders, such as mendicant friars, as well as by the deterioration of much of the church lands, termons etc. signifying general disorder in the territorial organisation of the church there.

At the lowest level in the territorial hierarchy are the townlands, many aspects of which remain puzzling. In their size and structure they appear to offer no patterns within the borderlands. In contrast to the parishes, some of the smallest units are found in the Gaelic lands of Monaghan. In the barony of Farney for example, mean townland sizes range from 160 acres in Donaghmoyne parish to 238 acres in Magheross. In Fews Upper on the other hand, the average townland is 376 acres in Creggan parish, 563 acres in Newtownhamilton and 922 acres in Ballymyre. In the barony of Clankee in east Cavan, townlands range from 225 acres in Drumgoon to 334 acres in Bailieboro. The manorial parishes of Louth, however, provide few clues – in Ardee barony, they range from 160 acres in Cappoge to 626 acres in Stabannan. In Dundalk Upper they range from 157 acres in Barronstown parish to 496 acres in Faughart. However, it is evident in the manorial lands of County Louth that there are much greater irregularities in townland structures than in the corresponding hilly regions of Armagh and Monaghan. So for example Drumcar parish's average of 310 acres is lowered to 250 acres if Drumcar townland (1,045 acres) is excluded. Similarly Castlebellingham townland's 1,038 acres (possibly comprising smaller medieval units) significantly skews the average size for Gernonstown and in Ardee parish whose townlands average 257 acres, if two large units of 1,568 acres and 739 acres are omitted, the mean size is reduced to 175 acres. These small townlands undoubtedly represent strategies for land assessment and valuation in medieval times. There seems little point however in looking for comparability between regions. Due to the inherent political fragmentation of medieval society in Ireland, it would seem that separate Gaelic territories evolved complex territorial orders of land assessment which did not bear the same relationship to their economic and demographic resources as the differently organised English or feudal districts.[16]

III

The territorial structures in the borderlands provide a fitting background to the evolution of settlement patterns in this region. Territorial organisation may reflect variations in land use and economy on both sides of the frontier – the cattle and creaghts of Farney for example, versus the common fields of Louth. The tates and ballybetaghs of Monaghan, farmed out in fractions among various septs, seem to represent one distinctive territorial approach to resource management which differed significantly from the feudal tenures of Louth. The classic view across the medieval frontier was towards an underdeveloped, sparsely populated Gaelic countryside from a comparatively densely populated, villaged manorial society. Were the outlying fringes of the Pale, however, under constant threat of pillage, quite so bustling or was settlement more dispersed and ragged in these transitional zones? Ellis points to the sophisticated regionalisation by the Pale authorities of the landscape around it, ranging through the 'maghery', to the 'marches' and the 'fasaghe' beyond. The 'maghery' was particularly important to the late medieval community of Dundalk and County Louth.[17] Most contemporary references to the northern fringes do suggest that vulnerable though the Pale borderlands were, they seem to have afforded continuing attractions to raiders from Gaelic territories right up to the beginning of the seventeenth century. In the 1580s and 1590s, black rent was being paid by the settlers in the Pale and there are constant references to raids on the English in Louth. In 1591, the archbishop of Dublin, recommending John Talbot of Castlering as a tenant to the earl of Essex drew attention particularly to his strategic occupation of a large 'scope of ground bounding on MacMahon's country and the Fewes . . . to the good hope and comfort of all that quarter of the English country . . [which] . . had recently suffered losses by fire'.[18]

Thomas Raven's 1634 survey of Farney gives some clues about the shape of settlement in this part of the borderland in the previous generation. By 1634 the countryside of Farney (about 70,000 acres) was comparatively underpopulated with extensive blocks of townlands being quite empty.[19] One must assume that the relative peace and stability of the previous thirty years led to some growth in settlement, so that for much of the sixteenth century the landscape of Farney must have appeared almost deserted, a picture which tallies with contemporary accounts describing the country as waste, unpeopled and unproductive. As with all such marginal regions, however, there were local exceptions to the general rule. Numbers of Pale families maintained fairly strong economic ties across the frontier. To a much greater extent in east Cavan than in Farney, Plunkets, Flemings and Talbots had been involved in land purchase throughout the sixteenth century and much of the confiscated church land in the Gaelic territories had been taken up (in title) by Palesmen.[20] In general, though, the south Ulster borderlands, apart from their inherently poor environment, because of their very situation between the O'Neills of Ulster on the one hand and the Pale on the other, were never in a position to sustain economic growth for long periods. The former's exactions in the sixteenth century were especially deleterious to the area and places such as Farney which were the first to bear the brunt of Tudor expansion plans into Ulster were not very desirable for either cattle or farmers.[21] Smyth's researches serve to pinpoint some of the processes which were to have a crucial impact on the south Ulster borderlands. In summary, his data depicts the Pale region of Louth as a well furnished economic region in the mid-seventeenth century, containing some of the most densely populated areas in the country and a diversified and complex settlement hierarchy of fields, farms, villages and towns.[22] In contrast south Ulster still showed many elements of a simpler less stratified society occupying a sparsely populated and underdeveloped countryside. The evidence, however, points to sweeping changes in north-east Ulster, where economic and cultural links with Scotland and northern England were being established. Smyth characterises a south-westward moving ethnic frontier in Ulster running up against an old Gaelic world and in the process deflecting older populations further south into places like the Cooley peninsula. The south Ulster interface was being born again and in it the conditions for eighteenth century rural sectarian conflict were being created.

Although from the seventeenth century, the borderlands were beginning to be integrated into the broader national economy,[23] this very process of settlement in the later seventeenth and throughout the eighteenth century served to prolong the process of differentiation within the borderlands. New settlements, new farms and new roads were established in formerly unsettled areas by either planter settlers or displaced Gaelic people from further north. Often as a result of these processes cultural and economic contrasts in the borderlands were renewed. Many other frontierlands have had the same experience through the modern period, with central governments exerting their influence by deliberate integration of the periphery.[24] But this very process of political, economic or cultural integration becomes a distinctive experience in itself, serving to underline the separate character of the newly settled region – reflected not only in enduring regional consciousness, but in structural elements like farm size, settlement patterns and communications.

In the south Ulster borderlands, new towns were created where none had existed before: Carrickmacross, Newtownhamilton, Castleblaney, Crossmaglen, Forkhill, Bailieborough, Bessbrook, Kingscourt, Cootehill, Virginia – some villages like Peterborough in Farney did not thrive beyond the seventeenth century and others like Jonesborough never developed. All of these were essentially intruded plantation settlements, in their very names symbolising a new era for this part of the borderlands. Here was an experience which sharply juxtaposed these districts with the older settlements and communities of Louth. In the countrysides of south Ulster, new settlers percolated: in parts of south Armagh they followed the new roads being built in the eighteenth century.[25] As with many border regions, pockets of more isolated less desirable lands were occupied by the dispossessed and displaced following the in-migration of settlers in the seventeenth century. It is no accident that many of the more famous tories of the later seventeenth century – most notably Redmond O'Hanlon – found succour in the hills and homes of south Ulster, eluding capture for many years and that the most serious conflicts with the authorities (represented by the Revenue police) in the eighteenth century took place in the same hill lands over the incidence of an appropriately marginal industry – illicit poitín distillation and the rural communities inevitably came to be represented by agrarian secret societies such as the Defenders.[26]

Smyth's mid-seventeenth century ethnic frontier is ultimately reflected in the religious affiliation of the people as it emerged in the 1861 census. From an overwhelmingly Catholic Louth (where only a handful of parishes had less than 90 per cent of their population Catholic), one moves north initially into a buffer zone of dominantly Catholic communities. Less than seven per cent of Creggan, Forkhill and the Farney parishes, for example, were Protestant. But a few miles further north, parishes such as Killevy, Newtownhamilton, Muckno and Ballybay had proportions from 30–50 per cent Protestant. The mechanics of the Ulster plantation which resulted in a degree of rural ethnic segregation (reflected today in 'Protestant' and 'Catholic' townlands) has given the borderlands a characteristically patchy and fragmented appearance. The maps produced for the Boundary Commission in 1921 provided such a detailed picture, which no doubt presented the Commission with problems akin to those faced by boundary arbitrators in post-war central Europe, whose ethnic borderlands and frontiers were uncannily similar to those around Ulster. The precariousness and the territorial fragmentation of the religious balance in the south Ulster borders provided ideal breeding grounds for the sectarian hostilities of the Peep O' Day Boys, Defenders and Orangemen during the land- and lease-hungry decades of the later eighteenth century with tensions high not only between Catholics and in-migrating Protestants, but also between Presbyterians and Anglicans.[27]

It was the farmed landscape maturing in the nineteenth century which most epitomised the borderland character of this region. As Crawford has demonstrated, a combination of pioneering land exploitation and agricultural development, and a booming cottage linen industry revolutionised the countrysides of this comparatively poorly-endowed region to the extent that the medieval dichotomy of a well-endowed Louth facing into northern wastelands was radically altered. Throughout Monaghan and south Armagh, lands were being extensively cleared and cultivated and by the second half of the eighteenth century the opportunities in linen spinning and weaving led to a period of frantic parcellation of land units. Surveys on the Bath estate in Farney, for example, show an enormous mushrooming of cabins and cabin clusters throughout the 23,000 acre estate between 1735 and 1777.[28] By the mid-nineteenth century the south Ulster borderland contained some of the most ubiquitously small farm landscapes in Ireland. In much of Farney, for example, less than seven per cent of holdings were more than thirty acres in extent. In south Armagh, bigger farms were equally scarce, with districts around Forkhill, Camlough and Crossmaglen having less than four per cent in the greater than thirty acres category. Crossmaglen district had nine farms out of 506 in excess of thirty acres; Cullyhanna had ten out of 220. Farms mostly clustered in the five to fifteen acres category. For example, of Jonesborough's 656 holdings, 313 were between one and five acres and 272 between five and fifteen acres. In Crossmaglen it was 135 and 237. Quite quickly south of the county boundaries, the farmscape changed: through north-west Louth where farms continued small to districts around Dundalk where one fifth and more of farms were over thirty acres in extent. This pattern was consolidated into mid-Louth. Apart from this there was a much more even spread of holdings between one and thirty acres. In Castlering, for example, which had 169 holdings enumerated in 1851, there were twenty three, fifty seven and forty two respectively in the size groups one to five, five to fifteen and fifteen to thirty acres.

Associated with this contrast in the distributions of farm size across the frontier, was the appearance in County Louth of significant populations of landless agricultural labourers, associated in turn with the striking emphasis on tillage once the Louth plain was reached. In the 1840s, almost half the rural population of Louth was landless, concentrated especially among the larger holdings of central and eastern districts of the county declining northwards into the zone of tiny family holdings. In Monaghan and Armagh the landless labourer was much less important though landlessness was by no means insignificant in such a land hungry and fragmented countryside in the 1840s.[29]

The report of the Railway Commission in 1838 adverted to many of those contrasts and in its maps underlined some of the borderland features already discussed. Interestingly, while the Commission (established to make recommendations for a railway system in Ireland) was anxious to provide for a rail link between Dublin and the growing city of Belfast, the evidence adduced by the Commission served to show the separateness of the borderlands, where traffic focused chiefly on Dundalk to the south and Newry to the north.[30] The rich and expanding merchant and industrial community of Belfast subsequently showed relatively little enthusiasm for communications south of the borderlands which seem to have marked the limit of their commercial interest, and the Belfast–Dublin line was not completed until the mid-1850s.

IV

Population distribution is the most sensitive indicator of spatial contrasts and variations in social and economic conditions. Population change also serves to epitomize the nature of the borderland shift in such areas as the economy, land use, settlement and landscape which occurred through the previous two centuries. From the poll tax returns of the mid-seventeenth century to the censuses of the early twentieth century, the borderland region was demographically transformed, with the changes rotating around a frontier fulcrum located along the Louth/Armagh/Monaghan borders. By the nineteenth century, the south Ulster borderlands were part of one of the most densely populated regions in Ireland, and map 2 of population density in the area in 1901 is a true illustration of a frontier

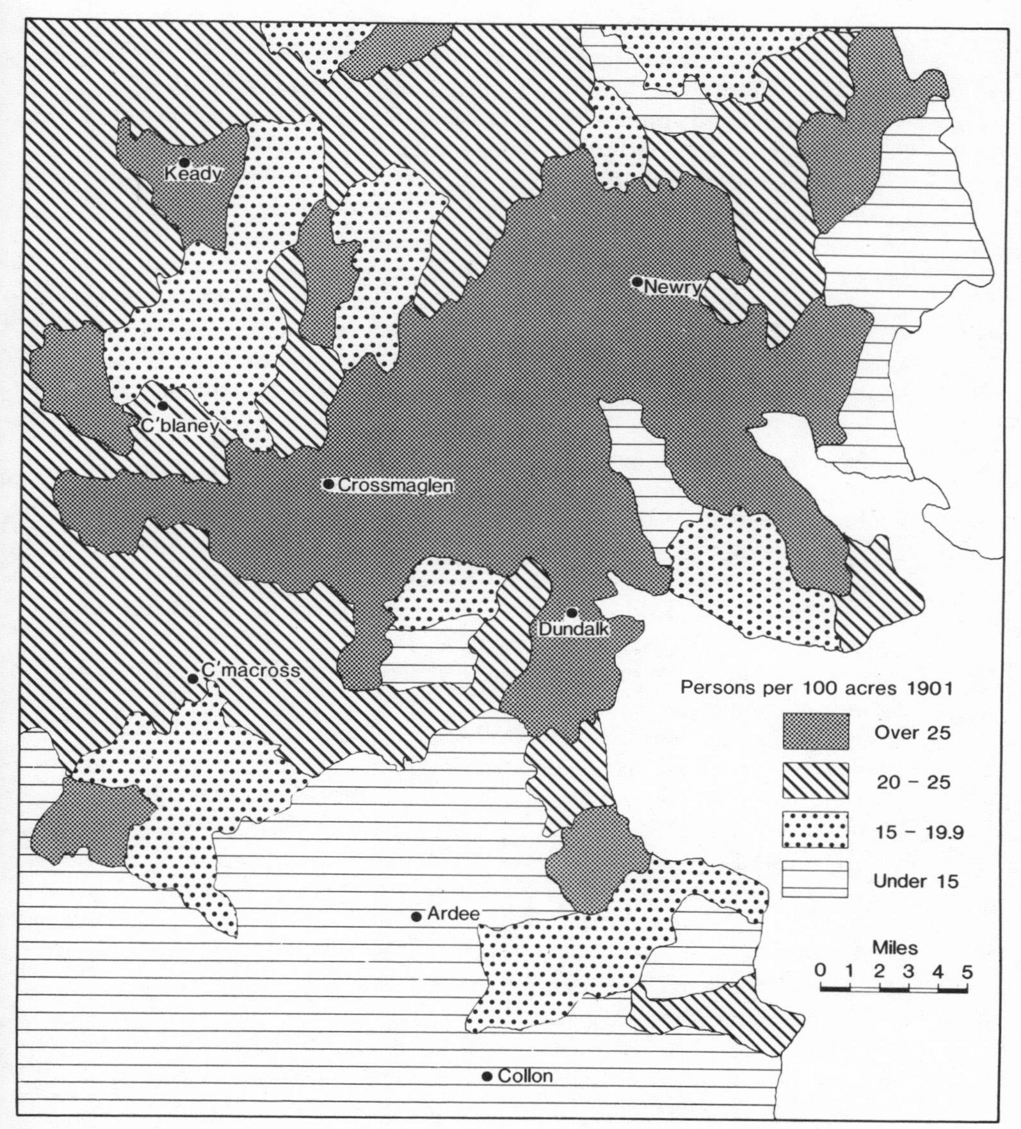

Map 2: *Population density, 1901.*

region – showing a transect across some of the lowest rural population densities on the island in north Meath and south Louth to some of the highest in south Armagh. Patrick Kavanagh was acutely aware of this crucial contrast and well he might, because his Iniskeen was almost literally on the edge of the small-farm, thickly-peopled drumlin frontier, looking down on the large and comparatively emptier expanses of Louth.

The unpublished enumeration schedules of the 1901 and 1911 censuses help to focus more closely on this demographic divide, looking for example at the structure of individual households at townland level. One would expect that different 'types' of household would reflect such things as occupational, class and religious differences. In Monaghan, for example, the pattern of land holding was evidently shaping the household demography and the twentieth century survival of many households was dictated by the constraints of living on, and holding onto, the small family farm.[31] Might one expect differences in household composition between farming and labouring families, or between big and small farms or between tillage and grazing farms?

Three main types of household are apparent in this borderland region, roughly classified on a townland basis: townlands where agricultural labourers (generally classified in the census as 'labourer' or 'cottier') form a significant proportion of the population alongside farm households; secondly townlands where the labourer households are more specialised and reflect a clear-cut link with a large farm or estate; thirdly townlands where small farm households formed the overwhelming majority. Additionally, one might separate townlands where Protestant households form a significant proportion.

The first group comprises a relatively simple composition of individuals, often elderly and often living alone or in an elementary nuclear family unit. Though the isolated cottier household was present throughout the south Ulster borderlands, it was most characteristic in the transition zone through north Louth into Monaghan and Armagh. These households often occurred in little clusters – rows of cottages or cabins on roadsides, reflecting earlier subletting practices or mill-working opportunities.

The second group generally comprised a large nuclear family, occasionally with third generation additions, probably reflecting the security of an established relationship with large landholders in the same or an adjoining townland as well as long-established kinship links with the large labourer community. Louth had many of these examples, where farms of sixty, seventy and over a hundred acres were associated with traditional loyal groups of labouring families.

The third group exhibited a much more complex range of types – from elementary young large households and three-generation households to bachelor-type households. The major characteristic of this demographic group, found abundantly through south Monaghan and Armagh, was its large size, often containing, in addition to many children, grandparents, maybe a nephew, niece or 'cousin' (born possibly in Glasgow or Boston) and often a lodger or hired 'servant'. The incomplete 'bachelor' type households remained large, consisting often of several brothers and sisters, past marrying age. As Bell has suggested,[32] hired labourers in small-farm south Ulster came generally from the small-farming class itself – the sons and daughters and relatives of small farmers in their teens and twenties hiring themselves out in hiring fairs such as Newtownhamilton in May or November. The demographic complexity of household structure in south Ulster, therefore, was due to this traditional type of arrangement between landholding families as well as the extensive kinship and mutual support system which was faltering into the twentieth century.

Comparatively few contrasts occurred between Protestant and Roman Catholic households, attributable no doubt to the fact that in this region both were ubiquitously small-farm families. In general, however, in the relevant districts of south Armagh, most of the hired 'servants' in Protestant households were Catholic, a reflection of the numerical dominance of the latter group in this region. Appropriately, also, one might draw attention to the transition in house quality across this socio-demographic frontier. The houses occupied by the families in south Armagh and Monaghan were demonstrably better than the general run of houses in the Louth plain, if the classification in the 1901 census is reliable. There were higher proportions of first and second class houses in the northern districts, a reflection perhaps of variations in proportions of landless people north and south as well as the legacy of agricultural and domestic industrial opportunities in south Ulster in the previous century.

Population decline and emigration which were the hallmarks of the post-Famine period especially were greatly altering both the distribution and demographic structure of the population. Emigration might be viewed as a differential response to economic and social conditions within the borderlands. Thus, for example, in the pre-Famine period, there was a significant drifting of labour southwards across the frontier to the large farms of east and south Louth to fill the harvest deficit in resident labourers (many of whom in turn had migrated for higher wages to Wales and England). The last half of the nineteenth century, of course, saw a weakening of the economic base of the borderlands, with consequent repercussions for the agricultural population. The labourers of Louth suffered a serious decline in job opportunities as both mechanisation and cattle numbers increased. The small farms of Monaghan and Cavan became increasingly unable to provide livelihoods for family members and seasonally-hired labour, and the spinning and weaving opportunities in south Ulster had progressively dried up as the industry concentrated in the Belfast region,[33] leaving large families to fall back on grossly uneconomic farmholdings. Emigration was facilitated by proximity to Newry, Dundalk and Belfast, with the latter having an expanding role as a magnet for many emigrants as rail transport consolidated its links with south Ulster. By the early twentieth century, the unremitting stream of rural out-migration was bringing about significant changes in household structure. The familiar isolated bachelor-type household of the later twentieth century was beginning to appear in Monaghan and Armagh – the result of the migration of farm family members in an unplanned fashion leaving households of unmarriageable siblings behind; the result also of increasingly uneconomic holdings preventing heirs from venturing into marriage. The small farm landscape was being maintained into the twentieth century, but its demographic structure was in the process of radical change. In contrast, the labouring communities of Louth were being decimated in the late nineteenth century. Whole families emigrated, so that overall Louth's rural population did not have as many depleted and unbalanced households as the predominantly small farm districts to the north. Kavanagh's poem *The Great Hunger* is an authentic elegy for the disintegrating communities of the south Ulster borders in the early twentieth century.[34]

V

The direction which political events on this island have taken in the twentieth century has meant that the borderlands of Ulster have undoubtedly attained more lasting significance than many other regions within Ireland, and the emigration and economic depression which have characterised these borderlands through much of the twentieth century have probably been exacerbated by their political peripheralisation. However, their significance is the consequence of a deep-rooted and region-specific historical process. Through much of the middle ages these borderlands were part of an important buffer zone arching around the English colony. The economic and environmental inferiority of the Ulster-Leinster border helped to shape its political destiny as a marchland between the Gaelic core in mid-Ulster and the colonial power in the Pale. O'Hanlons, MacMahons and O'Reillys emerged as minor lordships in south Ulster alternately supporting O'Neills and the English. Their landscape and territorial organisation reflected this borderland role. Through the revolutionary process of land settlement and economic integration in the seventeenth century, the region continued to occupy a peripheral position *viz-a-viz* the new Scottish and English 'pale' in east Ulster and its mixed cultural ingredients, symbolised in such figures as tories, priests, planters and poets reflect episodes in its evolution from the seventeenth to the nineteenth centuries. By the early nineteenth century it was emerging as an ethnic interface between Ulster and Leinster, a cultural divide which ultimately found itself on the margins of both the new states in Ireland in the twentieth century.

3 From the Darkness to the Dawn

The Later Prehistoric and Early Christian Borderlands

VICTOR M. BUCKLEY

The contemporary image of a border is often of a well-defined line drawn on a map or the physical manifestation of a 'frontier mentality', such as the Berlin Wall dividing East and West Berlin. The physical remains of a frontier from the protohistoric period, that is the third century BC until the eleventh century AD, the period with which we shall be dealing with in this essay, can still be found fossilised within the south Ulster-north Leinster landscape. These can be revealed through field surveys and excavation with fragments of documentary evidence used to fill in the gaps in our knowledge. They must, however, be seen in their social, economic and political context. If there was a border then there must also have been a heartland and a focus for the tribe or state and it is necessary to understand these if we are to appreciate the nature of the borders.

Our analysis of the border regions of north Louth, south Armagh and parts of counties Down and Monaghan begins in the third-second centuries BC, a period which has long been termed a 'Dark Age' by archaeologists but a 'Heroic Age' by scholars of early Celtic literature. The present border area of north Louth has close associations with the tales of the Ulster Cycle and the Táin Bo Cuailnge in particular. These tales contain accounts which are often anachronistic, sometimes didactic but encapsulate the clues to the creation and infrastructure of an embryonic state-like society in the north of Ireland in the centuries preceeding the birth of Christ.

The Táin, or Cattle Raid, is the nearest approach to an epic saga in early Irish literature.[1] Though the earliest surviving manuscripts are late in date, it has been suggested that they capture an essence of the pre-Christian Iron Age in Ireland, with similarities to the Celtic world described by Roman writers – a world of champions, chariots, head-hunting, totems and taboos, tinged with mysticism and the occult. Archaeological evidence for many of the things described in the Táin, such as scalloped-edged shields, swords and finery, chariots and royal houses is difficult to identify and they have been regarded, by archaeologists, as fanciful embellishments of the storytellers' imagination. However, there are many pieces of evidence from the placenames mentioned to set the bulk of the story in the present area of north County Louth. Many of these refer to topographic features, such as rivers, hills and passes – important landmarks in a mental map as we shall see later. Other names such as 'Smirommair' must be the large hilltop enclosure of Lismore fort at Smarmore townland, near Ardee. Other sections of text attempt to explain the derivation of earlier monuments such as the 'Lia Toll' – Pierced Stone – which is created when Cethern, in a rage, attacks a pillar-stone and pierces it with his sword. This must be the holed standing-stone of Hurlstone townland, the townland immediately adjacent to Smarmore townland. Though any interpretation of the saga is fraught with the problems in anachronisms, later remodelling and the additional Christianising of earlier oral tradition, the Táin is still a source which has a useful part to play in our analysis of the protohistoric period.

Antiquarians[2] and archaeologists[3] have long recognised the existence of large-scale linear earthworks forming defensive features in the north of Ireland. These 'linear earthworks', shown in map 1, consist of sections of banks and ditches running for long distances across the countryside which were assumed to be direct copies of the second century AD frontiers of the Roman Empire, such as Hadrian's Wall between the River Tyne and Solway Firth and Antonine's Wall between the Firth of Forth and River Clyde. These earthworks are known by a number of popular names in various parts of Ulster, such as the 'Dane's Cast' or 'Worm Ditch' which extends from south-west of Banbridge in County Down, for a length of six miles, to the north of Drumantine.[4] A similar earthwork, 'the Black Pig's Dyke' extends intermittently across the country from County Monaghan to County Sligo.[5] The traditions ascribing the construction of these massive sites to the headlong rush of a monstrous black boar and its subsequent demise are well documented.[6] Recent excavations on a section of the Black Pig's Dyke in Aghareagh West townland, near Scotshouse in County Monaghan revealed that the double-banked and double-ditched earthwork, with its northernmost bank invariably higher, was almost consistently constructed on the south-facing slopes of drumlins.[7] In the north bank of the site the finding of a palisade trench suggests a wooden breastwork on top of the embankment. The width of the trench would suggest timbers which would have stood to a height of three to four metres. From the finding of charred timbers during excavation it was concluded that the palisade had been deliberately burned down.[8] It can be assumed that this was during warfare rather than by accident because the timber had burned slowly down to below the ground level – an event unlikely to have been allowed to occur in an accidental blaze. The charred wood provided samples for 14C-dating, giving a date-range from 2240 ± 90 BP (GrN 12616) to 2165 ± 55 BP (UB 2600). These dates are in the first and second

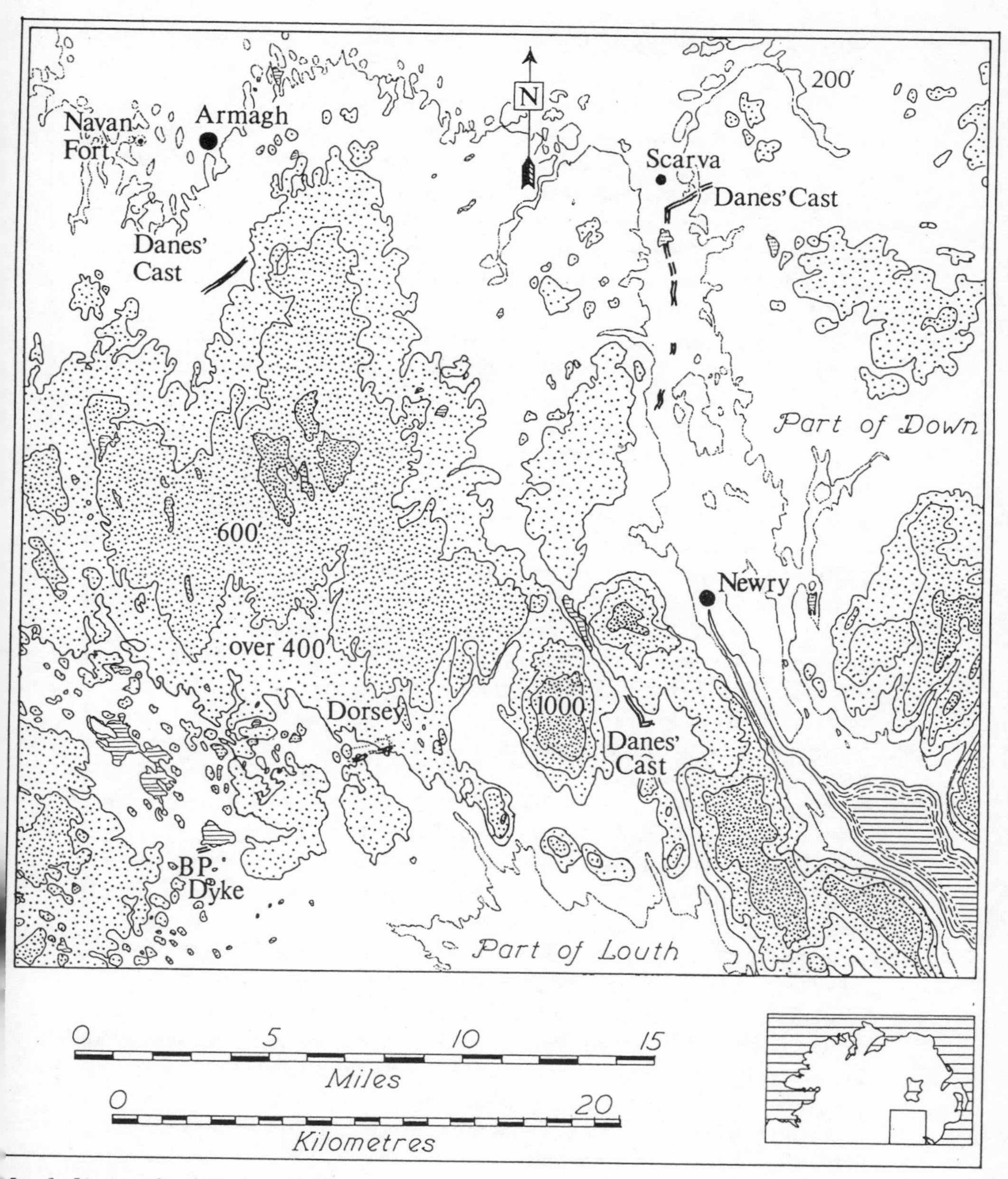

Map 1: *Linear earthworks in the south Ulster area.*

centuries BC, some two hundred years prior to the Roman frontier fortifications in Britain.

There is another linear earthwork, 'the Dorsey', near Silver Bridge on the main road from Newtownhamilton to Dundalk. The Dorsey (Map 2) consists of short sections of bank and a double-ditch with a boggy area in between.[9] This boggy area was bridged by a palisade or causeway of massive close-set oak piles. Some of these timbers were sampled during trial excavations and dendrochronologically (tree-ring) dated. The results suggest that the felling range for the timbers was 96 or 95 ± 9 years BC.[10] Recent sampling of timbers from the northern loop of the earthwork gives dates from slightly earlier than those published from the southern line of the earthwork. This suggests that the bank and palisade does not form a complete enclosure but are two separate phases of activity forming barriers across the route.[11] The fact that the original plan of the site mitigated the theory of an enclosed stronghold now appears to have been cast aside for that of routeway monitoring or checkpoint.

That these physical remains of a territorial frontier are intermittent can be easily explained in two ways. First, the ravages of land reclamation, both modern and in the past must have destroyed some areas. O'Donovan wrote in 1835, 'The people are plagued with it [the Black Pig's Dyke], striving to pay rent for it, they are labouring to level it with great industry, and it is completely defaced in some fields, but up the sides of barren hills it still shows its double ditch and broad rampart in all its pristine condition, defying, on its way through the plantation and across the summits of unprofitable hills the pick-axe of the covetous farmer at least for another century'.[12] The 150 years since O'Donovan has seen the development of heavy machinery which makes 'labouring . . . with great industry' very easily accomplished. Secondly, we can see from the Táin that natural landscape features such as lakes, hillocks and especially rivers were regarded as parts of the territorial boundaries. The meanings of place-names or onomastic lore in Old Irish tradition served as a mental map for warriors and herders alike.[13] Rivers in particular were of major significance, forming as they do, a long length of uncrossable barrier. At Drumsna, in County Roscommon a large linear earthwork, 'the Doon', cuts off a large promontory formed by a loop in the River Shannon.[14] The main bank of this earthwork, over a mile long, is up to six metres high and thirty metres wide and has two entrances with inward returns, reminiscent of British early Iron Age hillfort entrances. A flanking series of banks continues down the western loop of the Shannon and further river-bank stretches of earthwork are found up to three miles away. The Shannon Navigation maps show that there are a series of fordable points on this stretch of the river, with no other crossings for up to twenty miles either up or downstream. This creation of defended isthmus to cover all combinations of crossings is unique in Ireland in the early Iron Age. Thus fording places

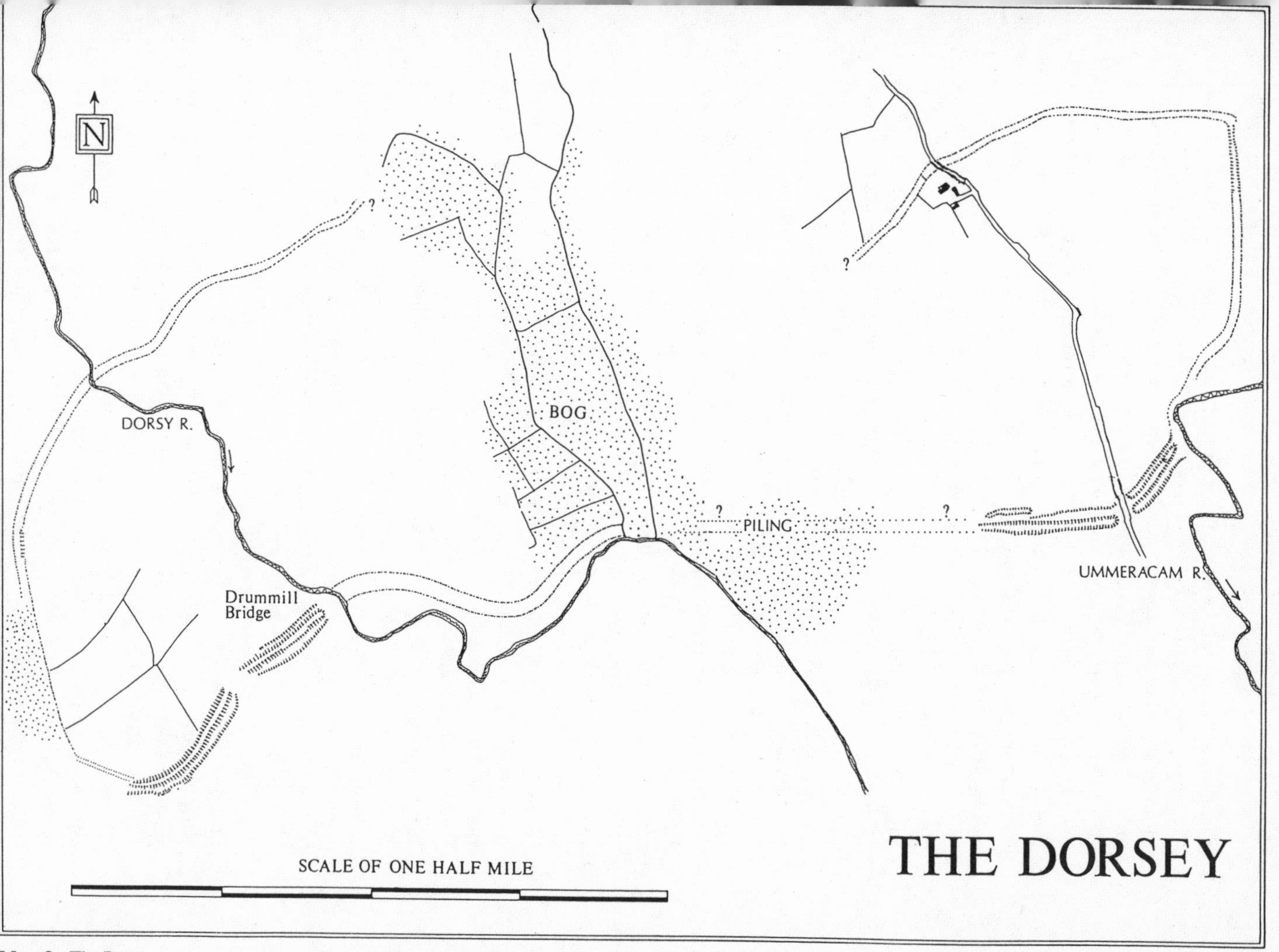

Map 2: *The Dorsey.*

assumed a status far beyond their present importance. In the Táin Bó Cuailnge, Cuchulainn uses a series of ritual ploys, such as the spansel hoop in order to delay and divert the Connacht army.[15] Cuchulainn is particularly noted as a mighty warrior in the water, especially when using his Gae Bolga (Spear Bag?). This weapon, concealed by the water, appears to have been lethal. Thus we can see that the border at this time was of a composite nature – massive earthworks, with their own version of the Berlin Wall's 'Checkpoint Charlie' and natural features, some impassable, others negotiable entrepots in trade and in war.

The old routes used by pedestrians, horsemen and armies were usually the ones which afforded the easiest passage, and it is interesting to note that the 'old coach road' to Armagh passed through the eastern section of the Dorsey. In the days prior to the rise of the Dublin–Belfast industrial axis, this was an important route. The Dorsey, with boggy hollows, drumlins and small lakes to the west and dominated by the Slieve Gullion range to the east is the only direct pass from north Louth into the plains of Armagh and thus to Emain Macha.

The building of massive, travelling earthworks to monitor traffic northwards needed a cohesive society behind it, be it a monarchy, democracy or theocracy, which could call upon a large manpower-base and utilise vast natural resources. If we assume the timbers from the palisade trench at Aghareagh West to have been two feet wide, then even the length of fifteen miles reputedly extant in the 1950s would have required 39,600 beams to have formed a continuous palisade.[16] The society as displayed by the Táin is violent, hierarchical and primitive, a regal tale of courts, favourites and champions. The underlying trend as with all 'heroic tales' is of a single person against the odds, however in his feats of single combat Cuchulainn is continually in conflict with the hosts of Connacht and when finally roused from the plains we can see the army of Ulster as a cohesive unit, even if the numbers of men given is suspect.

Research carried out on Navan Fort, the ancient site of Emain Macha has revealed an interesting correlation between the date of this site and the linear earthworks of the Dorsey and Black Pig's Dyke. The site of Navan Fort today, consists of an enclosure demarcated by a bank and ditch enclosing an area of some eighteen acres. The fact that the bank is external and the ditch internal is suggestive of some ritual or ceremonial function for the enclosure rather than a defensive one. In the interior is a large mound forty-five metres across, five to six metres high. Excavation of this area between 1963 and 1971 revealed a complex structure, forty metres in diameter, with a concentric arrangement of postholes which formerly held the large number of posts which would have been required in order to support the weight of this structure's roof.[17] The lack of everyday domestic occupation material from the structure suggests that it was not a house or even a palace but was for ritual use. In the centre of the structure was a massive post which has been firmly dated by dendrochronology to 95 or early 94 BC.[18] As stated before the timbers from the southerly section of the Dorsey dated to about the same period and the radiocarbon determinations from the Black Pig's Dyke fall within the same date-range. Thus we may have identified both the heartland of an incipient Ulidian polis or city-state and its frontiers, both bearing the signs of massive constructions which were major socio-economic undertakings.

At some time in the first century BC the entire structure at Emain Macha was filled in with limestone cobbles to form a cairn and the upper parts of the structure set on fire. Finally the cairn was covered over with layers of turf sods and soil. One suggestion is that this was a ritual preservation for eternity of their great temple by the people of Ulster.[19] Certainly the effort which went into the composition and construction of the mound is suggestive of ritual preservation rather than destruction in time of war. Tradition ascribes the end of Emain Macha and its subsequent burning to the advance of the Three Collas in 331 or 332 AD and how after the battle of Achad Leithderg, probably somewhere in County Monaghan, the Kingdom of Ulaidh was pushed back to counties Antrim, Down and the north of Derry, with Emain Macha, their hereditary capital, falling from their sphere of influence forever.[20] Another tradition records that St. Patrick visited Emain Macha and equates this with the decline of the Ulaidh and rise of the Airgialla as being fifth century in date.[21] Both of these stories were preserved in oral tradition and show the anachronistic casting into the past of the political situation at the time that these histories were written down. That the control of the old Ulaidh kingship declined and its power-base shrank is indisputable but whether the Airgialla were invaders or merely an internal confederation growing in stature is difficult to determine.

What is clear from the evidence of pollen analysis is that in the third century AD farming was reduced. This shows as a drop-off in the pollen-record of composites and a reduction in the amount of grass pollen. By 500 AD the appearance of sage, a cereal-linked weed, at such places as Red Bog near Ardee, County Louth suggests the large-scale renewal of settled farming. It has been suggested that the renewal of cereal-production with the consequent decrease in transhumance and the dependence on cattle as a major part of the subsistence economy may have begun as early as 300 AD.[22] If this is the case, then we can postulate that the more settled type of mixed farming practised would have had an effect on the population levels. The introduction of a more balanced diet coupled with a reduction in the possibilities of famine would have led to a healthier population, more resilient to disease and in particular an increase in the number of females liable to reach child-bearing age. This could in turn have led to an increase in births. As the population rose the pressure on the land rose and land-grabbing and wholesale tribal movement may have ensued. With these agricultural and socio-economic developments in mind one can easily envisage the wider implications for the tribal and political boundaries of Ulster. The tradition of St. Patrick at Emain Macha may represent a fictional claim to primacy within the territory of the ascendent Airgialla, but as we shall see at Faughart, County Louth, the 'Christianising' of earlier local power centres was the normal development in this transitional grey area before the dawn of the early historic period.

A few miles to the north-west of Dundalk, a small hill rises to a height of 376 feet – Faughart Hill. Though the hill is not significant when viewed today from the nearby main Belfast–Dublin road, this hilltop encapsulates the development of the north Louth borderland from the early Iron Age through to the seventeenth century AD. Perhaps significantly, it is designated on the Ordnance Survey six inch to the mile map as 'Site of many battles'.[23] The hill strategically commands entry of the passes to the north and has extensive vistas over the plains to the south and the Cooley Peninsula and Dundalk Bay to the west. The site today consists of the remains of a small early medieval church and graveyard with an Anglo-Norman motte nearby visible at ground level, but early historical literature and aerial photography combine to paint a prolonged and complex picture of the history of this site and the adjacent area.

The early literature records an onomastic link between Cuchulainn and the site. The placename is variously interpreted as being derived from various feats performed by him.[24] One version given for the origin of the name is that Cuchulainn cast a piece of split holly which hit Ferbaeth, Cuchulainn's foster-brother, in the neck and passed out through his mouth, hence the place became known as 'Focherd Mhuirthemne' – 'the Good Cast of Muirthemne'. Another tale suggests that because Cuchulainn killed fourteen men from this area in single combat, it became known as 'Focerd' – 'the Good Art' of the killing of fourteen men.[25]

These associations with the reputedly early Iron Age sagas need not be taken too literally, but they do suggest that the site was of some importance even at this early period. This fact is borne out by the archaeological evidence. An aerial photograph shows the small modern graveyard with traces of a large ditch continuing the line of the enclosure from the north-east around to the motte and across the road on the southern side of the site.[26] This black line, the remains of an extensive ditch, is visible from the air because of the susceptibility of crops to underlying features. In this case, the large ditch of the early monastic enclosure contains less-compacted soil than the surrounding ground and hence more moisture which allows crops to grow higher. This pattern of crop-differential is only visible from an elevated position. Beyond the traces of the early monastic enclosure showing on the photograph is a second large enclosing ditch. This is not concentric with the inner enclosure, and is further down the slope of the hill on the relatively steep north side. This enclosing ditch, possibly represents the remains of an earlier hilltop enclosure, probably dating to

Plate 1: *Faughart from the air.*

the early Iron Age. These hilltop enclosures such as Freestone Hill, County Kilkenny;[27] Rathgall, County Wicklow[28] or Dun Ailinne, County Kildare[29] can be seen not only as defensive structures but also as ceremonial and gathering points for the community.

Faughart also has close associations with two early saints, St. Moneena and St. Brigid, being recorded as 'Teampull Brighíde na hAirde Máire' in early records.[30] The use of the term 'teampull' or anglicised 'temple' in association with a townland name or early church site usually denotes a primary monastic foundation.[31] Thus the combination of 'teampull' with Brigíd may denote a very early foundation indeed.

In many instances power centres of kingdoms were handed over to the church,[32] as at Cashel by the Eoganacht kings of Munster, partly in order to gain favour with the church but also to stop these places falling into the hands of rival tribes whilst at the same time legitimising in the eyes of the church their claim to supremacy over an area. It is tempting to see this as having been the case at Faughart. The church at Faughart continued to be of importance through the medieval period, but by the twelfth century it comprised of little more than a simple, plain rectangular church with divided nave and chancel.[33] Though the church building itself was not grandiose, the events which occurred at the site bore out its savage reputation as a killing ground. In 732 AD Aedh Roin, king of Ulaidh was beheaded on the Cloch an Chommaigh, a rough granite boulder beside the church and later on 14 October 1318, Edward Bruce, last pretender to the Irish high kingship, was buried here following his death at the battle of Faughart. The site was thought by the Anglo-Normans of the late twelfth century to be strategically and psychologically significant for they built their motte, or raised earthwork castle, on what would have been the perimeter of the early monastic enclosure.

As we can see therefore the site or sites at Faughart not only shows the transition from a pagan early Iron Age with focal power centres to a changing less nucleated society with the adoption and adaptions of the intrusive element of Christianity, but also underlies the need to regard archaeological sites not as independent entities in time and space. They must be viewed not only as part of a landscape but as part of the society or societies to which they belong and as a changing element during their use by man.

The archaeological and documentary record for the Early Christian period is often much more extensive than that for the early Iron Age. The pattern of the landscape was to change with the introduction of a mixed-farming economy. There is little evidence from the early Iron Age about the settlements and burials of the ordinary people but with the coming of Christianity we see the development of a physical infrastructure linked to the church, which can be related to the historical record. Burials begin to be found in organised cemeteries, mostly associated with churches, and estimates can be made of the size of population and palaeodemographic studies carried out on life expectancy, male/female ratios and disease.[34] The evidence from pollen analysis, discussed above, suggests the introduction of large areas of labour intensive cereal crops throughout the country.[35] This in turn led to a less mobile society which, combined with rapid population increases in the fifth and early sixth centuries, must have led to pressures on land. It is possible to postulate the development, if not introduction, of legal and physical control of boundaries and ultimately frontiers at this period.

Can we find from the archaeological record any evidence to suggest a border as such in the Early Christian period? The historical record confirms that the Early Christian period had all of the components for borders to be drawn up – tribal groupings, with various sub-divisions, of people who felt that they were of a common kinship, allegiances and dynastic feuds coupled with land hunger. These ingredients are revealed in the early historical records which chronicle the decline of some kingdoms at the hands of others.

In the area that we are dealing with, there was the interface of three large tribal groupings. In the north of County Louth are the Uí Connaille Muirthemne, the O'Connells of the Plain, a group who felt themselves to be ethnically linked to the kingdoms of Ulaidh. The Ulidian sub-kingdoms, the principal two of which were the Dál Fiatach in north County Down and south Antrim and the Dál nAraide in mid-Antrim, believed themselves to be ethnically different from the other Irish tribes. They held that they were 'Cruithne' – Picts, more closely related to the kingdoms of eastern Scotland than to the other peoples of Ireland.[36] This ethnic alienation, proclaimed by the Ulaidh themselves, may be regarded as an attempt to foster a separate sense of identity by a beleaguered people who had found the kingdom of Ulster gradually pushed back to east of the River Bann by the Uí Neill from the west. In County Monaghan and mid-Louth the Fir Rios, a sub-kingdom of the Airgialla, which from the sixth century was allied to the Uí Neill were pressing the Uí Connaille Muirthemne from the west and by the eighth and ninth centuries we are to see the rise of the Bregan kingdom to the south of Louth.[37]

For the archaeologist the Early Christian period is characterised by the development of the ringfort, an earthen bank and ditch enclosing a circular area usually some thirty metres in diameter. These sites are the most common field monument found in Ireland, with some 30,000 examples recorded.[38] Using Ordnance Survey six inch sheet twenty one for County Cavan it can be seen that we have fifty-nine ringforts for 15,000 acres (over 6,000 hectares) which is a density of one ringfort to 250 acres (100 hectares).[39] There are a number of factors involved however, which make settlement distribution and density studies more complex than merely counting ringforts. First, ringforts may not have been occupied contemporaneously. It is suggested that in parts of the country ringforts continued to be used until well into the seventeenth century.[40] Secondly, the evidence from aerial photography has drastically altered our perception of the 'norm' in settlement types in the Early Christian period. In County Louth, some 160 ringforts are recorded as being extant, but a further 160 enclosures have been identified from limited aerial coverage by Dr. J. K. S. St. Joseph of Cambridge University in the late 1960s and early 1970s and by the Air Corps in the late 1960s.[41] Most of these sites, logically enough, have been discovered in the high-tillage areas of the mid and south county which has been intensively farmed for many centuries. The evidence from aerial photographs suggests that it is only the smaller enclosures/ringforts which have survived to the present day. Larger enclosures such as Edenakill, near Castle Roche, which measures 82 by 60 metres, and Whitecross, one mile east of Louth village, which has a circular enclosure, 47 metres in diameter enclosed within a large elongated area 138 by 82 metres, have been completely levelled.[42] Many of the other enclosures revealed by aerial photography show traces of annexes and attached field systems. It would seem from the evidence that archaeologists, particularly when dealing with the agriculturally intensive eastern counties, have adopted a 'ringfort mentality' when looking at the surface morphology of Early Christian settlement sites.

An analysis of the 162 sites in County Louth classed as ringforts by their surface morphology gives a breakdown into seven types.[43]

Table 1 Surface morphology of County Louth ringforts

	Type	Percentage	Number
A)	Single bank, no ditch	42.6	69
B)	Single bank and ditch	24.7	40
C)	Double bank with intervening ditch	13.0	21
D)	Bivallate, i.e. double banks and ditches	3.6	6
E)	Trivallate, i.e. triple ramparted	1.4	2
F)	Raised, interior 2 m above external ground-level	11.7	19
G)	Platform, 2.5 m high or more, with or without bank and ditch	3.0	5
	Total	100.0	162

Source: see note 43

If we analyse the distribution by types then it becomes clear that the percentage of type A is biased by the high preservation rate on the upland slopes of the Carlingford Peninsula. Here the ravages of reclamation have not been extensive and the predominant type of enclosure consists of a single earth and stone bank with no fosse, because of the shallowness of soil over the underlying bedrock. This same bedrock precludes the digging of ditches. Other types of ringfort are uniformly spread throughout the remainder of the country. Thus with the infilling of blank areas in the distribution by aerial photographic evidence and a detailed analysis of the physical remains from this form of settlement site, there is a relative cultural homogeneity which defies categorisation into borders, frontiers and heartlands for this type of settlement site.

The ringfort however is not, as the name implies, a purely military or defensive site, the majority being merely the enclosed farmsteads of a particular class of farmer at that period. Excavation of a number of examples, such as White Fort, Drumaroad, County Down have shown that these sites contained the houses and farm-buildings of an extended family.[44] It would be better therefore to view the enclosing ramparts not as defensive but as delimiting the extent of the home farm and as an effective means of keeping out wild animals, thieves and wandering farm animals.

In order to understand the tribal areas of the Early Christian period it is necessary to look at a site-type which is defensive in nature and could, when all factors are taken into consideration, be found throughout the country. In this respect the souterrain fulfills both conditions. Souterrains, an archaeological term derived from the French 'sous' – under, 'terrain' – ground, are artificial underground structures, built either of drystone-walling and capped by large stone lintels or cut into solid bedrock or boulder clay. Some examples built either partly or wholly of wood have been found, but being of a less durable nature these are rarer.[45] Souterrains, or 'uaimha' as they are referred to in early Irish literature are found throughout the country and are often referred to as 'caves' by farmers.

Souterrains are generally regarded as places of refuge in time of trouble – not as permanent or semi-permanent dwellings.[46] The early literary sources do suggest that they could be used for storage also, but always for storage of valuable possessions, such as food during a time of famine.[47] If ringforts were not primarily defensive structures, then the souterrain can be seen as the single most defensive structure of the Early Christian period. The overall distribution of souterrains in the nine counties of Ulster and in County Louth, as shown in map 3, show marked concentrations and marked blank areas. These cannot be fully explained away by the lack of archaeological fieldwork in some areas. Souterrains are usually found during the course of building or agricultural work, when a lintel is dislodged and reveals a long-forgotten cavernous void. Thus the pattern of discovery should be more uniform. Some areas had such a large number of souterrains however that they were used as ready-made quarries for building materials. The Ordnance Survey Memoir for Aghadowey records that many houses in Aghadowey and Macosquin were 'built of stones taken from caves and underground vaults with which the country abounds'.[48] Many souterrains were roofed with broad, flat stones which were convenient for corner stones for building school houses and churches.[49]

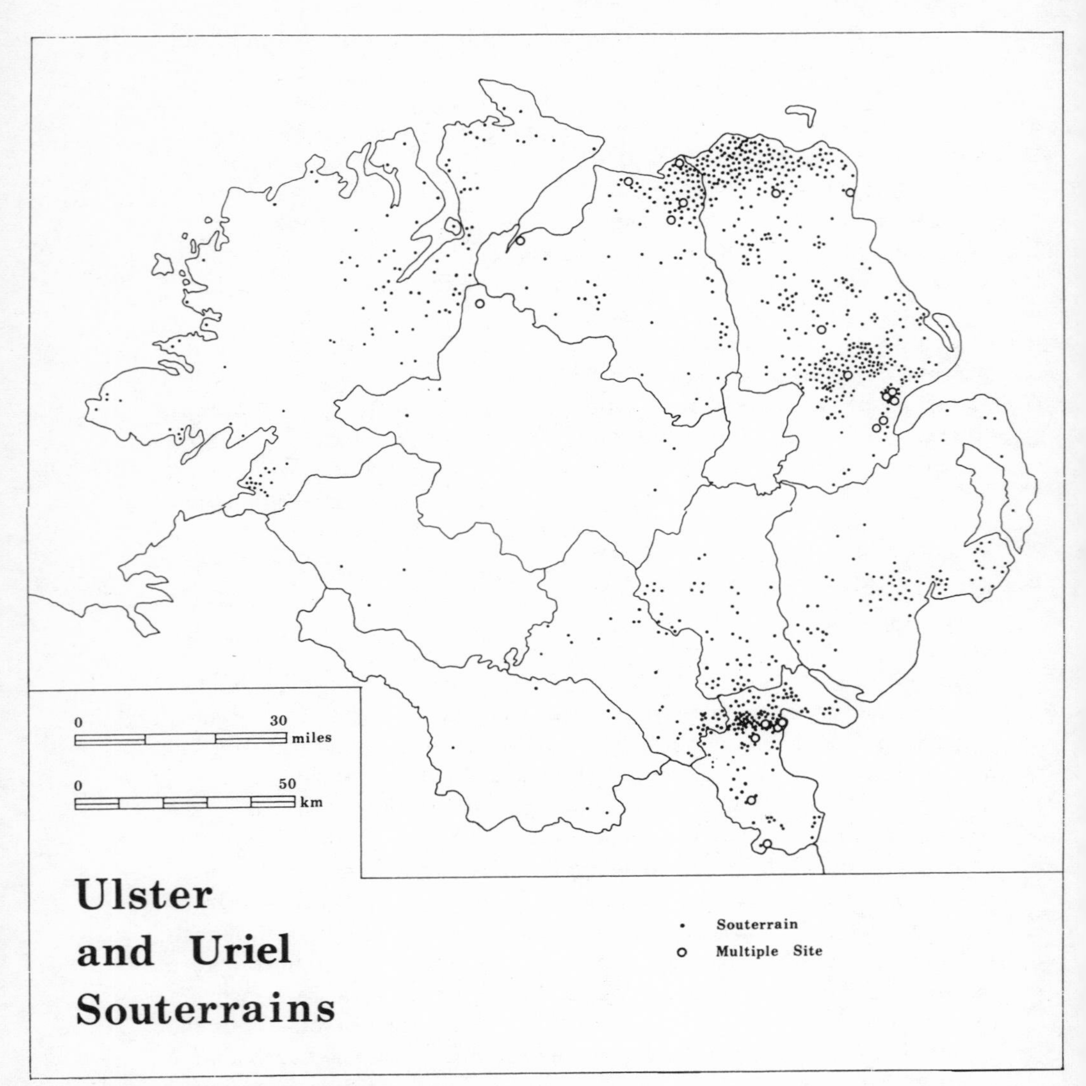

Map 3: *Distribution of souterrains in Ulster and Uriel.*

Souterrains are rare in counties Down, Fermanagh and Monaghan, but Early Christian settlement is dense in these counties, County Monaghan, for example, has 742 ringforts and enclosures.[50] Part of the reason for lack of discovery of souterrains in these counties may be the largely pastoral nature of the farming in these areas, however the reason may also be partly due to the nature of construction of many of the souterrains, as with the wooden-built example from Coolcran, County Fermanagh.[51] There are 151 recorded souterrains in County Louth and a further 139 possible examples, giving the county one of the highest concentrations in Ireland.[52] A close examination of the distribution map shows that the principal concentration is between the Castletown and Fane Rivers – the heartland of the Uí Connaille Muirthemne. There is a particularly high density around Dundalk town, with examples having been found, mainly due to construction work, at Demesne (three sites), Farrandreg, Dowdallshill, Crumlin, Priorsland, Marshes Upper (nine sites) and Ballybarrack (three sites). The density on the slightly rising ground to the west of the sloblands of Marshes North and Bellurgan townlands can be best explained by the estuary of the Castletown River which must have been a favourable site for fishing, trading and raiding.

Souterrains comprise of various combinations of passages, creeps and chambers and can vary from the very large and complex as at Balregan[53] and Donaghmore,[54] County Louth, down to the very simple, as at Cortial,[55] County Louth or Rossdreenagh,[56] County Monaghan. They did however represent a considerable financial outlay for the owner. A reference in the brehon laws notes the cost or fee of 'two cows for uamairecht [cellars?]'.[57] The next sentence continues 'two cows for causeways [toghers] and two cows for caiseals [stone enclosures]'.[58] These structures are engineering feats and it is hardly surprising that the literature refers to craftsmen, known as 'uamairecht', as being employed in their construction.[59]

Souterrains are often found in association with other types of sites such as ecclesiastical remains,[60] mottes,[61] which may be sited on top of pre-existing Early Christian ringforts, and of course ringforts themselves. Only 24.5 per cent of the Louth souterrains can be definitely proven to be within enclosures, though unpublished excavations at a number of sites such as at Ballybarrack by Mr. E. P. Kelly and Marshes Upper III–VII by Ms. Margaret Gowen have shown that what appear to be isolated souterrains were in fact within large enclosures which have since been levelled. Considering that souterrains are an appendage to a settlement site proper, it would appear that between one quarter and a third of the settlement in Early Christian Louth was enclosed. This situation is also true of other areas of the country.[62] Thus we are correct in not using our distribution pattern of ringforts to indicate borders or zones of conflict.

By contrast it is possible to see early frontiers emerging from the distribution map of souterrains. The line of the Six-Mile Water river in mid-Antrim, shows clearly that the souterrains are grouped to the north of the river, on the territory of Dál nAraide and centred around their capital at Rath Mhór. This territorial boundary was to be fossilised in the twelfth century AD as the ecclesiastical boundary between the dioceses of Down and Connor.[63]

In the case of County Louth there is a thinning out of the souterrains in the area to the south of the Fane River, and there are relatively few in the south of the county. We have to look for a more precise date for souterrain construction in order to ask questions as to what was happening in our area from the historical record. Only one souterrain, the timber construction from Coolcran, County Fermanagh has been precisely dated, by the use of dendrochronology, to 822 ± 9 AD.[64] However we do have indirect indicators to date souterrains. For instance, at Ballybarrack, near Dundalk, an ogham-stone has been re-used as a lintel. These commemorative slabs appear to date from the fourth to sixth centuries AD, and for it to have been reused in such a manner it is safe to assume that its significance was no longer valid, therefore a reuse of the stone any time after the eighth century can be postulated.

Another indirect piece of dating evidence is the Scottish–northern Antrim link of the Dál Riata. Though souterrains are very common in the territory of Dál Riata in the north of Antrim, they are virtually non-existent in the area of western Scotland into which this people expanded during the middle of the first millennium AD. This link between the Scottish and Irish Dál Riata was severed following the battle of Magh Rath in 637 AD, this must surely provide us with a date after which souterrains were introduced to Ireland.

The combination of these pieces of evidence suggest a date of the eighth century AD for the earliest constructions of souterrains in Ireland. Evidence from some excavations, such as at Ballybarrack, seem to suggest a deliberate policy of de-lintelling and backfilling of these sites by the Anglo-Normans, in areas within their sphere of influence, by as early as the thirteenth century. The use of souterrains by brigands and raparees made them an intolerable nuisance to the Anglo-Norman and late settlers.

An interesting confirmation of the late first millennium date for souterrains is found in the type of native pottery known as 'souterrain ware'. This pottery derives its name from the fact that it was frequently found by antiquarians in the course of investigating newly-discovered 'caves' during the nineteenth century. 'Souterrain ware' is a coarse, hand-made pottery consisting of a range of flat-bottomed vessels, either plain or sparsely decorated. The distribution of this pottery is from eastern Ulster and County Louth.[65] Although more sherds have been recovered during excavations since that date, these have merely served to fill out the pre-existing distribution. Apart from this area no pottery is known from Ireland at this period, and it can hardly be coincidental that the pottery is only found within the Ulidian sphere of influence. The north of County Louth and the tribe of Uí Connaille Muirthemne were, as stated before, by their own admission ethnically linked to the kingdoms of Ulaid. It would appear also that by the late eighth century, the growing sense of Ulidian independence was being documented in the historical record,[66] and with this 'siege mentality' due to pressure from the Ui Neill to the west and the Airgialla to the south-west, comes signs in the archaeological record of cultural difference and distinctive tribal areas in the form of defensive structures and distinctive pottery only to be found within one ethnic group.

An examination of the south Ulster–north Leinster region over these twelve hundred years shows the development of two different types of frontier. In the early Iron Age a physical barrier in the form of the Dorsey and Black Pig's Dyke with a central focus of power and a society in which ritualised concepts of frontiers were adhered to. It would be interesting to have seen how the history of Ireland would have developed if this had been followed to its conclusion. By the early centuries of the first millennium AD changes in agriculture, the economy and population movements led to the fragmentation of this society and the gradual rise of sub-kingdoms within over-kingdoms but with much more flexible boundaries and systems of allegiances. In the early Iron Age the geographic features of the mountains of south Armagh and the drumlin terrain of Monaghan served as part of a physical barrier between distinctive kingdoms but by the late first millennium north Louth was in allegiance with a territory to the north from which it was all but cut off by the mountains, an allegiance more probably for security rather than long-held ethnic links. The situation was to change yet again with the intrusive imposition of the Anglo-Normans on part of north Louth from the late twelfth century.

Plate 2: *Carlingford Abbey from* Dublin Penny Journal, *3 May 1834.*

4 The Medieval Border

Anglo-Irish and Gaelic Irish in late thirteenth and early fourteenth century Uriel

BRENDAN SMITH

Uriel, an area broadly coterminous with the modern County Louth, had been a border-zone or 'debatable land' long before the arrival of the Anglo-Normans, but it was only after their appearance that part of it became a march. Many of the earliest Anglo-Norman invaders came from Wales and they brought with them to Ireland the terminology and concepts which they had developed there. Thus the parts of Ireland which they penetrated were labelled by them as either *terra pacis*, 'land of peace', *terra guerrae,* 'land of war', or *marchia*, 'march'. The first they had already conquered, the second they had not. The third they believed they were on the point of subjugating. The use of 'peace' and 'war' in this context can be misleading. It was not necessarily the case that the 'land of peace' witnessed less violence and warfare than the 'land of war'. What those who used the terms wished to suggest was that one area enjoyed the 'benefits' of Anglo-Norman rule and the common law, while the other did not. The march, which separated these two areas, was thus a cultural frontier. It divided people who lived under different social, economic and political systems. In Uriel, therefore, the medieval border, the march, has no earlier (or indeed later) equivalents.[1]

The era of territorial expansion by the Anglo-Normans in Uriel was effectively ended by the failure to maintain a permanent military outpost at Clones after 1212. From the 1220's onwards the emphasis shifted to defending the marches. The march as a concept was given a physical shape at Castle Roche in 1236 and Donaghmoyne in 1244 and this defensive line held good for most of the next three centuries.[2] With a secure frontier thus established the problem which faced the Anglo-Irish in Uriel was how to exert sufficient control over the Gaelic-Irish clans in the neighbouring 'land of war' to prevent their own territory being attacked. In the period under review this control could be exerted by either the earls of Ulster, the Dublin government or the local gentry. Let us consider each in turn.

The area we now know as County Louth has ancient links with Ulster and even today, in many respects, seems more akin to that province than to Leinster. In the middle ages the Ulster connection was strong and varied. Carlingford and Dundalk, for instance, were included among 'the ports of Ulster' for accounting purposes at the Dublin exchequer.[3] The bond was even more obvious in the ecclesiastical sphere. The political and religious developments of the twelfth century left the southern boundary of the province of Armagh at the Boyne, permanently removing the southern part of the present County Louth from the ambit of the bishopric of Meath. Subsequent disputes for control of the area in the thirteenth century involved the archbishops of Armagh and their suffragen bishops of Clogher. There was no question of Uriel being transferred to the Leinster province of the archbishops of Dublin. The importance of Uriel to the archbishops of Armagh may be gauged from the fact that for the most part they lived at Termonfeckin, close to the Boyne.[4]

The intrusion of John de Courcy into Ulster in 1176 added a new dimension to its relations with Uriel. In the course of his turbulent career he came into conflict first with the native O'Carroll kings and then with their Anglo-Norman successors.[5] The first earl of Ulster, Hugh de Lacy II, who finally ousted de Courcy in 1204, had already received a grant of half of the de Verdun lands in Uriel by a marriage agreement of about 1195. By 1235 de Lacy had returned most of these to Roesia de Verdun, but the descendants of his wife, Lescelina de Verdun, continued to hold the manor of Carlingford and other lands in the Cooley peninsula until 1305. In that year these lands were acquired by Richard de Burgh, earl of Ulster, who marked the event by founding a Dominican friary at Carlingford under the invocation of St Malachy.[6]

Richard de Burgh, the 'red' earl of Ulster, was the most powerful man in late thirteenth and early fourteenth century Ireland. His power was based on his extensive landed possessions and on his control of the Gaelic-Irish clans of Ulster. Although Uriel was not part of his earldom he was a landowner there. He was also capable of exerting considerable pressure on the Gaelic-Irish who threatened the 'land of peace' in the area, the Mac Mahons and O'Hanlons. His influence in Uriel was demonstrated in 1305 when he requested and was given custody of Neylin, son of Gilpatrick Mac Mahon who was being kept in Dublin castle as a hostage for his father's good behaviour. De Burgh undertook to ensure that Gilpatrick would keep the peace and allow the men of Ardee to cut timber without hindrance. Should Gilpatrick misbehave, Neylin was to be returned to the castle.[7]

De Burgh's power was also to be feared by the Anglo-Irish of Uriel. In 1306 Nicholas de Verdun accused John del Aunee of having defamed him before the earl. As a result of this defamation, Nicholas claimed, 'the earl was moved beyond measure against Nicholas and had ill-will against him to his damage of £200'.[8] Another incident of the same year demonstrated that Uriel was well within the reach of the earl's vengeance. A valet of de Burgh's was robbed at Greencastle by a thief who fled south. The earl's men caught up with him near Drogheda and murdered him. De Burgh then proceeded to recover the stolen money in court.[9]

The early fourteenth century saw the earl of Ulster expand his landed interests in Uriel. In 1305, as mentioned above, he acquired land in the Cooley peninsula. In 1311 he was given a commission for the former Templar manor of Kilsaran and in 1315 he was made guardian of the royal manor of Ardee.[10] His growing influence in the area was shown in the aftermath of the de Verdun rebellion of 1312 when he obtained a partial pardon for a former sheriff of Uriel, Thomas de Stanley and his son Adam, both of whom had rebelled.[11]

The years immediately prior to the Bruce invasion of 1315 are generally regarded as marking the zenith of Anglo-Irish power in Ulster.[12] De Burgh simultaneously expanded his influence westward into the Inishowen peninsula in Donegal and southward into Uriel. Uriel, however, was not part of the earldom and had its own political and social dynamics which made it difficult for outsiders to control. De Burgh was unable to stop raids on the 'land of peace' in 1306 and 1310 and he was also powerless in 1297 when 'Cu Uladh O hAnluain, king of the Oirrthir and his brother and Aenghus Mac Mathgamna and many of the chiefs of his people were killed by the foreigners of Dun Dealgan, in returning to their houses from the earl'.[13]

Whatever de Burgh's ambitions in Uriel may have been, they were irrevocably dashed by the arrival of the Scots under Bruce in 1315, yet another casualty of that cataclysm which left the earl for a time 'a wanderer up and down Ireland . . . with no power or lordship'.[14]

De Burgh's pre-eminence in the northern part of Ireland influenced the attitude of the Dublin government towards Uriel. In 1600 the English observer John Dimmock wrote of County Louth that 'this county hath the most dangerous borderers and neighbours of any county'.[15] Three hundred years earlier the official perception was somewhat different. Uriel occupied a relatively low position on the government's list of military priorities, a list headed by the Leinster mountains and followed by the marches of Laois and Offaly.[16] The chief governor rarely visited Uriel. In the thirty-five years between 1295 and 1350 he came only fifteen times and strayed further than Drogheda on only two occasions, journeying to Ardee in 1303 and 1306. In comparison, Cashel received the chief governor nine times in the eleven years between 1308 and 1318.[17]

The situation in Uriel was seen as relatively secure. Most disturbances could be dealt with by the local gentry and the earl of Ulster. Generally, the government intervened only to fill the role vacated by one or other of these powers. In 1282 and again in 1334, for instance, the chief of the O'Hanlons was brought to Dublin to parley at the government's expense. On both occasions the earldom of Ulster was either vacant or the earl was absent.[18]

Royal armies were rarely seen in late thirteenth and early fourteenth century Uriel. There were expeditions in 1252, 1273-6, 1291, 1299, 1312 and during the Bruce invasion of 1315–8, but this hardly compares with the virtually annual campaigns of the chief governor and his forces in the Leinster mountains from the 1270s onwards.[19] When they did venture into Uriel, royal armies often behaved badly and were greeted with hostility by the local population. In 1252, for instance, The Galls of Ireland invaded Ulster in great force, when strife arose between the Meath and Munster contingents, and some of those of Munster were killed, at Dundalk.[20]

In 1301 a force on its way to Scotland, led by Peter de Bermingham, was attacked in Drogheda and several soldiers were killed.[21] Again in 1312 during the de Verdun rebellion, the community of the county of Uriel persuaded the Justiciar, John Wogan, not to lead a royal army into the county, arguing 'that by the coming of so great an army the faithful men of those parts would suffer greater evils than before'.[22] The behaviour of the government's forces in Uriel during the Bruce invasion fully justified the observation of the annalist that

> excepting homicides ... deeds no less evil were done by an army drawn from different parts of Ireland to do battle with them [the Scots] in the districts through which the units passed.[23]

The crown was not a major landowner in Uriel. In the original grants of the 1180s it had retained for itself half of the barony of Louth but in the 1250s Lord Edward granted this to his cousin, Geoffrey de Luzignan. The French wars of the 1290s, however, led to the confiscation of this property and it remained in the king's hands for several years before being delivered to Geoffrey's nephew and heir, Drew de Merlow.[24] In 1302 the crown became responsible for another large portion of Uriel when Ralph Pipard transferred his Irish lands to the king in return for land of equal value in England.[25] In Uriel this consisted of the barony of Ardee and land in east Monaghan. Thus, the early fourteenth century saw the crown acquire control of the parts of the 'land of peace' in Uriel most liable to attack from the neighbouring march. This in turn necessitated an unprecedented degree of government involvement in the affairs of the county.

As far as possible, the government attempted to exercise its newfound responsibilities in Uriel through the local gentry. In 1308, for instance, Milo de Verdun was given a commission to parley with the Gaelic-Irish of Meath and Uriel.[26] The government was also fortunate in being able to call on the services of Richard d'Exeter, who was not only one of the leading men in Uriel, but also one of the highest officials in the Dublin administration. D'Exeter's father, also Richard, had twice been deputy chief governor briefly in the 1270s and was the first justice of the justiciar's court. He also acquired large grants of land in Connacht.[27] Richard d'Exeter junior was a lawyer by profession and after serving as a justice itinerant in the 1290s was made a chief justice of the bench in 1302.[28] He also served as constable of

Roscommon castle and as collector of the fifteenth in Uriel.[29] His lands in Uriel centred on the manor of Darver, but also included land in Philipston Nugent and Stackallen.[30] He was connected by marriage to the de Verduns and the de Lacys. His links with the latter family led to charges being levelled against him in the 1320s of treason during the Bruce invasion, but he survived these and finally died *c.*1330.[31]

The Dublin government made use of Richard d'Exeter's services on three occasions between 1306 and 1310. Sometime before 10 January 1306, Doneghuth O'Reilly stole cattle from Nicholas de Netterville's manor of Dowth and pastured them on the lands of Stephen d'Exeter. De Netterville sued against O'Reilly in the county court and succeeded in having him outlawed because he did not appear to answer the charges. Execution of the outlawry, however, was suspended by the justiciar 'for the good of the peace' after friends interceded on Doneghuth's behalf, testifying that he 'was a faithful man of Theobald de Verdun'. A commission to examine the case was then made for Richard d'Exeter and Thomas de Snyterby, another justice of the bench who also held land in Uriel. They devised an agreement whereby Doneghuth was to compensate Nicholas de Netterville with Gilpatrick Mac Mahon providing his pledges. Doneghuth, however, subsequently defaulted and de Netterville sent his son Luke with an armed band to recover the cattle. Their efforts were resisted by a force led by Stephen d'Exeter, possibly a relative of Richard's. A fight ensued and several footmen and Luke de Netterville were wounded. In 1308 the case was finally settled in favour of the de Nettervilles.[32]

Later in 1306 d'Exeter's arbitration was again required. He was given a commission 'to treat with Brian Mac Mahon for reformation of the peace'. He succeeded in having Mac Mahon pay a fine of sixty cows in return for the king's peace. The Mac Mahons, along with 'the English of those marches' also agreed to a mutual return of goods taken by either side since the previous July. D'Exeter himself stood as pledge for Brian's compliance with these terms and was later held accountable for their fulfillment.[33]

In 1310 the government called on d'Exeter's services for the third time.

> Because Maghoun Mac Maghon, an Irishman of the said county [Uriel] and all the Irishmen of his sept and Maghoun Mc Keygh O'Reilly of County Meath and all the Irishmen of his sept openly put themselves at war against the king on account of divers dissensions between the Irish and English of their marches now arisen anew, by which it was feared great damage might easily come if such dissensions should not somehow be allayed, Richard d'Exeter, one of the justices of the bench, was commanded to treat and parley with the said Irish to see if he could find a reasonable measure to make amends as well to the king as to others of the marches of said Irish for the damage done by the said Irish.

The 'reasonable measure' found by d'Exeter was to have Mac Mahon pay a fine of £10 for the king's peace. A number of natives of the marches 'as well English as Irish' were to be chosen to decide complaints against the Mac Mahons 'provided that the Englishmen satisfied them in turn'.[34] This rather sophisticated settlement has parallels in medieval Wales where border disputes were defused in 'march days' without recourse to violence.[35] The good will to make d'Exeter's agreement work, however, did not exist in Uriel. Soon after Mac Mahon came into the king's peace one of his men was murdered in Ardee by some of its inhabitants, 'by which the whole peace of those marches is disturbed to the common ill of the Englishmen of those parts'. The Ardee men were subsequently acquitted when it was adjudged that the dead man had been a common robber.[36]

These three incidents show the variety of problems which faced the Dublin government in Uriel. It often found it easier, for instance, to impose its will on the Gaelic-Irish than on the Anglo-Irish communities it was supposed to be defending. Another difficulty was caused by the fragmented nature of authority within the most important Gaelic-Irish clan of the area, the Mac Mahons. Within four years Richard d'Exeter had to deal not only with Brian Mac Mahon, king of Uriel, but also Gilpatrick and Mahon Mac Mahon. This situation arose because of what Dr Simms described as 'a well developed system of appenage whereby the ruling Mac Mahon allowed his kinsmen to hold considerable sections of such territory as vassal chiefs under his dominion'.[37] An agreement between the Mac Mahons and Nicholas Mac Maol Iosa, archbishop of Armagh, in 1296 shows the system in operation. Letters notifying the agreement were sent out under the name not only of Brian Mac Mahon, king of Uriel, but also under those of Ralph his brother, lord of Dartry, Mahon Mac Mahon, chief of Molfhinn, Patrick (Gilpatrick) Mac Mahon, of Farney and several other sub-chiefs of the Mac Mahons.[38] Brian Mac Mahon, who ruled from 1283 to 1311, often saw his authority ignored by his family. The Angus Mac Mahon murdered in Dundalk in 1297, for instance, had some years previously been granted the 'kingship' of the barony of Cremorne by Ralph Pipard and had acknowledged the overlordship of Eachmharcach O'Hanlon.[39] This multiplicity of Mac Mahon rulers made it difficult for the government to deal with one individual, but it also enabled it to exploit the internal divisions of the lordship. In 1302, for instance, Brian Mac Mahon received 40*s.* from the government to defend Castle Frank 'against the Irish'.[40]

Another method employed by the Dublin government to control the Mac Mahons was the taking of hostages. In 1304 Gilpatrick Mac Mahon was taken to Drogheda castle and forced to surrender his son as surety that he would pay rent owed to the crown since 1302 and that he would guard the king's workmen of Ardee.[41] Presumably this hostage was the Neylin son of Gilpatrick Mac Mahon entrusted to the care of Richard de Burgh in 1305.[42] In 1306 the same Gilpatrick agreed to give pledges for the behaviour of Doneghuth O'Reilly 'except that the body of Gilpatrick be not taken'.[43] In January 1315, Achy Mac Mahon left his wife and three of his sons as hostages in Dublin castle to ensure his payment of thirty cows to the king and also as an incentive to capture 'or at least kill' a notorious robber in his area, Philip O Scethel.[44] Two years later it was Achy himself who, as *obsidem nostrum*, was led by an armed posse from Castle Roche to Dublin castle.[45]

Uriel represented an unsought and unwelcome additional commitment for the Dublin government in the early fourteenth century. The crown's acquisition of the Pipard lands in 1302 coincided with an upsurge in the level of conflict between Anglo-Irish and Gaelic-Irish in the Ardee area. The government responded wisely (and economically) by acting through important men with local connections such as Richard d'Exeter. The policy of hostage-taking was probably effective in limiting the raids of at least some of the Mac Mahons, although its impact may have been reduced by the fragmented political organisation of that clan. The greatest vindication of its efforts lies in the fact that the Mac Mahons took no part in the Bruce invasion.

Relations with the Gaelic-Irish of the 'land of war' in Uriel were, in general, of peripheral concern to the earldom of Ulster and the Dublin government. To the Anglo-Irish who inhabited the neighbouring 'land of peace' however they were of primary importance. Not surprisingly these relations were extremely complicated and often appear contradictory. 'It is possible, nevertheless, to find in them a general consistency if the following points are borne in mind. First, the O'Hanlons and Mac Mahons were prepared to operate within the feudal structure used by the Anglo-Irish to the extent to which this benefited themselves or to which the Anglo-Irish could force them to do so. Second, the inferior position which the Gaelic-Irish occupied in this feudal structure *viz-a-viz* the Anglo-Irish was not necessarily reflected in the balance of power in the area. In other words the ideal represented by these feudal arrangements was often at variance with reality. Finally, the tone of relations between the two cultures in Uriel was one of deep hostility which transcended the many links which joined them.

The original land grants in Uriel in the 1180's to Bertram de Verdun and Gilbert Pipard included areas deep in Monaghan and south Armagh thus in theory making the Gaelic-Irish of these parts tenants of Anglo-Irish lords. The Mac Mahons and O'Hanlons probably owed the de Verduns rent from at least the middle of the thirteenth century.[46] That the Mac Mahons also owed rent to the Pipards is suggested by Gilpatrick Mac Mahon's promise to the king in 1304 to pay rent owed since Pipard transferred his land to the crown in 1302.[47] These rents were probably paid only when sufficient force existed to collect them. Part of the agreement reached by Richard d'Exeter with Brian Mac Mahon in 1306 stated that the de Verduns might keep 'the goods which they took from the Irish for rent due to them or that the Irish may pay their rent and have restitution'.[48]

The Gaelic-Irish of the 'land of war' used systems of lordship and land-ownership far removed from the feudal practices of the Anglo-Irish.[49] This did not prevent the Gaelic-Irish, however, from entering into arrangements of a feudal nature. Sometime between 1284 and 1297, for instance,

Ralph Pipard granted Angus Mac Mahon the kingship of Cremorne free of rent and certain other lands at their usual rent. Dr Simms has discussed elsewhere the many problems raised by this interesting and difficult document but what is significant for Uriel is the divergence the agreement reveals between theory and practice in relations between the two cultures. On one level the document seems to demonstrate the full integration of Mac Mahon into feudal practice, all be it in a subservient position dictated by his race. It was Mac Mahon who received the grant from his Pipard lord. In return he was obliged to guard Ralph's men and surrender hostages as guarantee of his behaviour. Quite a different picture emerges, however, on going beyond the form of the document to its context.[50]

Ralph Pipard had little time for his Irish possessions. He visited the country on only six occasions between 1265 and 1302. In the latter year he finally divested himself completely of his Irish interests by transferring them to the crown in return for land of equal value in England. By the time he granted Cremorne to Mac Mahon it was no longer under his control. The indenture merely formalised this situation. Thus Mac Mahon acknowledged Pipard as his lord while undermining the basis of that lordship, the control of land.[51]

Form and fact appear even further divorced in a document in the Dowdall collection dated 1 May 1335 in which Donal O'Hanlon, king of Erthir, granted the tenements of Drumgaha and Doolargy to Walter Dowdall senior and Geoffrey, son of Elias.[52] The grant was strictly feudal in its arrangement, even down to the affixing by O'Hanlon of his seal at the bottom of the document. It is this adherence to feudal practice which makes the grant all the more extraordinary. It was as *rex Erthir* that O'Hanlon made his grant to Walter and Geoffrey, yet O'Hanlon owed rent to the de Verduns and their successors who were in turn lords of the Anglo-Irish grantees. However, these superior lords are nowhere mentioned in this agreement. In typical feudal fashion O'Hanlon also promised to warrant Walter and Geoffrey against all men, but this would have been impossible if, as seems likely, O'Hanlon did not have the use of the common law.

The background to this grant was Donal O'Hanlon's desire to improve relations with the Anglo-Irish of Dundalk.[53] That he was in a position to grant lands so deep within the 'land of peace' demonstrates how far the position of the Anglo-Irish had been eroded. O'Hanlon made the grant in Dundalk and had it witnessed by some of the leading men of the town, suggesting that both sides wished to see its terms fulfilled. In order to achieve a settlement, both sides were willing to adhere strictly to feudal forms while ignoring the inconvenient theories these implied.

Another Anglo-Irish practice shared by the Anglo-Irish and the Gaelic-Irish was the naming of pledges to guarantee agreements. In 1310, for instance, Magnus and Nicholas O'Carrol and Gilletyrny Mac Mahon stood as pledges for the payment by Mahon Mac Mahon of £10 to the crown in return for the king's peace.[54] More significantly, Anglo-Irishmen of Uriel were, on occasion, prepared to act as pledges for the Gaelic-Irish. In 1306 Richard d'Exeter stood as pledge for Brian Mac Mahon and in the same year Nicholas de Verdun performed a similar function for a son of Cu Uladh O'Hanlon.[55] Baldewyn le Fleming acted as surety for Gilpatrick Mac Mahon in 1304 and 1306 and had to pay a large sum when Gilpatrick defaulted on the latter occasion.[56] To stand as pledge for a man was a responsibility not undertaken lightly and it might be argued that its frequency in Uriel implied the existence of a degree of trust between some of the leading men of the two cultures. That the Gaelic-Irish often defaulted on their payments, leaving their Anglo-Irish pledges to pay instead, however, suggests that the latter took the practice more seriously than the former and that theory and reality were again at odds.

The Anglo-Irish also kept certain of the Gaelic-Irish under their avowry. In 1306 Doneghuth O'Reilly was described as 'a faithful man of Theobald de Verdun' as was Gilpatrick Mac Mahon.[57] In 1313 Molsathlyn O'Reilly was said to be 'a *hibernicus* of Theobald de Verdun'.[58] Normally, *hibernicus* should be translated as 'betagh', but O'Reilly enjoyed a higher status than the unfree manorial labourers who comprised the betagh class. Ironically, it was these Gaelic-Irish who were in the avowry of Anglo-Irish lords who in Uriel often caused warfare among the Anglo-Irish.[59]

The Anglo-Irish of Uriel sought to involve the Gaelic-Irish in feudal arrangements which *per se* emphasised the theoretical superiority of the former over the latter. The Gaelic-Irish acquiesced in this while steadily eroding the basis of Anglo-Irish power, control of land. That the Anglo-Irish realised the limitations of their strategy was shown by their increasing recourse to extra-legal methods of control and more particularly to assassination. In 1297 Cu Uladh O'Hanlon and Angus Mac Mahon were murdered by the men of Dundalk.[60] In 1321 'Niall O'Hanlon, lord of Orior, was treacherously slain by the English of Dundalk', shortly after blinding his predecessor Manus, probably with Anglo-Irish connivance.[61] In 1331 Murrough Mac Mahon was slain 'by John Mac Mahon and the English of Machaire Oirghiall'.[62] Such dissensions among the Gaelic-Irish made it easier for the Anglo-Irish to retain some influence in their affairs.

It would be a mistake to underestimate the success of the settlers in containing the threat from the 'land of war'. The de Verdun rebellion of 1312 and the Bruce invasion of 1315–8 presented the Gaelic-Irish with opportunities to wreak havoc in the 'land of peace' which were not taken. Neither the O'Hanlons nor the Mac Mahons created any disturbance in 1312 and during the Scottish invasion the Mac Mahons were quiescent while the O'Hanlons could make little headway against the men of Dundalk.[63]

Relations between the two cultures in early fourteenth century Uriel reached a virulence scarcely matched elsewhere in the lordship. No attempts to maintain the peace could restrain the deep mutual antipathy which existed at the time. This hostility was to be found at different levels of society. The de Verduns and O'Hanlons, for instance, pursued a bitter feud in these years, possibly as a consequence of the murder of Cu Uladh O'Hanlon in Dundalk in 1297. In 1316, one year after the town had been burnt by the Scots, Manus O'Hanlon attacked Dundalk but was repulsed. He did succeed, however, in killing Robert de Verdun, brother of Theobald II, Nicholas and Milo and leader of the rebellion of 1312.[64] The de Verduns were in a position to exact revenge. In October 1316 the justiciar, Edmund Butler, was ordered to ascertain[65]

> whether the release of Mora, wife of O'Hanlon, from prison in the town of Drogheda, where she was placed by Nicholas de Verdun, by whose men she was captured in war would be injurious to the king or to the disturbance of the peace and if he finds that she can be released safely to deliver her to Nicholas to make his profit of her and if not to make *gratium* (?compensation) with Nicholas for what pertains to him for her capture.

In the following year the prior of St Leonard's of Dundalk lost two horses to the O'Hanlons while collecting rents from the de Verdun lands around Dundalk. Had Mora O'Hanlon not been in custody he might have lost a great deal more.[66]

The feud continued after the Bruce invasion. In 1321 Manus O'Hanlon was blinded by his kinsman, Niall, with Anglo-Irish support and in the same year Niall himself was slain 'by the English of Dundalk'.[67] The 1330's saw an improvement in relations, apparently at the instigation of Donal O'Hanlon. In 1333 he went to Dublin for discussions with the government and two years later granted land near Dundalk to Walter Dowdall and Geoffrey, son of Elias.[68] This *rapprochement* with the Anglo-Irish was formalised by a peace agreement, drawn up at Kilsarin in 1337, between Donal and the leading men of Anglo-Irish Uriel. This ended the period of O'Hanlon raids on the 'land of peace'.[69]

Below this level of 'aristocratic' antipathy there existed the hostility of the common folk of Anglo-Irish Uriel to the Gaelic-Irish of the 'land of war'. The authorities at times found this impossible to control. The earl of Ulster lost two allies in 1297 when O'Hanlon and Mac Mahon were murdered by the men of Dundalk. The murder by the men of Ardee of a supporter of Mac Mahon in 1311 wrecked an agreement fashioned by Richard d'Exeter 'to the common ill of the Englishmen of those parts'.[70] In the same year Robertston, nearby in County Meath, was burnt by Mathew O'Reilly in revenge for a cattle raid instigated by Henry de Cruys.[71]

This hostility to the Gaelic-Irish resulted from the frequent attacks from the 'land of war' which often involved not only cattle raiding but also murder. In 1278 Walter O'Carrol, a sub-chief of the Mac Mahons, 'wretchedly killed' Robert Gernon and in the same year Nicholas Crossath and Robert Cachepol were murdered by Rory O'Hadhlan while attempting to raise hue and cry after William Wyot had been robbed of sixty cows.[72] In 1306 Maoliosa O'Reilly came into the 'land of peace' specifically 'to slay Peter le Petit and other faithful Englishmen'.[73]

In many instances it was not the leading Gaelic-Irish clans who were responsible for such raids but the criminal bands who lived on their lands and over whom they had little control. The Mac Mahons might be held responsible for the activities of 'notorious felons' such as Philip O'Scethel and Conlyth Mac Neill, but in reality such men could do much as they pleased. Mac Neill seems to have acknowledged the lordship of Mac Mahon only when it suited him. His felonious activities were also facilitated by the behaviour of the Anglo-Irish. In 1311 Walter Gigg was hanged for leading him to steal in Ardee but shortly before this Mac Neill had been captured by the sheriff of Uriel. He escaped because the constable of Drogheda castle would not accept him as a prisoner and so had to be kept in Ardee. Internal dissensions were not peculiar to the Gaelic-Irish.[74]

When it was not used in reference to the betagh class, the term *hibernicus*, 'Irishman', was usually applied in the context of destruction. The lands of the late Benedict Pipard in Pipardstown could not be extended in 1316 'because they have been totally burned by the Irish'.[75] In 1317 the barony of Louth was said to be worth nothing 'because it is totally destroyed by the Scots and Irish'.[76] In 1332 Castle Roche was described as having no buildings within it *quia castrum cumbustum per Hibernicos*.[77] Paranoia seems to have crept into Anglo-Irish attitudes during the Bruce invasion with Milo de Verdun reporting rumours to the king that the Scots intended to conquer the country 'with the help of the Irish of Ireland'.[78] It was this deep distrust and hostility which the archbishop of Armagh, Richard Fitz Ralph, himself a Dundalk man, condemned so strongly in the 1340s.[79]

What impact did such attitudes have on Anglo-Irish society in Uriel? Ironically, warfare did a great deal to bring the two cultures closer together. March warfare, which consisted in large part of cattle-raiding, encouraged techniques which both sides employed. Raiding parties went 'well-armed and on equipped horses' to harry the lands of their victims.[80] Nor were these raiding parties always organised along racial lines. In 1314, for instance, Mahon Mac Mahon and several members of the de Netterville family were ordered to appear before the justiciar to answer certain charges which apparently arose from a joint raid they had conducted.[81] In official terminology, no distinction was drawn between the *sequela*, 'following', of the Gaelic-Irish felon and that of his Anglo-Irish, counterpart, suggesting that both in composition and in purpose they were identical. In 1278 Aulef Mac Finan *cum sequela sua* robbed the town of Ays, while in 1295 Peter le Petit and other Uriel men 'with their following' stole sheep from Castleknock on their way to fight the Gaelic-Irish of the Leinster mountains.[82] Again, in 1306, Brian Mac Mahon and *sequela sua* were admitted to the king's peace while in 1312 Robert de Verdun and his *sequela*, 'both English and Irish', rebelled against the king.[83] Finally, warfare also gave rise to customs such as avowry, hostage-taking and pledging, all of which acted as bonds between the two cultures.

In certain fundamental ways, however, the Anglo-Irish of Uriel were less willing than their counterparts elsewhere in the lordship to compromise with the culture which faced them. In their attitudes to the Gaelic-Irish they were extremely conservative, not to say reactionary. That variety of compromises with and adaptations to native practices which characterised the Anglo-Irish lordship from the late thirteenth century onwards and which a disapproving government labelled as 'degeneracy' was less obvious in Uriel than in any other area which contained a march.[84] There is little evidence, for instance, of intermarriage among the aristocracies of the two cultures. On the other hand, the names Ralph Mac Mahon and Mahon Cruys may suggest that gossipred was, on occasion, used to link certain families together.[85] In the sphere of family organisation, extended kin groups did not flourish. By the early fourteenth century *cognomines*, 'surnames' or *nationes* 'nations' had become common among the Anglo-Irish. These were extended families under their own 'captains', which often operated as fighting units. The Harolds and Lawlesses of south Dublin and Roches, Cauntetons and Christophers of Cork and Waterford are just some examples of this phenomenon.[86]

In Uriel there are virtually no examples of Anglo-Irish *cognomines*. In 1319 John de Cusak, sheriff of Uriel in 1316 and 1329, stated that he had had with him 'the best of his own surname and lineage' at Faughart when Edward Bruce was killed, but other examples of a de Cusak 'lineage' are lacking.[87] The low level of kin awareness in Uriel was well demonstrated by Roger Gernon in 1299 when he admitted to being unaware of the existence of three other Roger Gernons in the country at the time.[88] Following the de Verdun rebellion of 1312, 104 men were charged with involvement. The family most strongly represented was that of Teling of Sidan in County Meath with five members involved. No Uriel family, including the de Verduns themselves, had more than three members indicted.[89] If we compare this with the disturbances between the Roches and Cauntetons in Waterford in 1311, when over fifty Roches were involved, we see clearly that extended families were relatively unimportant in Anglo-Irish Uriel.[90] Ten members of the de Bermingham family were indeed murdered at Braganstown, but this apparent exception to the rule only serves to confirm it. The de Berminghams were from the marches of Offaly, not Uriel. Their assailants, who represented the cream of Uriel society, did not come in large family groupings to murder them in 1329.[91] Why Uriel should eschew extended family organisation is unclear. Illegitimacy, on which the system was based, was apparently not as common in Uriel as in some other parts of the lordship. The answer perhaps lies in the fact that Anglo-Irish Uriel was more densely colonised than other regions where *cognomines* flourished and that this feeling of strength in numbers made adaptation of the family unit less crucial to survival.

Another manifestation of 'degeneracy' which Anglo-Irish Uriel did not display was the keeping by its leading men of kernes. These were the lightly armed mercenary troops who formed the core of both Gaelic and Anglo-Irish armed forces throughout Ireland. They were deeply unpopular with the common folk because of the system of billeting by which they were maintained. Theobald de Verdun allowed his *hibernici* such as Doneghuth O'Reilly to pasture their cows on his lands, but these *hibernici* were neither betaghs nor kernes. The earliest use of the term 'kerne' traced in Uriel was in 1329 when twenty-nine of 'the satellites of the lord, John de Bermingham, earl of Louth, who are called kernes' were murdered by the inhabitants of Ardee in the prelude to the Braganstown massacre. It is very likely that de Bermingham imported these kernes from Offaly when he was made earl of Louth in 1319.[92]

The leading men of Uriel also avoided 'degeneracy' by not patronising the Gaelic learned classes. Uriel as a whole, indeed, seems to have been something of a cultural backwater at this time, with only a handful of praise poems surviving in honour of the Mac Mahons and O'Hanlons and none at all addressed to the Anglo-Irish gentry of the area. The single example of Anglo-Irish patronage of Gaelic learning is again provided by John de Bermingham. He was being entertained at Braganstown by the best harpist of his day, Mulroney Mac Carrol, when his angry and murderous tenants arrived at the gates.[93]

The Braganstown massacre of 1329 provides a fitting conclusion to this essay, illuminating as it does some of the important themes in the nature of relations between the two cultures in this period of Uriel's history. The local resentment which in part led to de Bermingham's murder, was fuelled by what the Anglo-Irish of Uriel saw as his willingness to compromise with Gaelic-Irish practices. His use of kernes and his patronage of the Gaelic learned classes were habits acquired in the marches of Offaly. What was acceptable there was intolerable in Uriel.[94] What gave Uriel its special character at this time was not the fact that it contained within it a march or border, as these were to be found in many other parts of Ireland. Nor was it because its Anglo-Irish inhabitants were self-reliant and hostile to outsiders, be they Gaelic-Irish chiefs, Dublin government officials or 'blow in' Anglo-Irish magnates, although it may have exhibited these characteristics more strongly than other areas of the lordship. Finally, what made medieval Uriel so remarkable and so unusual was the fact that the march strengthened rather than lessened its resistance to compromise.

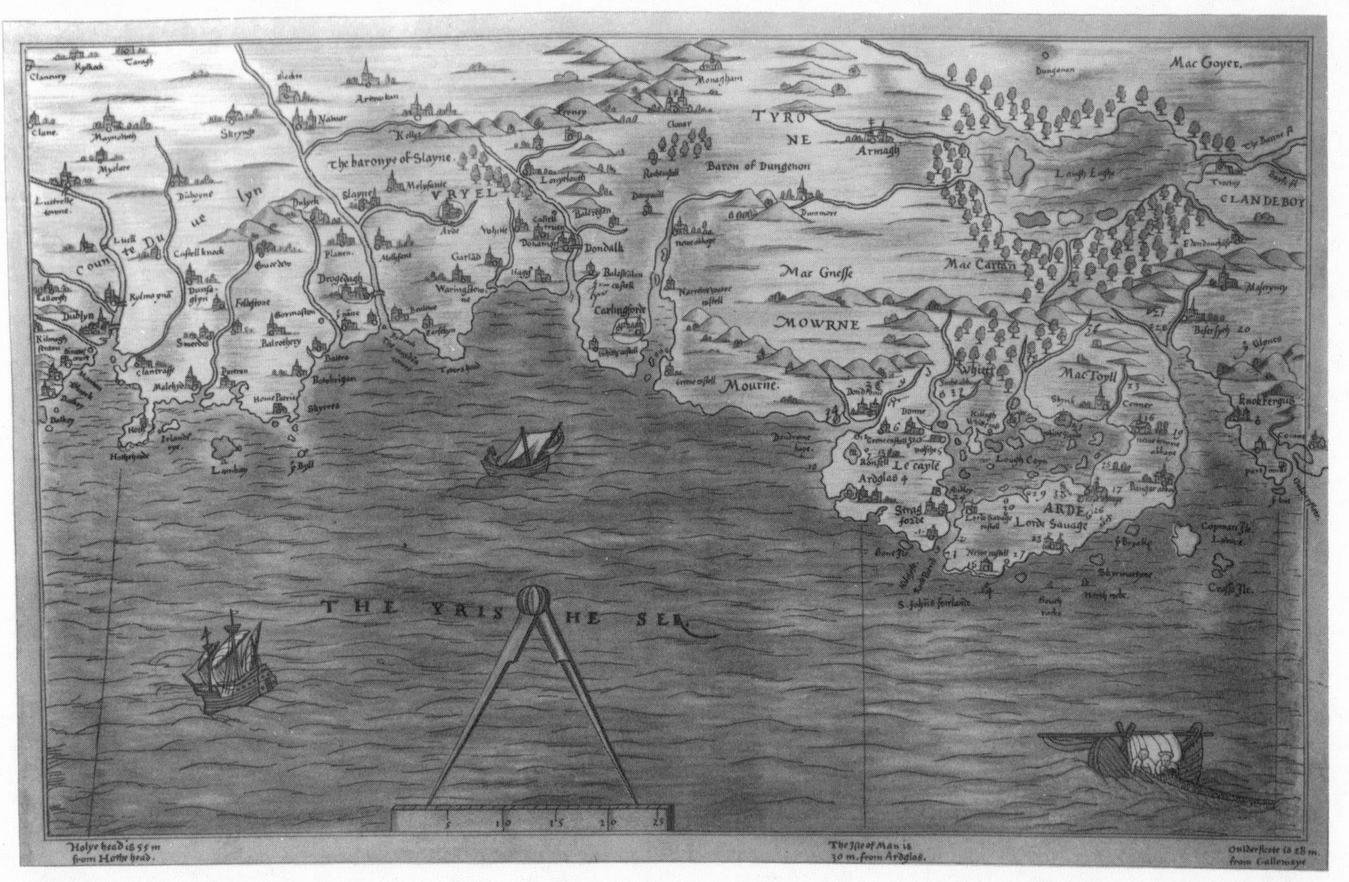

Map 1: *Late sixteenth century map of the north-east coast of Ireland from* Facsimiles of national manuscripts of Ireland, part IV (London, 1882), compiled by J. T. Gilbert.

5 The March of South-East Ulster in the Fifteenth and Sixteenth Centuries

A Period of Change

HAROLD O'SULLIVAN

Whether Ireland in the early part of the fifteenth century could have been described as a nation, as that word is understood today, is debatable.[1] What is certain however is that even if it could have been so described, it lacked political focus and direction. Responsibility for this can be traced to the failure of the twelfth century plan for Ireland contained in the papal bull Laudabiliter and which envisaged the king of England, Henry II, entering 'the island of Ireland in order to subject its people to law and to root out from them the weeds of vice'.[2] The high hopes entertained by the pope in this grant of the lordship of Ireland to Henry II were never to be realised largely because, apart from few exceptions, his successors rarely became involved in Irish affairs. Instead of providing a united body politic with a common system of government and order, the country evolved into a patchwork of semi-autonomous Irish and Anglo-Norman lordships, acknowledging a nominal fealty to the king, as lord of Ireland, but who were left to shift for themselves, as a succession of English kings spent their time either in continental wars or in internecine conflict.[3] By the end of the fifteenth century the lord's writ barely ran outside the capital city and surrounding areas of Dublin, described as the loyal shires of the English Pale. At the northern end of the Pale, the county of Louth, or English Uriel, stretched as a finger of land into south-east Ulster, constituting a march or divide between that county and the native Irish of the north.

The conditions which prevailed in the march at this period were not fundamentally different from that found in those other marches, the English borders with Scotland and Wales, where two sets of social, economic and political orders met. For most of the fifteenth century England itself had been engaged in a succession of civil wars which had reduced that country to a state of disorder and which was only brought to an end in Henry Tudor's victory on Bosworth field in 1485.[4] For Ireland as much as for England a new era had begun. The early Tudor period in England had coincided with the introduction into that country of the 'new learning' of Renaissance Europe out of which came many new philosophical concepts regarding the role of the state, of religion and of the relationships of individuals, to each of these and to each other. It was to come into Ireland later on in the sixteenth century under the guise of 'English civilitie'. By that time however, Henry VIII's breach with Rome had been accomplished and England turned irrevocably to protestantism. From these developments came a new gentry class, which had been enriched by the dispersal of the confiscated monastic properties and whose principal characteristic, apart from loyalty to the crown and an aggressive protestantism, was an acquisitiveness for landed estate.[5]

The 'new order' was readily exported to Wales where the Welsh origins of the Tudor line facilitated the Act of Union of 1536. Under this Act the legal distinctions between the Welsh and English nations were abolished. The English common law, including systems of land tenure and inheritance were introduced, replacing the existing laws of gavelkind. A local system of self government entitled the Council of Wales and the Marches was also introduced for the Principality. While full legislative union between Scotland and England did not take place until 1707, the accession of James VI of Scotland as James I of England in 1603 was to provide a common bond between the two kingdoms.[6] In Ireland no such commonality existed and after the fall of the house of Kildare in the 1530s, no other strong centre was available to make common cause with the new monarchy of Tudor England, while the European struggles of the Counter-Reformation made rapport between the 'New English' agents of the crown and the indigenous populations progressively more difficult.

At the beginning of the fifteenth century, south-east Ulster was much as it had evolved, after the first impact of the Norman settlements in the east Ulster coastal areas of Antrim, Down and Louth, the territory of the medieval earldom of Ulster. The latter, having gone into decline by the middle of the fourteenth century, occupied only a few coastal peripheral areas in the counties of Down and Antrim, while the county of Louth, although still nominally in Ulster, had from a very early period come under the central administration of Dublin and the English common law.[7] The Anglo-Norman settlements in Ulster had a very profound impact on the native Irish. The break-up of the kingdom of the Uladh, in the late twelfth century saw the end of the O'Hatty line in Uí Eachach, to be replaced by that of the Magennises and the MacCartans, of the newly emerged lordship of Iveagh.[8] Of even greater significance was the ousting, in 1241, of the O'Loughlins of the northern Uí Neill by the O'Neills of Tullaghoe in County Tyrone. By their claim to the over kingship of Ulster, as the successors of the Uí Neill, they kept alive the notion that all the other Irish lordships in the province were their vassals or Oir-Righthe. Due to pressure from them, the MacMurphys of Muinntir Bearn in Tyrone and the O'Hanlons of Oneilland in north Armagh migrated into south Armagh in the early thirteenth century where the latter settled in Airtir or Orior, the southern border of which abutted onto north Louth.[9]

To the west the O'Carrolls of Oirghialla or Oriel had been replaced, in the thirteenth century, by their near relations the MacMahons of Monaghan, a family which by the beginning of the fifteenth century had become divided into three distinct lines, the principal or 'lucht tighe' at Monaghan; Darty in the Newbliss area and Farney which bordered with the western part of County Louth.[10] This tendency to family division also reflected itself in the other Irish septs of the march and was to be one of the principal causes of the dissensions and disorders of the period. By the middle of the fifteenth century the O'Neills had encroached further into south Armagh under their lord, Eoghan, who in 1444 attacked and burned the Sraidbhaile of Dundalk having agreed to spare the walled town on payment of sixty marks and two tuns of wine.[11] The land upon which this encroachment took place became known as the Fews, the lordship of which first passed to Eoghan's second son Hugh in 1455.[12]

In the southern march lay the county of Louth or 'English Uriel', so called to distinguish it from the 'Irish Uriel' (Oirghialla) of the MacMahons, to the west.[13] Settled since the late twelfth century, the English colony of Louth, which it had become by the beginning of the fifteenth, was not less anciently established than their neighbouring Irish lordships. By the fifteenth century, the picture which the colony presented was that of a long established, tightly knit community, dominated by an elite gentry class and regulated by the common law of England.[14] By this time also the county appears divided into two fairly distinctive parts; to the south and east of a line from Dundalk to Ardee and thence to the County Meath border at Drumconrath, lay the English Pale; protected and fortified by the two walled towns and a string of castles or tower houses with a delineating pale ditch, some remnants of which can still be traced.[15] Within this area, especially in the extreme south, around the town of Drogheda, relatively peaceful settlement and order prevailed. To the north and west of this line lay the areas known as the march and maghery.[16] Of the latter at least two existed, possibly from before the coming of the Normans. To the north, the flat country south of the Armagh borders and around Dundalk was the Machaire Connaille, while to the west of Ardee, along the borders of Monaghan and Louth lay Machaire Oirghialla (anciently Machaire Rois). In County Louth, the march was the area immediately contiguous to the Pale, including the southern parts of the Carlingford peninsula, and while parts of the maghery, particularly Machaire Connaille, were included within the march, it seems likely that the maghery, being further north and west, constituted the Irish section of the march. These were the areas which suffered most from the endemic disorders which were to prevail throughout the century.

Although easily identified in historical, as well as in topographical terms, the machaire, (of which there were several others skirting the English Pale), also had a legal identity, as they were regarded as being part of the 'land of peace' within which the lordship's writ was intended to run. For example, at a parliament held in Drogheda in 1488, before the lord deputy, Gerald earl of Kildare, the Act of marches and maghery was passed making it a felony to take 'coign and livery' within the maghery of the English Pale.[17] The nature, as well as the timing, of this legislation is suggestive of a resurgence of English power and influence in the Pale borderlands, throughout the fifteenth century, and which seems to be borne out by events in County Louth from this time forward. The taking of 'coign and livery' was an Irish practice which had been adapted by the Anglo-Norman marcher lords, enabling them to quarter their troops in an extortionate manner on a local population and had been made the subject of excommunication at a provincial synod of Armagh in Drogheda in 1495.[18] That the practice of coign and livery may still have been in vogue during the sixteenth century may be evidenced by the fact that, in 1559, Joan the widow of Sir James Dowdall of Termonfeckin, took an action against a Christopher Dowdall, who had 'forcibly' entered on the estate of the former and 'had taken the issues and profits thereof ever since, and oppresses the said Dame Joan's farmers of the premises with coign and livery to their utter undoing'.[19] As late as the 1570's the Bellews had a clause in their tenancy agreements whereby the tenant was required to provide them with accommodation for their horses and 'horseboys' in accordance with 'the custom of the country'.[20]

As with the rest of County Louth the machaire had been reduced as 'swordland' by the Anglo-Normans. This may have been the reason why in the subsequent centuries the northern Irish never seriously attempted to recover them, ceding to the colonists, a right under Irish custom to acquire title and to settle there. This may explain why the MacMahons never questioned the King's claim to the lordship of Farney in County Monaghan. This territory had been designated the manor of Donaghmoyne, probably in the late twelfth century and may have formed part of the area, together with the adjacent barony of Louth, which was reserved to the king, in the grants made at the time by King John to the Pippards about Ardee and to the De Verdons in north Louth and Ferrard. An attempt to sub-infeudate Farney having failed, the king recognised the MacMahons as 'farmers of the territory of Farney' in 1401, at an annual rent of £10, an arrangement which was continued until the late sixteenth century when the territory was granted to Walter Devereux, earl of Essex.[21] A similar situation also existed in the nearby manors of Louth, Castlering and Ash, in the barony of Louth, which in the early Norman period had passed through several tenancies, including Geoffrey de Lusignan, half brother of Henry III in 1256. They were in the king's hands in 1300 when John de Somerset was allowed a fee of £33 to maintain them, but which included a payment of forty shillings to Brian MacMahon 'to defend them against the Irish'. Subsequently the combined manors passed through several tenancies until 1341, when they were passed to Sir John Darcy who was justiciar in Ireland in 1323 and again in the years 1333–40. He died in 1357 and was succeeded by his son John, second Lord Darcy of Knaith in Lincolnshire. His younger son William was the founder of the Darcys of Platten, a family which, by the sixteenth century, had also acquired the manor of Stonetown in the borders of the barony of Ardee and County Monaghan.[22] The manors of Louth, Castlering and Ash remained as part of the estates of the Darcys of Knaith, who were absentees, until 1465 when they were acquired by purchase by Thomas Talbot of Malahide. In 1539 they were held by Sir William Talbot who in that year had been knighted by the lord deputy, Grey, after the battle of Bellahoe. He was succeeded by his son John 'of Castlering' who was one of those knighted by Essex in 1599. In 1591 he was described as having 'of late years inhabited a great scope of land bordering on the MacMahons and the Fews and had built a house of strength on the borders'.[23]

As in Machaire Oirghialla in the fifteenth century, so also was it in Machaire Connaille, a territory in north Louth which formed part of the land grant, made by John as earl of Mortain, to Bertram De Verdon in 1190, described in a Charter of Bertram's son Nicholas as the cantred of 'Machwercunvilla'.[24] In its original extent it may have included parts of the lands of County Monaghan about Inniskeen and of Armagh south of Slieve Gullion. After the partition of the De Verdon lands in Ireland in 1332, the Furnival purparty, constituting the manors of Castletown and Roche, with the chiefry of the ville of Dundalk passed by purchase, in 1366, to John FitzJohn Bellew of Duleek, County Meath, described as 'lord of Dundalk, and le Roche'. He was succeed in the estate by his younger son John who was, in turn succeeded by his son Richard.[25] The latter proved to be a man of action who, by 1449, had wrested a substantial part of the lordship of the Fews, described as the 'five townlands of the Fews' from the O'Neills. Legality for this action was given, by a Statute 'removing O'Neill and his power from certain lands of Bellews of Roche, called the Fews, into which they forcibly entered'.[26] Bellew fully succeeded in consolidating his position within Machaire Connaille. In 1463 he obtained a subsidy of £10 to repair his castle at Roche 'on the frontiers of the March' and in 1467 he obtained a further £10 'to erect a tower and pile at Castletown', which has survived.[27] Another example of English intrusion into the machaire was in 1481 when Alexander Plunkett made a claim to the manor of Dungooly 'near the Roche', which he claimed had been held by his family 'since beyond the time of the memory of man' [i.e. since the conquest], with the custom of 'wey silver', a levy imposed on all Irish coming into or very near English lands. Plunkett's claim may not have succeeded as Dungooly was comprised in lands held by the earl of Kildare in the sixteenth century.[28]

Thus in the fifteenth century English Uriel experienced a period of expansion into the machaire, a position which was to be further extended and consolidated in the century which followed. This happened notwithstanding the periodic driving off of tenants (who were themselves for the most part Irish) by invading Irish, leaving the land they occupied waste, a condition which was particularly noticed in the Kildare and Bagenal estates in Dungooly and Omeath.[29] In the sixteenth century the heavy impositions of cess to pay for the army garrisons, which grew progressively larger as the struggle with the northern Irish increased, though a source of constant complaint, did not impede the growth in prosperity, while the merchants of the walled towns were able to extend their trading hinterlands deep into the Irish territories, where they were often suspected of giving support to the 'Irish rebels'.[30] In addition to the various families of the Pale area of Uriel, who succeeded in establishing themselves in the machaire, such as the Bellews of Roche and Castletown, the Darcys of Platten, the Dowdalls of Castletowncooley, the Gernons of Killencoole, and the Taaffes of Braganstown and Cookestown, cadet branches of such other families were also established there. In addition to the Talbots of Castlering these included the Flemings of Laggan and Bellahoe related to the lords of Slane, the Clintons of Nistlerath, related to the Clintons of Stabannon, the Bellews of Lisrenny and Graftonstown and of Thomastown, related to the Bellews of Duleek and perhaps the most important of all the Plunketts of Tallonstown, a cadet branch of the Plunketts of Beaulieu.[31] To these must be added a few of the New English who had settled in the county with the advance of the Tudor power in Ireland such as the Moores of Mellifont who had acquired the confiscated properties of the Cistercians of Mellifont and Crutched Friars of Ardee and the Bagenals, Nicholas and his son Henry, who acquired the properties of the Cistercians of Newry and Dominicans of Carlingford. The Plunketts of Tallonstown, created Barons Louth in 1541, also benefited in these confiscations, by the acquisition of the properties of St. Mary's Abbey of Louth.[32]

The opening years of the sixteenth century saw both the Irish and the English of the march in an extraordinary combination, under the lord deputy, the earl of Kildare, against MacWilliam Burke the lord of Clanricard of Galway.[33] The cause of the dispute is obscure and may have had little to do with an affair of state but the significance of the participation of the Irish lords, Art O'Neill the tanaiste of Tyrone, Donal Magennis of Rathfriland in Iveagh, Eochy O'Hanlon of Orier and Ross MacMahon of Farney, then the chief of the MacMahon sept, lay not so much in their alliance with the lords of the Pale as in the fact they were able to coalesce with each other. Only a brief ten or fifteen years earlier they had been engaged in a bitter internecine conflict.[34] Of those who participated in the lord deputy's army against Clanricard, Art O'Neill of Tyrone was perhaps the most eminent, suggesting that the outcome of the earlier conflict was the supremacy of the Tyrone O'Neills over the northern Irish. It was to be a supremacy 'with opposition' and throughout the rest of the century the loyalty of the Irish lords along the march, including the O'Neills of the Fews was a wavering one, reflecting the predicament of a people cast in the immediate path of opposing and increasingly violent forces. When in 1531 the viceroy Sir William Skeffington led a force into Tyrone, Niall Mor O'Neill lord of the Fews, joined him.[35] It was the beginning of a fitful alliance between the south Armagh O'Neills of the Fews and successive Dublin administrations which had the effect of providing the former with a strong counterpoise against the growing influence and power of the Tyrone O'Neills, who on many occasions sought to bring the recalcitrant sub lords to heel. In the closing years of the century the dominance achieved by Hugh O'Neill, earl of Tyrone, brought them back, however unwillingly, into the fold. However when O'Neill travelled southwards to Kinsale, Turlough MacHenry of the Fews did not accompany him, remaining instead in south Armagh. After the defeat at Kinsale, he gained a pardon from the crown and in 1603 obtained a grant of the 'country of the Fews' from James I.[36]

Art O'Neill who succeeded as the head of the O'Neills in 1509, was not of the principal line of the O'Neills and after his death in 1513 the succession reverted to the former. Art's descendants continued the line, which became known as the O'Neills of the Fews.[37] The succession was not without contest but thanks to the intervention of the lord deputy, the earl of Kildare, it was accomplished without bloodshed. The probable reason for this intervention was that the successor, Art Oge, was the son of Conn Mor, by his first marriage and who had married secondly Eleanor Fitzgerald, the earl's sister. Eleanor was his mother's niece, his father Henry having married a daughter of Thomas the seventh earl. This Kildare connection was to have its implications later on for Eleanor's son, Conn Bacach, who succeeded Art Oge in 1519.[38] His succession coincided with the recall of the earl to London being replaced in the following year as lord lieutenant by an Englishman, Thomas Howard, the earl of Surrey.[39] The latter, in a manner that was followed by many of his successors, set about his task of reducing the country to submission and order, by a series of military campaigns which proved, in the main, fruitless. One such was a progress northwards into Farney in retaliation for an earlier raid by Conn Bacach into the Pale and which was concluded with a verbal submission by O'Neill.[40] In 1523 Kildare returned to Ireland and from then until his final departure in 1534 the march was relatively quiet, the only significant events which occurred, in the years 1531–1532, were when Skeffington, acting as lord deputy, campaigned in Ulster against Conn Bacach.[41] On these occasions he was to receive, in addition to the support of the O'Neills of the Fews, that of the MacMahons and others of the northern Irish.

The insurrection of 'Silken Thomas', earl of Kildare, in 1534 ushered in a further period of tension between O'Neill and the lord deputy, Skeffington, during which the former carried out raids into County Louth, but a peace was patched up when, in July 1535, Conn came to Drogheda where he took an oath of allegiance.[42] Amongst other things it was agreed that any O'Neill involved in a wrong doing within the 'obedient districts' would be tried by English law, that any subject of the king taken in the Irish quarters would be reserved for royal consideration and not put to death, that O'Neill would continue to receive his 'black-rent', but that none of his people were to levy any other Irish exactions or graze their cattle in the English districts. It was also agreed that the English would enjoy freedom of trade into Tyrone and that O'Neill would serve the lord deputy in any hostings he might be called upon to serve in. All things considered it was an agreement which gave O'Neill some valuable concessions and recognition, but with the appointment of Lord Leonard Grey as deputy in 1536 a new era was at hand.[43]

In 1538 and again in 1539, Lord Deputy Grey led plundering raids into the north, at first against the Magennises of Iveagh and the Savages in Lecale and later against the MacMahons of Farney. His attack on the MacMahons was based on his claim that they had failed to pay their annual rent of £10. Although the MacMahons had been forewarned by their near neighbours in the English march (probably the Gernons of Killencoole), Grey managed to take away some 500 cattle and other animals. The result was a counter-attack into County Louth by O'Neill who complained that his black-rent had not been paid. The townspeople of the walled towns of Drogheda, Dundalk and Ardee rallied to a hosting called by Grey and O'Neill withdrew. It was however only a stand-off on his part. Joining with O'Donnell of Tir Conaill, in what became known as the Geraldine League, they invaded Louth accompanied by others of the northern Irish, including the MacMahons and some of the Magennises led by their chief, Murtough, the lord of Iveagh.[44] Significantly, neither the Fews O'Neills, nor the O'Hanlons of Orier participated, suggesting that the objectives of the MacMahons and Magennises may have had to do with retribution for what Grey had done to them the year before. They swept southwards through the western parts of the machaire, captured and sacked Ardee, then Navan and on to Tara where they turned back laden with booty. While these events were taking place Grey was in Dundalk, where he immediately rallied all available forces. He succeeded in intercepting the Irish, on their withdrawal northwards at Bellahoe, on the Lagan river boundary between Louth and Monaghan. The lords and gentry of the Pale and march, including the Flemings of Slane were with him. They routed the Irish who fled in such disarray that they left most of their spoils behind them.[45] Grey followed through his victory by advancing on Monaghan where he burned the local monastery and secured the submission of the MacMahon chieftains. Thereafter, not alone those of Farney, but also of the lucht tighe of Monaghan, found it to be more in their interests, to side with the English than with the Tyrone O'Neills.

Murtough Magennis, lord of Iveagh, had been captured after the battle of Bellahoe by the Louthmen, who it was said 'treacherously slew him at the instance of a party of his own tribe, who had bribed them to put him to death'.[46] This allegation pointed the finger at the Rathfriland Magennises, whose Donal Oge succeeded to the lordship, but not without opposition from Art of Castlewellan, a near relative of Murtough. During his stay in Dundalk, Grey plundered the Franciscan friary, already earmarked for confiscation, leaving only the bell tower standing. Despite his military achievements Grey had many enemies in Ireland and after his recall in May 1540, he was impeached by the Irish Council. Among the many charges laid against him was that of unlawfully invading Farney in 1538. After trial he was executed in May 1541.[47] Grey's conduct of affairs in Ireland had been an aberration, in that a movement for liberal reform had already begun under Antony St. Leger, who had headed a commission during the years 1537–38 to inquire into the state of Ireland. He succeeded Grey as lord deputy in 1540 and was soon at work implementing the new constitutional arrangements, at first by securing legal recognition for the king as the 'supreme head of the church in Ireland' and in 1541 by the enactment by Parliament of an act declaring the king of England to be also king of Ireland. Other enactments made during this period were the denial of the authority of the 'bishop of Rome', the suppression of the monasteries and the confiscation of their properties. It was also at this time that the policy of 'surrender and re-grant' was introduced.[48]

In the conduct of his reforms and in securing rapprochement with the Irish of the north St. Leger was assisted by two County Louth men, George Dowdall and Sir Patrick Gernon of Killencoole. The former was the prior of the monastery of the Crutched Friars of Ardee, the dissolution of which he had resisted. Nevertheless, after the death of Primate Cromer in 1543, he accepted nomination to the vacant see, by Henry VIII, against the papal provision of Robert Wautchope, who never succeeded in occupying his diocese before his death in November 1551. Dowdall was therefore the effective primate, his episcopacy spanning the remaining years of Henry VIII. He was deposed for a time during the reign of Edward VI and after restoration, with papal approval, in the reign of Mary Tudor, he served until his death in 1558.[49] Sir Patrick Gernon, with some members of his family had been implicated in the insurrection of Silken Thomas and later took refuge with O'Neill, but in 1541, having given assistance to St. Leger, in the latter's dealing with the Magennises, he received a royal pardon.[50] He was therefore a person who enjoyed the confidence of all the people of the march as well as of the crown administration in Dublin. His involvement with the Magennises arose from the disputed succession, following the death of Murtough, when the tanaiste, Art Oge of Castlewellan, disputed the succession of Donal Oge of Rathfriland. After a meeting between the disputants and St. Leger at Maynooth the matter was referred to the arbitration of Art Mac Prior Magennis and Sir Patrick Gernon.[51] Their findings were that Art Oge should be exempted from the jurisdiction of Donal Oge, but should he die before Art, then the latter would succeed him. This did not happen and therefore the succession lay with the Rathfriland Magennises, despite interference by O'Neill and by the crown administration in Dublin later in the century. No small part of the problems of the Irish lordships arose from instabilities of this kind which were brought about by the methods used by them in choosing the successor of the lord or chief. Theoretically the tanaiste was the elected or chosen successor but in fact any near relative of sufficient strength and following could challenge him and in the conflict which might ensue the strongest would prevail. Thus throughout the sixteenth century, in particular, the Irish were a much divided community into whose succession conflicts the Dublin administration constantly meddled in order to ensure that the succession would go to the most 'dependable' person.

The constitutional reforms, ushered in by St. Leger, proceeded apace. With an accommodating episcopacy the monastic foundations were closed down and their confiscated properties made available for distribution. Only in the case of the Franciscan friaries in Dundalk and Monaghan was violence resorted to and then only perhaps for the plunder they afforded Grey. In dealing with the Irish, conciliation was the approved policy, as much by Henry as by St. Leger, a process which was facilitated both by the ready acceptance by all of Henry's accession to the kingdom of Ireland and by the policy of 'surrender and re-grant' in respect of land tenures. The latter was an attempt to bridge the gap caused by the refusal of the fourteenth century lordship to allow the extension of English law relating to land tenures to the Irish.[52] The result was that two distinctly different systems operated. The English held their land of the king in right of conquest and in feudal tenure, according to English law, with inheritance by primogeniture, while the Irish held theirs by ancient custom. In their case the land was held in common by the sept, with the immediate demesne of the lord liable, upon his death, to partition amongst his next of kin, in accordance with the law of gavelkind, a system similar, though not identical, to that which prevailed in Wales until the Union of 1536.

The policy of 'surrender and re-grant' envisaged the Irish lord relinquishing his title, under Irish law, to the crown, in return for a grant of title from the king. This carried with it the implication that with his surrender the lord passed title to the king, a title which was not his to surrender in the first place. The implicit change in the relationships between the lord and his subjects which 'surrender and re-grant' carried was never fully thought out, or even understood, with the result that the latter continued with the old customary law, aided and abetted by whoever might oppose the lord's succession. Initially however, the new policy was readily resorted to by all of the Irish lords of the march, the MacMahons, the O'Neills of the Fews, the O'Hanlons and the Magennises.[53] Only the Tyrone O'Neills held out. St. Leger's response was to launch a campaign against Conn Bacach and in this he was supported by all of the Irish of the march. Tyrone was invaded with O'Neill in turn invading Louth, but he was driven off by Oliver Plunkett, the newly created Baron Louth. After two further attacks by St. Leger, O'Neill capitulated and signed articles of surrender in Dundalk on the 28 December 1541.[54] They provided for the ritual renunciation of his obedience to the 'pope' of Rome, and recognition of the king as the supreme head 'under Christ of the church of England and Ireland'. He also pledged himself to live under the 'laws of my most serene lord' and to pay an annual rent in respect of his lands. He also renounced his claim to the black rent of Louth. By the beginning of the following year the Irish Council made the rather premature pronouncement that 'Ireland was at peace'.[55]

The period of St. Leger's lord deputyship was, as far as the march was concerned, one of consolidation. There was little opposition to the new constitutional reforms and for a time the clergy and laity had no difficulty in accepting the changes made in the king's titles, including those relating to religion. This applied equally to the Irish lords, who also accepted, without any apparent reservation, the full implications for them of their new titles, under the 'surrender and re-grant' policy. For a time the new constitutional framework offered the prospect of long-term peaceful development. That this did not happen was due to a variety of circumstances. In the first place, the policy of 'surrender and re-grant' never developed below the level of the lord, while the succession was regularly liable to challenge and dispute. This resulted very often in two persons claiming the chieftainship, one resting his claim on the customary laws of the sept, the other on inheritance through the English common law. Secondly, the mild theological changes in regard to religion, during Henry's reign, gradually gave way to a more defined theological protestantism, with the introduction of the Book of Common Prayer in Edward's reign and even more so throughout the Elizabethan era. The innate conservatism, which both sides of the ethnic divide shared, especially below the levels of the higher lords and gentry, was opposed to innovation and change whether in land titles or religious worship. Thirdly a succession of English lord deputies brought with them a regular accretion of newcomers, the product of the new gentry class of England and Wales, who gradually took over the positions of power and influence in the crown administration, squeezing out the old elite of the Pale. It was however a gradual process which waxed and waned according to the constantly changing policies of successive administrations in Dublin and which wavered between the benign policies of a St. Leger to the outright thoroughness of conquest pursued by Mountjoy in the closing years of the century and which was in turn a response to the final great challenge of the Irish under O'Neill. That challenge was weakened by the disunity within the Irish themselves and nowhere more than in the march where support for O'Neill was at best lukewarm. This division was to reflect itself in the policies of government in the early decades of the following century. Compared with the root and branch confiscation and plantation of the escheated territories of the departed earls, the territories of the Irish of the march were not confiscated and so remained substantially in Irish hands. Their respective lords together with their immediate relations became assimilated to the new gentry class, holding their tenures in freehold according to the laws of England.[56]

It is possible that, left to themselves and without the dynastic turmoils which regularly beset the Irish, the people of the march might have been able to establish a modus vivendi. That this was not to be arose from the decision to grant Conn Bacach O'Neill the earldom of Tyrone with remainder to his son Matthew Ferdorcha. This was accomplished when Conn visited the king at Greenwich in October 1542 where he agreed to accept the king's 'clemency', to give him 'what name, state, title, land or living' it should please him to confer on him. It was as ample a surrender as could have been made. The disorders which it introduced into the family of O'Neill, were however, to continue for decades. Meanwhile, during the lord deputyship of St. Leger, which continued until May 1551, relative peace was maintained in the march. The only problems which arose concerned the boundaries of Conn's domain with his neighbours, including those between Tyrone and the O'Neills of the Fews, where raiding had begun between them. The matter was settled by an agreement drawn up at a parliament in Trim in June 1542.[57]

Conn O'Neill had several children, very many if his son Shane is to be believed. Of these only two can be identified as having been legitimately born to him and Matthew Ferdorcha was not one of them. The two were his daughter Mary, who was married to Sorley Boy McDonnell and his son Shane. The grant of the remainder and succession to the earldom to Matthew was never accepted by Shane and when he was of age and had the necessary following, he harried both his father and half-brother, chasing the former from his earldom and eventually killing his arch rival Matthew in Dungannon in 1558. The latter had been recognised until he was sixteen years of age as the son of Kelly, a Dundalk blacksmith, who upon the demise of the latter was brought, by his mother Alyson to Dungannon, where she presented him to Conn as his son. Incredibly not alone did Conn accept him but he also nominated him as his heir. As Shane himself explained it, Matthew's mother 'for vain glory and for a name to herself declared him to be O'Neill's son, alleging and boasting of her unhappiness, how that O'Neill lay once with her. And O'Neill being a man that never refused no child that any woman named to be his, as he had divers besides the said Matthew, accepted and took him to be his son'.[58] Within ten years of Conn's creation as the earl of Tyrone he had lost control in his lordship, so much so that Croft, the lord deputy (who had succeeded St. Leger in May 1551) removed him to Dublin leaving Ferdorcha, now the Baron Dungannon, and others as a commission to 'see for the defence of the country and quiet of the people, whereby the country was kept from such raven as before was used'. For the next seven or eight years, until Shane's death in 1567, all Ulster including the march was in turmoil. The only respite occurred when Shane visited Elizabeth at Whitehall in the early part of 1562.[59]

A leading opponent of Shane O'Neill was the New English settler in the Carlingford Lough area, Nicholas Bagenal, a native of Staffordshire. The first account of Bagenal, in Ireland, was as a fugitive from justice, who having fled to Ireland, found succour with the ever gullible Conn Bacach O'Neill. If the Irish Privy Council of the time is to be believed, Conn petitioned a reprieve on his behalf from Henry VIII, which was successful.[60] His career in Ireland rapidly prospered after this. After military service in France in 1547, he was created marshal of the Irish army and in 1550 was appointed to the Privy Council. From then until his death in 1590 he was to be the most powerful of the English in the march. Writing of him in 1575 Lord Deputy Sidney reported

> I found such good policy and order in the country where the marshal dwelleth, his lands so well manured, his tenants so well cherished and maintained, the town so well planted with inhabitants and increasing in beauty and building as he is much to be commended as well as he useth his tenants to live so wealthily under him, and his own bounty, and large hospitality and housekeeping, so able and willing to give entertainment to so many and chiefly to all those who have occasion to travel to and fro northwards, his house lying in the open highway to their passage.

The town mentioned was Newry, which was a small village adjacent to the Cistercian abbey at the time of Bagenal's acquisitions in the Carlingford Lough area, but which had become the most important town and garrison of the march by the end of the century, eclipsing Dundalk. The reason for this was strategic in that Newry provided a direct access into the heartlands of south Ulster and a jumping off point into Tyrone and Iveagh, thus avoiding the wooded fastnesses of the Fews and Orier of south Armagh. This development also had the effect of increasing the importance of Carlingford, where because of the deeper water, heavy ships could be unloaded of their reinforcements and supplies for onward transportation by smaller vessels to Newry. Bagenal's estates incorporated the town and lordship of Newry; Greencastle and the lordship of Mourne; Carlingford and the adjacent lordships of Carlingford, Cooley and Omeath. This was an estate estimated in 1568 at 120,637 acres inclusive of mountains.[61] The lordship of Newry alone amounted to 31,030 acres described as 'good arable ground, [with] meadow and pasture and woods for fires'. Like the rest of the march and the adjacent lands of the Irish, his estates suffered much at the hands of Shane O'Neill. In 1566 Bagenal having been evicted by Shane, who maintained a castle at Fathom in the upper reaches of the lough, complained that the country was 'so out of order, robbery, stealing, and killing throughout the English Pale'. With the death of Shane in 1567 Bagenal's fortunes as well as his estates were recovered and the process of re-tenanting the latter commenced. They were a mixture of Irish and Anglo-Irish of the march, including native Irish from the nearby lordships of the Magennises, the O'Hanlons and the O'Neills. Included also were many Welsh settlers, probably ex-soldiers brought in during the Shane O'Neill uprising. As well as the traditional pasturing of cattle and sheep, grass was saved for hay and the arable land used to grow corn such as wheat, rye, oats and barley. By 1575 a mill had been erected in Newry where in that year 541 pecks of corn and malt were processed.[62]

With the death of Shane O'Neill in 1567, the crown determined upon a policy of plantation in Ulster using as pretext the act of attainder of O'Neill and the pretensions of the crown to the medieval earldom of Ulster, with all its 'lands rights and titles'. The land was granted as part of a series of plantation schemes in counties Antrim and Down and Walter Devereux, earl of Essex, who was made general captain of all Ulster in 1573, obtained a grant of the lordship of Farney in County Monaghan.[63] On the basis of the act of attainder, the lordship had been declared forfeited and regranted to Essex in 1576, but before he could do much about his new acquisition he died. The result was that while the lordship remained as part of the Essex estate a MacMahon, Ever MacCon Uladh, was in effective occupation as tenant to the former at a rent of £300 per annum. The O'Hanlons were also made the subject of forfeiture, but for what reason is unclear, except that they too were comprised within the O'Neill attainder. Their territory of Orier was granted to a captain Chatterton who undertook that, within five years, he would not have an Irishman as tenant.[64] The MacCartan lordship of Kinnelarty was also granted to a captain Nicholas Malby (later president of Connacht), the condition of which was described in 1575 as

> 'that country was all desolate and waste, full of thieves, outlaws and unreclaimed people. None of the old owners dare occupy the land, because it hath pleased her majesty to bestow the same upon Captain Malby (who was) tied to such observation of covenant as Chatterton had his'.[65]

The unsettling effects of these grants, upon the Irish of the march, must have been readily apparent to Sidney, who returned to Ireland as lord deputy in 1575. In his subsequent progress in Ulster he had them revoked after O'Hanlon had refused to come to him lest he should be persuaded to accept Chatterton's title. Upsets of this nature, however, had the effect of making the Irish of the march extremely wary of English blandishments.[66]

During Shane O'Neill's ascendancy the town of Dundalk was an important place of refuge for his rival Matthew. The latter had three sons Brian, Art, who was born in Dundalk and may have been illegitimate, and Hugh. While Shane was in England visiting Elizabeth in 1562, his tanaiste Turlough Luineach, came on Brian between Omeath and Carlingford and killed him, not far it was said 'where his father had the like friendship of his men'. Art, who was the father of Owen Roe O'Neill, was the eldest and held a captaincy under Sir William Fitzwilliam, the treasurer-at-war.[67] In all likelihood therefore, Art participated in the defence of Dundalk against Shane in 1566 when Fitzwilliam repulsed the latter with severe losses.[68] By this time however Shane's last remaining rival for the succession to the earldom by Tyrone had been spirited away to England. This was Matthew's youngest son Hugh who also spent some of his life in Dundalk, before being brought over to England, at the age of nine, in 1559 by Sir Henry Sidney. His upbringing in England, first in Ludlow castle in Shropshire and later in London, Kent and Norfolk was to be a Protestant one and within the ethos of aristocratic English 'civilitie'. As Sir John Dowdall of the old Pale elite was to comment, with more than a hint of jealousy, the 'rascal horseboy' had been lifted up 'by the heat of her majesty's favour unto nobility and councellors with other great men and captains'.[69] Hugh O'Neill returned permanently to Ireland in the spring of 1568 as Baron Dungannon, his patron Sidney returning in the following October as the lord deputy. Later in 1579 O'Neill joined the Dublin forces in their campaign in Munster against James Fitzmaurice of Desmond. He was carefully biding the day when he should succeed to the fullness of his inheritance in Tyrone including his English earldom. His only opposition was Shane's successor, Turlough Luineach who had succeeded as The O'Neill following Shane's death.[70]

The appointment of Essex as captain of Ulster in 1573 and as the main settler in the proposed plantation of Antrim marked the commencement of a period of instability as the latter sought to make good his claims. He was resisted at first by the Clandeboy O'Neills of Antrim and then by Turlough Luineach, but on all occasions, until Essex's mandate for plantation was withdrawn in 1575, he enjoyed the support of Hugh, Baron Dungannon.[71] By this time the latter had made some recovery of the Tyrone estates in Oneilland and had his residence in Dungannon. In 1575 and again in 1579 his name can be found in lists of supporters and contributors to the English cause in Ulster against Turlough Luineach, along with the MacMahons of Farney and Dartry, the Magennises and the MacCartans, the O'Hanlons of Orier and the O'Neills of the Fews. The parochial and perhaps dynastic nature of the participation by the latter, against Turlough, may be gauged by the fact that when Essex called on the support of the Pale, only the

Flemings of Slane responded; complaining instead against the excesses of the cess being imposed upon them. As Essex saw it 'they think to have greater thanks for denial to go with me, than for their forwardness in this service; they do so often and so openly exclaim and complain unto me and I am not able to address it, as I am truly weary of myself'.[72] It was but a reflection of the growing disenchantment of the Pale elite with the New English, albeit that in the final struggle with O'Neill, few of them failed their side.

The growing strength of Hugh O'Neill especially after Turlough's submission to Essex in 1575 made it inevitable that his objective would be successful. In March 1584 he was appointed tanaiste to Turlough and in the following year he attended a parliament in Dublin as the earl of Tyrone. Agreement was also reached with Turlough as to the partition between them of the Tyrone lands and in 1587 Hugh received his patent as earl.[73] Meanwhile, probably as a counterpoise, Sir Nicholas Bagenal of Newry was appointed Commissioner for Ulster. O'Neill was soon to be in dispute with this family. In 1591, shortly after Sir Nicholas's death, he abducted his daughter Mabel and by means of a pre-arrangement, married her in Dublin.[74] It was an act for which Mabel's brother, Sir Henry, who had succeeded his father as marshal of the army, never forgave him. O'Neill had been married twice already, his second wife was dead but his first wife was still living and although the possibility of marriage to Mabel had already been broached, Sir Henry was adamantly opposed. As he put it 'I can but accurse myself and fortune that my blood which in my father and myself hath often been spilled in repressing this rebellious race, should now be mingled with so traitorous a stock and kindred'.[75] It cannot have improved relations between O'Neill and Bagenal that within a few years of the marriage Mabel was dead, allegedly through neglect. By this time O'Neill's loyalty to the English had become firmly suspect, a development which Bagenal did everything to encourage.

In 1589 another dynastic struggle developed in Monaghan where the lord of the MacMahons, Sir Ross Bui having no son to succeed him and in an endeavour to keep the succession in the lucht tighe group against the tanaiste Brian MacAodh Oge of Dartry, made a surrender of his lands to the crown, receiving a re-grant in English tenure and nominating his brother Aodh Rua to succeed him. Upon the death of Ross Bui, Aodh Rua hastened to Dublin to get confirmation of his inheritance.[76] After an initial reluctance this was acceded to and Aodh was sent back to Monaghan with a force of soldiers to back him up. The result was open warfare between the tanaiste, Brian MacAodh and Aodh Rua, during which the English of the march, under Lord Louth, invaded Dartry, but were repulsed. In August the English soldiers under Aodh Rua's command were heavily defeated in a battle at Clones after which, Brian MacAodh held the ascendancy with Aodh Rua having to content himself with cattle raiding into Dartry and

Farney. Meanwhile the lords of these areas Brian MacAodh Oge of Dartry, Ever MacCon Uladh of Farney and MacArt Maol of Monaghan schemed with the lord deputy to have their respective territories granted to them by way of surrender and re-grant. The obstacle in the way was the previous grant of all Monaghan made to Aodh Rua, even though Fitzwilliam the lord deputy was anxious to subject Monaghan to such a sub-division. Subterfuge had to be resorted to. A condition of the grant made to Sir Ross was that he (and his successors) would not wage war on the Queen. Aodh Rua's cattle raiding was to be so defined. The latter was arrested in Louth in 1589 and arrangements were made to bring him to trial for treason. In 1590 he was tried at Monaghan before a packed jury, found guilty and executed. The way was now clear. Following his attainder the lands of Monaghan were declared forfeited to the crown and a partition effected, Farney only excluded, being legally the estate of the earl of Essex. While most of the land was divided among the various branches of the MacMahon family, substantial grants were also made of Church lands which had also been forfeited, Bagenal getting some 3,000 acres in Muckno. Other beneficiaries were Roger Gernon of Stabannon, Thomas Clinton of Dowdstown and John Talbot of Castlering. It was the end of the MacMahon lordship of Monaghan as well as a precursor of a similar partition of the Magennis lands in Iveagh early in the following century.[77]

O'Neill's drift into insurrection seems to have commenced in the early part of the 1590s, earlier even if spies' reports are to be believed. He must have been unsettled by Essex's brutal attempts at plantation in the north and Fitzwilliam's equally brutal and treacherous behaviour in Monaghan, all of which happened within the traditional area of influence of the O'Neills. At this time also the Counter-Reformation movement was growing in strength in Ireland and when the newly appointed Catholic archbishop of Armagh Edward MacGauran arrived at Drogheda, in 1593, he carried promises of military aid from King Philip of Spain. It may not be without significance that he had his first contracts and conferences with the Irish at Ballymascanlon, at this time part of the estate of Garrett Moore of Mellifont, but almost certainly held in tenancy by his close friend Hugh O'Neill.[78] When it did come the insurrection was not begun by O'Neill but by Maguire and O'Donnell in west Ulster. At the outset he was opposed to it, being with Bagenal in Fermanagh in September–October 1593 where he was slightly wounded in the battle of the Erne Fords in October. By May 1595 however he had well and truly joined in the insurrection when he signally defeated Bagenal in the famous battle of Clontibret. The lord deputy, with 3,000 men, then set out for the borders and in June, by the Market Cross of Dundalk, O'Neill and other Irish lords of the north were proclaimed traitors.[79] The die had at last been cast.

At the outbreak of the insurrection, the Fews O'Neills and the Farney MacMahons sided with the insurrectionists, but not so O'Hanlon or the

Magennises of Iveagh. Sir Hugh Magennis of Rathfriland and lord of Iveagh held his lordship, as also did Ever MacRory of Kilwarlin by letters patent from the crown but upon the death of Sir Hugh in January 1596 a dispute ensued as to his succession. His son Art, who was married to O'Neill's sister Sarah, had the right by English law but he was opposed by Glassney MacAholly of Clanconnell, who strangely enough was supported by O'Neill who had appointed him tanaiste.[80] Art appealed to Dublin where he stood upon his right to succeed. The dispute dragged on throughout the rest of the century, neither side being strong enough to oust the other, albeit that Art came back in favour with O'Neill, who married his sister Catherine in 1598. The O'Hanlons under Sir Oghie, conscious perhaps of their exposed position, pursued a neutral course, but when in June 1595, the Lord Deputy Russell led his forces on an expedition into Armagh and Monaghan his guide and standard bearer was Sir Oghie who on the return journey was shot in the foot in an engagement near Newry.[81] He too had family relations with O'Neill being married to his sister, but like Magennis, favoured the maintenance of good relations with the English. As Captain Lee was to comment '. . . and if this affinity were not, the manner of the Irish is always to the part they see strongest, and when your majesty shall prevail, they will then seek favour and make offer of much service, but seldom or never perform any . . .'.[82] It was to be so throughout the Nine Years' War.

The Nine Years' War, begun in 1594, brought devastation to all parts of the march and to the nearby territories of the Irish lordships, more especially in the period of total war, begun by Mountjoy in 1600, when a deliberate policy of induced famine left whole areas depopulated. Until then O'Neill had carried on a desultory campaign, punctuated by periods of truce which were usually negotiated in or about Dundalk but after O'Neill's victory in 1598, over his great opponent Sir Henry Bagenal, at the battle of the Yellow Ford, in which the latter was killed and after the failed Essex expedition of the following year, it was inevitable that a Mountjoy should appear on the scene. The English of the march for the most part supported the crown, notably Lord Louth, the Gernons, Flemings and Darcys but the very weight of the reinforcements sent in from England in the wake of the Yellow Ford gave the closing years of the campaign a peculiarly New English character. In this the Pale elite played but a small and insignificant role, being in part suspect as to the totality of their commitment to crown policy.

When the war was over many of the New English soldiery remained on to found families and estates throughout Ulster, not alone in the escheated counties but also in the border areas of Monaghan and Down in many cases by buying out the native proprietors. Examples include the Blaneys of Castleblaney in County Monaghan: the Trevors of Rosetrevor, the Hills of Hillsborough and the Cromwells of Lecale all in County Down. They were to be the forerunners of the British colonial settlements in the Ulster plantations of the early seventeenth century. In time these were to be further extended into County Louth, following the Cromwellian confiscations of 1652–54 by which time the greater part of the gentry of English Uriel had become 'Irish rebels'.

Plate 1: *King John's Castle, Carlingford from Thomas Wright* Louthiana: or, an introduction to the antiquities of Ireland *(London, 1758)*.

6 The Transformation of the Borderlands, 1600–1700

RAYMOND GILLESPIE

In 1744 Walter Harris writing his *Antient and present state of the County of Down* observed that

> 'Newry is a borough town and sends to parliament two burgesses of whom the inhabitants . . . are electors and the seneschal of the manor the returning officer. Being a frontier town it was often exposed to the ravages of events but in the intervals of peace and by its own happy situation of trade it as often revived.'[2]

He recorded a rise in the town's fortunes in the early seventeenth century which were reversed by the rebellion of 1641 and the trade depression of the 1650s but which recovered with the Restoration of Charles II in 1660. A slump followed the burning of the town in 1689 in the wake of the advance of the Williamite forces under Schomberg but following the Williamite settlement the town again thrived, becoming by Harris's day 'the largest and most trading town in the county [of Down]'. By the middle of the eighteenth century a description of Newry as a frontier town might seem inappropriate. The colonisation of Ulster by English and Scottish settlers in the seventeenth century had brought it into a wider economic and social world governed by the central administration from Dublin and by 1700 it appeared an integral part of the island of Ireland.

Harris's description might appear more appropriate to the middle of the sixteenth century when Newry marked the limits of the English penetration into Ulster. It was then a small, fortified town built in the 1550s by Nicholas Bagenal, a Staffordshire man, later marshal of the Irish army, as part of an effort to prevent military incursions of the native Irish into the Pale. Further attempts were made to block other entrances to the Pale in, for example, 1576 when the earl of Essex was given the strategically located barony of Farney in County Monaghan to settle. Another attempt was made in 1572 when Queen Elizabeth granted the lands of Orior, the Fews and the gallowglass country in south Armagh to Captain Thomas Chatterton on condition that he would settle the area within seven years. No progress was made and the grant was revoked. The aim of these measures was, as Sir Nicholas Malby put it to Lord Burleigh, the principal secretary of state in England, to stop 'the murders of the good subjects on the borders by the men of the Fews, Farney, MacMahon's country, the Dartry and O'Reilly's country'.[2] Controlling movement and preventing raids across the border was a continual problem and was taken seriously. The native Irish chronicler who described Red Hugh O'Donnell's journey north after his escape from Dublin castle in 1591 referred to his journey through Dundalk northwards and the dangers of the 'watches and ambuscades set by the English on the border in every remarkable pass and each road by which they thought Aodh O'Donnell would come to them'.[3]

The Ulster-Leinster border of the sixteenth century was a debatable land, akin to that of the Scottish or Welsh borders, which could be controlled by whoever had enough strength to dominate it. The families who lived on the border were forced to ally themselves with whichever power block had sway in the area at any one time. Hugh O'Neill, for example, spent a considerable amount of effort in the late sixteenth century to ensure that families such as the O'Neills of the Fews were subservient to him but by 1597 they were fighting on the English side during the Nine Years' War. By 1599 they were back on the O'Neill side again.[4] The history of the allegiances of the Magennises in south Down during the Nine Years' War shows a similar pattern of vacillating loyalties. That war also demonstrated the position of the Ulster-Leinster border as a frontier between the two conflicting groups which neither could completely control since it was here the two sides met on 'neutral' territory to agree temporary truces. In September 1599 O'Neill met the earl of Essex at Aclint on the Louth–Monaghan border and in 1596 the Annals of the Four Masters record the meeting of O'Neill, O'Donnell and the earl of Ormond at Faughart to agree a truce. Among the terms of the truce was the condition that O'Neill's authority in Ulster would be confirmed and 'that the English should not encroach upon them beyond the border' and that no taxes would be imposed on Ulster.[5]

The defeat of O'Neill in the Nine Years' War meant that the authority of the Dublin administration became effective over the whole island for the first time and it was expected that the line of demarcation between the native Irish territory of Ulster and the Dublin administration's area of influence in the Pale would decline. In 1605 a proclamation declared that all the inhabitants of Ireland were now the king's subjects and not tied to any great lord such as the earl of Tyrone. Tyrone had received a regrant of his lands as part of the treaty of Mellifont, which ended the war in 1603, but his powers were nonetheless considerably curtailed from those which he had exercised in the 1590s. From 1605 settlers from England and Scotland began to arrive in Ulster, first as part of the privately sponsored settlements of Antrim and Down and later as part of the more formal scheme laid down for the Ulster plantation. Thus the ethnic cohesion of late sixteenth century Gaelic Ulster which apparently marked it off clearly from the Anglo-Irish Pale community began to change.

This new political orientation began to draw the borderlands of south Down and south Armagh into a wider economic world. In the sixteenth century there had been important economic and social contacts between Dundalk and its hinterland. Art Mac Baron O'Neill, for example, protested against Hugh O'Neill's plan to destroy Dundalk in 1595 on the grounds 'that their ancestors and especially themselves for the most part had been bred and brought up there. The earl confessed it to be true and said that he loved it best of any town in Ireland but nevertheless he would destroy it'.[6] Tenants also moved between the Pale and south Ulster in search of land and there was trade between the borderlands and the merchants of towns such as Dundalk, Newry and Carlingford. The peace agreed between O'Neill and Ormond in 1596 had recognised the requirements of trade and had stipulated that the English were not to enter Ulster 'excepting those who were in Carrickfergus, Carlingford and Newry who were at all times permitted to deal and traffic'. Newry merchants had also begun to purchase lands from the Mac Mahons in Monaghan by the 1590s thus opening up the area to new economic influences.[7]

Many of these economic links were based on a traditional sixteenth century Ulster trade which was orientated north–south. Carrickfergus, the main port of east Ulster, had traded mainly with Dublin and England rather than with the local Irish hinterland and according to Sir Henry Sidney most of the ecclesiastics and lawyers of the Pale who travelled to Ulster went to Carrickfergus. Also many of the Anglo-Irish families of the Pale were related to Anglo-Irish families who held land in east Ulster. The opening up of south and west Ulster after 1603 meant that the trade of Ulster became more internally integrated. By 1611, for example, Sir Thomas Phillips considered it feasible to use Lough Neagh to ship goods from Tyrone and Londonderry to Newry from where they would be sent to Dublin. Similar proposals were made in the 1640s and in 1703. The proposal was to see its most complete fulfilment in 1742 with the opening of the first summit level canal in the British Isles, the Newry navigation, which opened western Ulster up to the Dublin trade.[8]

If the aim of the seventeenth century settlement of Ulster was to remove the old sixteenth century demarcation between south Ulster and north Leinster by reducing Ulster's ethnic distinctiveness and its independence from the central government, it certainly failed. The idea of a border between the two areas persisted, as evidenced by Walter Harris's mid-eighteenth century description of Newry as a frontier town. Harris was not alone in making such comments. Owen Roe O'Neill, for example, wrote from Cavan to the earl of Ormond in 1646 'My lord, I had of long written to your excellency since my coming into the field had I not been assured that your lordship was daily expected with some forces upon the frontiers towards Dundalk'.[9] Even Owen Roe's adversary in Ulster, Robert Munroe, the commander of the Scottish force there, seemed to recognise the existence of a border around Dundalk since he never led his force south of the town during the seven years he was in Ireland. Later in the century Oliver Plunkett, the archbishop of Armagh, noted an apparent incompatibility between Ulster and Leinster, 'Leinstermen and Ulstermen will never agree' he wrote in 1672 'nor Munstermen and Connachtmen. Spaniards and Frenchmen would more readily agree or Poles with Germans'.[10]

South Ulster and north Louth continued throughout the seventeenth century to be an important interface between two regional cultures. The colonisation of Ulster in the seventeenth century had not made it more uniformly English as the administration had hoped but had brought together Scottish, English and Gaelic Irish cultures which were forced to make accommodations and in doing so created a unique regional society which was markedly different from the Anglo-Irish culture of the Pale.[11] The Dublin administration regarded many features of this regional society with deep suspicion. This was not principally because of any Gaelic characteristics which persisted, some new elements aroused equal unease in the Dublin government. One particularly important feature was the emergence of a large body of Presbyterians in Ulster. The attitude of the administration to the Presbyterians was ambivalent. While they denied the king the role of head of the church and did not accept the established position of the Church of Ireland, they were nonetheless Protestant and acted as an important balance to the Catholic Irish of Ulster. Thus they were tolerated within Ulster but the Dublin government was determined that the Presbyterians should not be allowed to expand outside the borders of the province. As a result the south Ulster borderland became an area of friction between the Presbyterians and the representatives of the Established church.

An Independent congregation had been established at Dundalk, with the Englishman Joseph Bowesfield as its minister, during the religious toleration of the 1650s. With the amalgamation of the English Presbyterian church and the Independents in the 1690s the Dundalk church became a Presbyterian one. The timing of the change was opportune since the Scottish dominated Presbyterian church in Ulster had resolved most of its internal problems and expanded outside the province by the 1690s. As a result Bowesfield's successors in Dundalk, John Simpson and Patrick Simpson, came from the Ulster church. The missionary intention of these men is indicated by the fact that both were able to preach in Irish. In 1700 a separate Presbyterian congregation was established at Carlingford.[12] Attempts to push further south than this border were resisted by the Dublin authorities. In August 1708 a minister from the Lurgan congregation, James Fleming, was sent to Drogheda to preach to about 200 dissenters in the town. He was summoned before the town council and warned to desist. However, he persisted and consequently was sent for trial before the Assizes. In October similar action was taken against William Biggar, a Presbyterian minister from Limerick, who had come to the town. The English government did not wish to alienate the political support of Presbyterians and so no prosecution was taken and the Presbyterian congregation was left in peace. It was clear, however, that while a congregation was acceptable in Dundalk this was not the case in Drogheda. A mental boundary of the limits of Ulster Presbyterian influence had established itself in the minds of early eighteenth century contemporaries. It was not just in the east of Ireland that this had been established. In 1712 an attempt by the Ulster Presbyterians to establish a new missionary congregation at Belturbet in Cavan met with the same degree of resistance as had been seen at Drogheda. According to one contemporary the Presbyterians were trying 'to make a Drogheda of Belturbet'. The outcome was similar to that of Drogheda with the Presbyterians being allowed to establish a congregation outside the town.[13]

Somewhere, therefore, in the region of south Ulster and north Leinster during the seventeenth century there lay a border in men's minds between the regional cultures of Ulster and Leinster; a border which was different in nature from that of the sixteenth century and affected the settler community also. This mental border was further demonstrated in the topography of the borderlands which tended to emphasise the separateness of Ulster and Leinster. In the seventeenth century there were only two main roads which ran through the borderlands. One ran from Dundalk to Armagh but avoided the main upland region. The other was the road which ran from Dundalk to Newry through the 'gap of the North' which formed the main entrance to Ulster. This was an old well established route and, as Sir William Brereton commented in 1635, it was 'stony, craggy, hilly and uneven, but a way is nothing difficult to find' which meant that it compared favourably with much of the Irish road network. Not until the early eighteenth century were the uplands of Carlingford and south Armagh penetrated by a road system.[14] This lack of internal communications within the borderlands led to the area being difficult of access for trade. The town of Carlingford itself, though a good part of and of considerable importance in the Dublin–Ulster trade of the sixteenth century, had little contact with its hinterland because of the poor road system. Archbishop Oliver Plunkett commented in 1670 that Carlingford was 'celebrated for its fine seaport . . . the seaport is capable of holding a thousand large ships but because of the roughness of the roads the ships go rather to Dundalk or Drogheda, which are less secure'.[15] As a result the town stagnated and there was little development after 1600 leaving many of the medieval buildings intact into the present century. A similar argument had been made by Charles Monck, the surveyor general of the customs, in 1637 who pointed out that while Carlingford was the appointed port for the region most merchants landed their cargoes at Greencastle or Newry and the officers at Carlingford could not get to these ports. As a result Carlingford was eclipsed as a port in the course of the seventeenth century so that by 1683 it was observed that it was 'inhabited with few fishermen' despite the fact that it was 'a fair and large harbour for shipping and a great plenty of sea fish'.[16]

Such difficulties with communications and particularly the lack of a port which had contact with Scotland meant that the area was little settled by the colonists who began arriving in Ulster from the middle of the first decade of the seventeenth century. Newry, for example, was described by Brereton in 1635 as 'a poor town and is much Irish'. In Dundalk, Brereton recorded that 'the greatest part of the inhabitants of the town are popishly affected . . . abundance of Irish, both gentlemen and others, dwell in this town'.[17] Dundalk was to receive a substantial immigration in the 1650s and 1660s so that Oliver Plunkett commented in 1670 that of 2,000 people in the town only 500 were Catholics.[18] In the borderlands to the north of Dundalk, by contrast, the population remained mainly native Irish. There were important pockets of British settlement on some estates, such as that of Thomas Ball of Glassdrumman or Toby Poyntz's land of Ballymoore, both in south Armagh, but the overall situation was of dominance of native Irish. The 'census' of 1659, in reality a poll tax return which recorded males and unmarried females over the age of sixteen, recorded the ethnic origin of the population and demonstrated a clear pattern in Ulster as set out in Table 1.[19] In the northern baronies of counties Down and Armagh the ratio of Irish to British settlers was low, never exceeding two and usually under one. The same is true of the southern baronies of Louth, although the barony of Ardee is unusually low because of the settlement of Cromwellian soldiers there. The figures for Dundalk barony are distorted because of the inclusion of the town. It is in the baronies touching the Ulster-Leinster provincial boundary that the ratio of Irish to British is highest, over two in all cases and over four in Newry and south Down. This does not mean that there was no immigration into the area or that the population did not grow. Although there are no sources which would enable a calculation of population size at different points in time, a comparison of the native Irish surnames in the Creggan area of south Armagh and north Louth in the 1659 census with those in the pardon granted to the followers of Sir Turlough O'Neill in 1602 shows that many of the 1602 surnames had disappeared by 1659. New surnames, such as McPartland, were among those most common in 1659 although they had not been present earlier. This suggests that in the first half of the seventeenth century the Ulster-Leinster borderlands saw an influx of native Irish from other parts of Ulster. This was not an uncommon feature of many areas of marginal land in Ulster.[20] The migrants were drawn from that group of native Irish who were unable to manipulate the changed circumstances of the seventeenth century to their

Table 1 Composition by barony of borderland population, 1659.

Barony	A English and Scots	B Irish	Total	B:A
COUNTY ARMAGH				
Oneilland	1,269	1,366	2,635	1.1
Armagh	450	891	1,341	2.0
Tiranny	108	546	654	5.1
Orior	193	694	887	3.6
Fews	373	858	1,231	2.3
	2,393	4,355	6,748	1.8
COUNTY DOWN				
Castlereagh	1,363	950	2,313	0.7
Ards	1,447	984	2,431	0.7
Kinelarty	693	763	1,456	1.1
Lecale	1,071	1,631	2,702	1.5
Upper Iveagh	448	2,149	2,597	4.8
Lower Iveagh	1,352	1,381	2,733	1.0
Newry	166	785	951	4.7
	6,540	8,643	15,183	1.3
COUNTY LOUTH				
Louth	39	1,019	1,058	26.1
Dundalk	327	2,209	2,536	6.8
Ferrard	115	1,675	1,790	14.6
Ardee	356	2,345	2,701	6.6
Drogheda city	958	647	1,605	0.7
	1,795	7,895	9,690	4.4

Source: S. Pender (ed.), *A Census of Ireland circa 1659.* (Dublin, 1939).

own ends, for example by being unable to pay the rapidly increasing rents demanded of tenants in seventeenth century Ulster. This process continued into the later part of the century as the settler population rose, especially in north Armagh and the Lagan valley, and demand for land increased thus forcing up rents. By the 1690s the poll tax returns show the density of settlement in the borderlands to be greater than many parts of west Ulster but considerably less than that of the Pale or north Armagh.[21]

The characteristics of this population growth had significant effects for the borderlands. Since population increase was one of the principal engines of economic change in early modern Ireland the failure of the local population to grow significantly had important economic repercussions. Archbishop Oliver Plunkett, for example, in a survey of his diocese in 1670 commented on the differences between the heavily settled northern part of County Armagh and the less densely settled south. 'The country around Armagh [city] for twelve miles to the north is all flat, and it abounds in fruit, wheat, fish, animals and every good gift of God. To the south it is rather hilly and full of herds, pigs and tribes of horses'. The Civil Survey of 1654 described a similar situation.[22] The contrast between the labour intensive northern economy and the livestock dominated economy of the south of the county which required little labour is clear. The relative trade of the two main ports in the 1620s (set out in Table 2) for which the borderlands were the natural hinterlands, Carlingford and Dundalk, in comparison with the adjoining ports of Drogheda and Lecale show clearly the economy of the borderland region. No grain was exported from the borderland ports as most was needed for local consumption. Neither were beef or live cattle significant elements in the trade although tallow and hides were of considerable importance. This suggests that cattle were slaughtered locally for food and the non-food parts of the beast exported. By contrast in the Lecale ports tallow and hides formed a relatively minor part of the trade but live cattle were a significant element in trade.

Perhaps the most striking feature of the Carlingford trade is the large part which linen yarn played in the trade. The production of linen yarn was not uncommon in south Ulster in the sixteenth and seventeenth centuries. This was not worked into cloth but was sold locally to merchants who shipped it to north-west England where it was woven into linen cloth. Some yarn was woven locally producing narrow bandle linen to meet local needs but this was of too poor a quality to meet the needs of English markets. Thus the yarn provided the cash element of the borderlands economy for the payment of rent which was usually collected in a mixture of cash and goods.

During the late seventeenth century in north Armagh this economic situation began to change. Arthur Brownlow at Lurgan began to encourage his tenants to weave their linen yarn into cloth and usually into fine linens. He did this in a number of ways, the most important being his promise to purchase all the linen sold at his market at Lurgan so guaranteeing that the weavers could not lose.[23] In the borderlands of south Armagh there was no such landlord supported development. The reasons for the failure of linen

Table 2 Composition of exports, 1621–22. (Percentages)

	Dundalk	Drogheda	Carlingford	Lecale & Clandeboy
Oats	—	—	—	10.9
Cattle	—	1.3	1.2	33.5
Beef	0.4	1.3	—	—
Tallow	10.1	17.4	10.7	0.5
Hides	33.5	27.2	20.4	1.3
Horses	8.0	2.0	7.2	53.2
Fish	—	18.4	4.6	—
Yarn	48.0	32.4	55.7	0.5
Total:	100.0	100.0	99.8	99.9

Source: P.R.O.N.I. T2860/13. Exports have been valued at rates given in *Cal. S. P. Ire., 1663–5*, pp 694–7.

weaving to spread into a marginal economy in poor land such as the borderlands, where it would have given much needed diversification in the economy, provide the key to some of the central features of the economy of the borderlands in the seventeenth century.

There were at least three influences at work in encouraging the growth of the linen industry in north Armagh in the late seventeenth century; the rapid growth of the population and the consequent need to provide employment, the encouragement and support of the local landlord and the development of a marketing system by which the linens could be sold to the wider world. The scale of population growth which other areas of Ulster experienced and which provided the impetus for economic diversification to prevent pauperisation was not matched in the borderlands. Also unlike other areas of Ulster no large estates, managed as economic entities, emerged in the borders. In the early seventeenth century, much of south Armagh was granted as part of the plantation scheme to Sir Turlough O'Neill of the Fews but like many of the native grantees he found himself in debt by the 1630s and was forced to sell parts of his land thus fragmenting the estate. Most of the rest of the Ulster part of the borderland was granted in small proportions to native Irish landowners with only a few larger estates reserved for newcomers.[24] In other cases many of the borderland landowners were absentees. The Books of Survey and Distribution record that the main landowner in the part of Creggan and Iniskeen parishes in County Louth in 1641 was the absentee Sir Christopher Bellew of Castletown. Again, the land of Carlingford parish was held by inhabitants of Dundalk and Patrick Bellew of Verdonstown. Much of this area was assigned to the Duke of York as part of the Restoration land settlement thus depriving it of any effective resident landlord capable of initiating change.[25]

There were some local attempts to establish markets in parts of the borderlands. In the early seventeenth century Sir Turlough O'Neill of the Fews had taken out a patent for two fairs at Glassdrumman, the location of one of his main castles. In the later part of the century patents were taken out for fairs at Crossmaglen in 1672, Cullyhanna in 1674, Mullaghcrew in 1684, Poyntzpass in 1685 and Jonesborough in 1705.[26] Fairs were seasonal events requiring almost no investment or town development but were simply meeting places to sell cattle. Markets were more regular affairs, usually weekly, and thus required the economy to be producing enough of a surplus to sustain such a development. The economy also had to be sufficiently commercialised to generate enough business to ensure a profitable turnover if it were to be worth the landlord's while investing in the infrastucture required for a regular market. The local economy was such that few south Ulster landlords were prepared to do this and only Crossmaglen received a patent for a market as well as a fair in its grant. Most landlords could see little immediate return from this economically marginal area and preferred to rely on the more speculative development of seasonal fairs.

A further feature retarding the development of markets was the difficulty of access to the area. This meant that few merchants from the port towns ventured into it and consequently there was insufficient demand for large quantities of goods brought to market. Landlords in seventeenth century Ulster who tried to establish markets without local merchant involvement soon found that their scheme was not viable and failure usually followed.[27] In the borderland area most of those who established markets or fairs were not local landowners. Only Thomas Ball, who tried to establish the market at Crossmaglen, could be described as an improving landlord. Ball was a Cromwellian lieutenant who was granted part of the lands of Sir Turlough O'Neill of the Fews and tried to develop them. According to the 1659 'census' there was a high concentration of British on his lands which would suggest that he was attempting to attract tenants from elsewhere in Ulster to settle and improve his estate. Over the borderland as a whole there were few men with either the resources or initiative to undertake the sort of projects which were being developed elsewhere in Ulster and which transformed the economy of much of the province.

This fragmentation of landownership and lack of control by one, or a few, powerful landlords to promote development, which characterized the borderlands in the seventeenth century, had implications beyond the sphere of economic development. The landlord and the large tenants on any estate were not only the main promoters of economic change they were also the basis of the local government structure. They acted as agents of the central government by serving in the offices of sheriff, sub-sheriff, justice of the peace and, at a lower social level, parish constables. The absence of a group of ready made office holders meant that law enforcement was poor and social control weak. Consequently, it was towards areas such as the borderlands that the tories, or bandits, of the late seventeenth century gravitated. This fact had an economic cost for the area in its quest for wealth. The jury at the Dungannon Assizes in 1667, for example, reported that, as a direct result of the activities of the tories, beer and ale sales had fallen by one third. Merchants were afraid to come to the market which resulted in lost sales of £10,000 a year in the cattle trade alone. Oliver Plunkett, the Catholic archbishop of Armagh fully appreciated the effect of toryism on the borderlands commenting that 'nobody would come to buy from them or sell to them for fear of bandits'.[28] The south Armagh area became well known as a centre of outlaw activity through the spectacular, and well documented, career of Redmond O'Hanlon who used south Armagh as his base during the late seventeenth century.[29] However, the problem of bandits in this area was not a new feature in the late seventeenth century. A description of Ireland in 1598 commented that 'Fews bordereth upon the English Pale . . . it is a very strong country of wood and bog peopled with certain of the O'Neills accustomed to live much on the spoils of the Pale'. Louth was described as bordering on the baronies of Fews and Farney 'by means whereof it is exposed to the incursions of the rude people who in times past kept a great part of the country lying next to them waste'.[30]

This type of raiding was part of traditional Gaelic Irish society in which a man's influence was extended not by conquest and encastellation but by cattle raiding and acquiring new followers, which were the main measure of a man's status. Thus in 1609 the solicitor general Sir Robert Jacob, commented of Turlough Mac Henry O'Neill of the Fews that 'he hath linked himself within the most powerful men in that country. This man is very much to be suspected, for he has 100 men at his command, and gives meat and drink and wages (which they call bonnaght) to idle and loose persons which has always been a course held amongst the Irish to make themselves great'.[31] Changing social standards during the seventeenth century led to a decline in this practise as status became determined by landholding rather than followers. Many of these swordsmen found employment elsewhere, including the armies of continental Europe and two of Sir Turlough's sons served in the army of Spanish Flanders, but the problem of idle and 'masterless' men remained throughout the seventeenth century.

It would be wrong to see the woodkerne and tories of the seventeenth century as the direct counterparts of these swordsmen. Some certainly were but others had more varied careers moving in and out of robbery as needs required it. Donel Oge O'Coney from Mayo, for example, was described in 1627 as a schoolmaster yet his earlier career had included a period in the Low Countries and as a woodkerne.[32] The seventeenth century also saw the opening up of new opportunities for theft. In the sixteenth century most ill-gotten gains, such as cattle had been eaten as part of a feast, kept for their milk or as a demonstration of a man's wealth. The opening up of a network of markets and fairs in seventeenth century Ulster presented the possibility of selling stolen cattle or other goods at a fair and purchasing other goods. One deposition of Brian O'Hogan in 1627 recorded that a number of native Irish bandits in County Tyrone stole cattle from settlers and sold them to a butcher in Armagh called Roger Russell.[33]

Late seventeenth century banditry was the successor to the activities of the woodkerne in the earlier part of the century. It became a much more obvious problem than it had been earlier. One reason for this was a change in the tactics of the late seventeenth century tories. The late seventeenth century bandits were much better organised than their earlier counterparts, operating in large groups commanded by one leader and so were much more obvious and menacing. 'This new way of torying' according to Sir George Acheson, in an account of the Ulster tories compiled for the duke of Ormond in 1667, 'was first brought in among them and shown them by such as had been abroad to foreign wars . . . the like practices being too much used abroad, and permitted the soldiery by military convenience'.[34] The second development which made the tory problem more obvious was the success of the Dublin government in spreading its authority throughout the whole country during the late seventeenth century. Early seventeenth century Ulster had been composed of a number of large power blocks in which the local landowner, whether newcomer or native, had reigned supreme, acknowledging the authority of the Dublin administration only when it suited. This situation changed in the 1650s when a combination of debt, heavy taxation and strong central government had broken the authority of the Ulster lords.[35] Only in areas such as the borderlands where authority had been always weak did government penetration continue to have little effect. These regions remained open to whoever could muster enough power to command them. The reorganising of the tories gave them that power. It was the presence of these bands which more than anything else gave the Ulster borderlands the appearance of being uncivil and barbarous regions. Sir George Acheson, for instance, referred to the hideouts of the tories as 'those mountainous and boggy and coarse lands inhabited only by natives'.[36]

This was not simply the view from the central government. The Catholic church under Archbishop Oliver Plunkett, was trying, as part of its reform to reshape Irish society along the standards of Counter-Reformation Catholic Europe. This was as much a secular as an ecclesiastical matter. According to one early seventeenth century bishop the role of the Counter-Reformation was to 'eliminate barbarous customs, abolish bestial rites and convert the detestable intercourse of savages into polite manners and a care for the commonwealth'.[37] For Plunkett the survival of toryism within his own diocese was a grave embarrassment and he attempted to stamp it out. In 1670, for example, he acted as intermediary with the Dublin government to persuade twenty-six tories to surrender with pardons, eight being of the gallowglass family of MacDonnell in south Armagh. Persuasion had only limited success and Plunkett took stronger measures condemning the tories at the Synod of Ardpatrick in 1678. As a result of his actions Plunkett was physically attacked by tories.[38]

In the final analysis the tory problem survived in the borderlands, and other remote areas of the country such as Connemara, after it disappeared from most of the rest of Ireland because the tories could count on local support in areas with no alternative leadership and because the traditions of these areas gave sanction to their actions. As Acheson commented in 1667 one encouragement of the Ulster tories was 'the foolish ancient way of hospitality to receive and give food to all comers of their nation [the native Irish] not enquiring the cause of their coming or business; so that they continue wandering from house to house as long as they will'.[39] This support was not confined to material possessions. The Irish poets of the borderlands composed poems in praise of the tories in the way native Irish lords would have been praised in earlier generations. There were also a number of Franciscan clergy who were involved with bands of tories in the borderlands. As the duke of Ormond put it they were 'told by their spiritual misleaders that the course they are in is little worse than spoiling the Egyptians was in the Israelites'.[40] However, it was not that these men were in some way ideologically opposed to the government of seventeenth century Ireland; Redmond O'Hanlon even offered to assist the government in hunting tories at one point. Moreover they were not a coherent body and many of the large bands fragmented as smaller groups established their own operations. They existed because they were part of a society which was not yet integrated into a market economy and in which wealth was redistributed in ways other than through the market, such as the cattle raiding which was ubiquitous in late sixteenth century Ulster. The large bands were only the tip of the iceberg and there were many smaller groups who attracted little attention but were engaged in similar activities. The poet Philip Mac Giolla Gunna who spent some time in Carlingford during the late seventeenth century referred to thefts of small items by tories in the area: hens, blankets, bags of corn and flax, turf, potatoes, nails, eggs and a butcher's knife for example.[41] Inevitably in a relatively poor area there was little to steal but small regular theft was in itself a method of exchange, albeit one not approved of by the central administration striving to maintain law and order on a uniform basis throughout the whole island.

The maintenance of law and order was not simply a secular matter. The seventeenth century also saw an attempt by the Catholic church to impose ecclesiastical discipline in the borderlands. Two complementary types of ecclesiastical jurisdiction existed in the archdiocese of Armagh. The southern part which lay within the Pale was characterised by a well-developed parish network served by secular clergy who were subject to a bishop. In the area within Ulster the parish network was poorly developed and the spiritual needs of the population were served mainly by regular clergy from religious orders, particularly the Franciscans. These two regimes were a reflection of the divergent historical development of the two regions. The Anglo-Norman settlement of the Pale had an established parish structure which had not been matched in Ulster. However it was the parish structure with a parochial clergy which was the norm of the Counter-Reformation movement in sixteenth century Europe and one aim of the Irish Counter-Reformation movement was to establish this structure in Ireland. The Synod of Drogheda, which promulgated the decrees of the Council of Trent in the diocese of Armagh in 1614, assumed that the parish would be the basis for the reconstructed Catholic church in the diocese. The issues at stake were greater than a theoretical model of how the church would operate since the right of the parish priest to officiate at funerals and baptisms carried with it payments of dues. The rights claimed by the religious orders to income from such sources undermined the parish priest's entitlement to parochial dues. There were acrimonious debates between the secular and regular clergy about these rights in the early seventeenth century. The parish system did develop in the northern part of the diocese of Armagh but in the borderlands although a parish system was present the clergy occupying the cures were members of religious orders and therefore technically not subject to the archbishop. In the early seventeenth century the Catholic archbishops of Armagh were not yet in a strong enough position to exert their authority over the religious orders. Some progress was made in promoting Counter-Reformation structures in the early seventeenth century but much of this achievement was undone during the 1650s and a description of the diocese in 1660 makes it clear that most of the ecclesiastical structures had collapsed.

The appointment of Oliver Plunkett as archbishop in 1669 saw a concerted attempt to restructure the diocese on approved Counter-Reformation lines. He ordained a large number of secular clergy to assume responsibility for parishes previously held by Franciscans. Plunkett was not enamoured with the friars as they did not fall under his jurisdiction. He referred to those in Ireland as 'dissolute friars' who had disturbed the peace of their orders' houses abroad and so had been sent home to Ireland. On more than one occasion he regarded the friars as overstepping their authority in matters such as dispensations on degrees of affinity in the case of marriage and demanded that this authority should be reserved to the local bishop. The bishops agreed but the religious orders refused to accept the ruling and appealed to Rome. What irked Plunkett most was the refusal of the regular clergy to accept his authority as archbishop over them.[42] The point was well made in the 1670s over the debate on questing, the right to gather alms after mass, between the Franciscans and the Dominicans who had recently arrived in the Carlingford area after a long absence. Plunkett himself had little sympathy with the dispute. He felt that questing, for instance, for barley, corn, lambs, geese, hens and money at the altar should not be allowed as it prevented parishioners attending mass. Moreover the alms were used by the friars, he alleged, to 'buy fine horses, fine clothes, Dutch cloth etc, they hire a servant and the luxury in these things is intolerable'. He also regarded it as contrary to the degrees of the Council of Trent which laid down that friars should not quest at the altar.[43] Despite these objections in 1671 he was appointed adjudicator by Rome in the dispute between the Franciscans and Dominicans. In October 1671 he ruled in favour of the Dominicans. The Franciscans refused to accept his ruling and appealed directly to Rome in March 1672 thus again undermining Plunkett's authority locally. The Propoganda Fide in Rome confirmed Plunkett's ruling in 1678 but the harm had already been done. Feelings between the Franciscans and Plunkett ran high and the guardian of the Franciscan friary at Dundalk threatened Plunkett to his face that they would treat him like Archbishop Richard Fitzralph in the fourteenth century 'whom they caused to be summoned to Avignon where he died of sorrow'.[44]

One other aspect of the clergy worried Plunkett; their quality. He complained in 1673 that there were too many clergy who were independent of the bishop but dependent on local gentry. At the Synod of Ardpatrick in 1678 the first three decrees all concerned the appointment of clergy and denying the laity a role in this process which they clearly enjoyed in south Ulster. The decrees restated the power of the bishop over the appointment of clergy and attempted to control the activities of the regular clergy.[45] Such controls were badly needed since with lay control the bishop could not vouch for the quality of the clergy. His concerns were legitimate. One tract composed about 1680 in south Ulster, the *Comhairle Mhic Clamha ó Achadh na Muilleann*, was scathing about the quality of the clergy, accusing them of ignorance and avarice. Seminary education to the required standard was only available abroad but few of the clergy had any continental education; only one priest in County Armagh had been ordained on the continent according to the 1704 returns of Catholic clergy. Moreover, according to the 1704 returns the clergy of the borderlands tended to be older than in the surrounding areas. In Louth, for example, the average age of the four clergy who operated in the north of the county was fifty-seven years as against an average age of forty-seven for the rest of the county. In south Armagh the average age of a cleric was fifty-five years in contrast to fifty years in the rest of the county.[46]

The controls which Plunkett devised to counter this situation particularly affected the religious orders and their alienation from the archbishop grew greater over time as he attempted to impose his ecclesciastial authority on the borderlands. It is significant that those who accused Plunkett of plotting rebellion during the Popish plot in 1681 were drawn from the Franciscans and others of whom Plunkett would not have approved from south Armagh. Edmund Murphy, for example, was parish priest of Killeavy where he had been born. Plunkett was dissatisfied with him, removed him from his native parish in 1674 and sent him to Salamanca where he remained until 1678. The two other main accusers of Plunkett, John Mac Moyer and Hugh Duffy, were Franciscans and had both studied on the Continent; Mac Moyer having been in Rome, Prague, Louvain and Madrid. Both were Edmund Murphy's curates in the parish of Killeavy.[47] While their annoyance at Plunkett's attempted reforms may not have been their main reasons for levelling their accusations it was certainly a contributory factor.

A third aspect of the society of the borderland in the late seventeenth century which resulted from its lack of firm landlord control and its status as a border between two regions was the existence of a strong tradition of spoken Irish and a flourishing poetic tradition which continued into the eighteenth century. The economic growth of seventeenth century Ulster resulted both in a rise of literacy and the increased use of English with a parallel decline of the Irish language. This change was, in the main, functional since the language of business and the law was English and the ability to read, and possibly write, in English became increasingly important in the transaction of business. As the native Irish were drawn into this commercial world as tenants or tradesmen they began to acquire a better knowledge of English. William Brooke noted in his 1682 description of Oneilland in north Armagh that 'Those few Irish we have amongst us are very much reclaimed of their barbarous customs, the most of them speaking English, and for agriculture they are little inferior to the English themselves'.[48]

The slow pace of economic change coupled with the relative scarcity of settlers using English in the Ulster-Leinster borderland meant that there was little incentive for the acquisition of English. Indeed, in 1680, when the Franciscan John Mac Moyer and others went to London to give evidence against Oliver Plunkett, who was being tried for treason, their evidence had to be taken down by a London schoolmaster 'by reason of their deficiency in the English tongue'. Irish continued to be the normal language of the borders and it was, of course, used by the local Catholic clergy for preaching.[49] It is natural therefore that most of the literary work to have survived from this area in the late seventeenth and eighteenth centuries was in Irish. The literary activity of the area is exemplified by the compositions of two late seventeenth century poets Séamas Dall Mac Cuarta and Pádraig Mac a Liondáin.[50] Many of the themes which cccur in these poems are traditional ones found in Gaelic poetry from earlier generations. They indulged in debates over the relative merits of Ulster and Leinster, a theme which can be paralleled in earlier poetic debates about the importance of Leath Modha and Leath Cuinn and the position of the Shannon. Laments in a traditional caoineadh metre were also an important feature of the poetry of both men, and are evidence that these poets fulfilled a social function by lamenting the death of significant individuals much as earlier generations of poets had done in respect of the native Irish elite. Pádraig Mac a Liondáin was a relatively wealthy farmer and was able to provide hospitality for visiting poets and musicians at his house in imitation of the older tradition of patronage and hospitality. Although the language and metre was simpler than in the works of the professional bardic poets, some of the works of the poets of the borderlands were emulating the earlier themes. The poetry of Séamas Dall Mac Cuarta included classical references and allusions to the mythological history of Ireland which were frequently used by the traditional poets.

The works of Mac Cuarta and Mac a Liondáin thus reflected aspects of the traditional literary values of the elite society of Gaelic Ireland. There were, however, some significant differences. Lacking training in the skills of the bardic poets, they were unable to reproduce the highly technical language and standard motifs of the traditional bardic schools. There was little need to do this in any event since the genre fulfilled a specific propaganda purpose in traditional Gaelic lordship society in which poems were commissioned and poets patronised by great lords. The replacement of lordship society by a different form of social organisation which had little use for traditional forms of political propaganda led to a decline of this sort of poetic patronage. Instead patronage was applied to other activities such as the writing of history and the commissioning of transcriptions of earlier works. Rather than cling to old metres, the poets of south Ulster developed their own style, and a favourite blend of the old and the new was the 'rann agus Amhrán' metre which was particularly popular in the borderland area. The poets of the borderlands preserved the memory of early Gaelic traditions in their compositions, but their poems had to be relevant to their own place and time. Thus for example, a lament or a praise poem composed by a late seventeenth century poet from the borderlands was more likely to relate to a bishop – Archbishop Hugh Mac Mahon, Bishop James O'Sheil who was a Franciscan, or to a priest – Fr Phelim O Hanlon, Fr Philip O Reilly – or an English style landlord such as the baron of Slane, than to the descendants of the old Gaelic nobility.[51] There were many innovative developments in the subject matter of the poetry, especially in the area of political poetry but even here in supporting the Jacobite cause the poets were following a pattern traceable to the early seventeenth century of accepting the Stuarts as kings of Ireland. These poets were also in part the inheritors of another older tradition of poetry, that of the 'file an tslua', poets who had written not for great lords but for more popular consumption. In this tradition the works of the south Ulster-north Louth poets reflected not the political and dynastic preoccupations of aristocractic society but included drinking songs, love songs and humorous poems. In this ways the themes of traditional poetry were blended with new innovations to reflect the needs of a survival of traditional Gaelic society. Some of the poems reflect other features of borderland society which were a blend of traditional values brought by the native settlers and adaptations to local conditions. There are poems in praise of tories and while there is a considerable body of religious poetry, with particular emphasis on devotion to Mary and on the passion of Christ, and poems in praise of selected members of the Catholic clergy, significantly there are none in praise of Oliver Plunkett, archbishop of Armagh who wished to change the religious and social structure of the region to bring it into line with a wider world.[52]

By 1700 the border between Ulster and Leinster had not disappeared despite the change within Ulster as a result of plantation and colonisation over the previous century. The reasons for the continued existence of a border were very different in nature from those which had delineated the separateness of Gaelic Ulster from the Anglo-Irish Pale in 1600. The changes of the seventeenth century had maintained the distinctiveness of Ulster through the colonial experience. Ulster was now Presbyterian, rather than Catholic, and the government was anxious to contain Presbyterianism within what they perceived was the boundary of Ulster. The growth of Presbyteriansim was only part of a wider change in Ulster society. Population rose dramatically in the seventeenth century, mainly as a result of colonisation. This colonisation began in the areas nearest the main ports of Londonderry and Donaghadee and pushed south and west bringing with them new ideas about economic organisation, estate management and new cultural values. In the process the native Irish either absorbed these new ideas or retreated before them. By the end of the century they had been pushed to the southern boundary of the influence of Ulster where it met the already commercially well developed area of the Pale. The result was an economic borderland of poor, little developed, land with limited contact with a wider commercialised world. It was certainly not impossible to develop this land as the eighteenth century experience was to show. Similarly the spread of the authority of central government, intimately associated with colonisation, left the borderland isolated and apparently more violent than the surrounding area. The frontier was not simply an economic and political one since the border towards which the old order had been pushed was also a linguistic one of long standing. As a result the economic border became coterminous with a linguistic one where a pocket of Irish speaking survived, and which produced a considerable volume of literature in Irish. The changes of the seventeenth century were not only economic and cultural. The Catholic church was also attempting to develop the island along the lines of the continental Counter-Reformation. Here again the Ulster-Leinster border was an area which could not easily be integrated into a wider ecclesiastical world, being caught between the well-developed medieval parish structure with secular clergy in the Pale and the system in Ulster which still favoured the religious orders. The result was tension between the secular and regular clergy where the two contrasting traditions overlapped and the difficulties were expressed in particular in the disputes between the archbishop of Armagh, Oliver Plunkett, and the Franciscans. These various features were not isolated elements randomly occurring in the borderland area. Rather they were all manifestations of the characteristic workings of a borderland society which evolved as a result of economic, political, cultural and religious changes introduced in the course of the seventeenth century in an area which was already a distinctive frontier zone in the sixteenth century. In the longer term the borderland was to become integrated into a wider political, economic, cultural and religious world but the experience of the seventeenth century determined that subsequent integration would not be without its own difficulties which would continue to isolate the borderland.

7 The Reshaping of the Borderlands *c.*1700–1840

W. H. CRAWFORD

Although the inhabitants of the region, comprising south Armagh, south Down, north Louth and east Monaghan, became increasingly amenable to control by the Dublin government and the common law during the seventeenth century, the early eighteenth century countryside was still regarded as a desolate wilderness, sparsely populated. It might have continued long in that state if the mountain mass of Slieve Gullion and Carlingford had not separated Dublin and the Pale from the developing economy of central and eastern Ulster. More than ever before, gentry and merchants found it necessary and profitable to traverse the mountains, and so they became promoters of schemes to drive roads through the glens as well as suppressors of the robbers, or tories, who molested travellers. Subsequently, it was the growing prosperity of the ports of Newry and Dundalk that was to provide the capital to colonise the mountainous region with men skilful and energetic enough to reclaim farms from the heathy moorlands and to establish new market centres and lines of communication throughout the region and with the countryside beyond.

By the end of the seventeenth century there were two major routes through the region from Dundalk to Newry and Armagh respectively. The more important was the great road from Dundalk to Newry. Successive English armies in the campaign against Hugh O'Neill in 1600–1 negotiating the Moyry Pass, the 'Gap of the North', found 'naturally one of the most difficult passages of Ireland' that wound among rocks, bogs, and dense woods. A century later a new and more direct road from Dundalk had been opened through the glen where the railway now runs.[1] At its highest point stood the new village of Jonesborough for which a patent for four fairs had been taken out in 1705 by Roth Jones,[2] a Dublin lawyer who had purchased the lands related to the Moyry Castle. Although there were many long ascents and sudden descents on this road it became the coach road linking Dublin to Belfast later in the eighteenth century. For the other major route from Dundalk to Armagh a contemporary traveller has left this account dated August 1708:

> We designed for Armagh [from Dundalk] and went sixteen miles towards it, mostly on the very wild mountains, the Fews. These mountains are of a boggy, heathy soil, the road through them of a rocky gravel; in all this way met but one house and nothing like corn, meadow, or enclosures. We baited [fed the horses] on them at the second house, which is called Black Ditch, where is also a small foot barracks, but without any soldiers. Here was miserable entertainment, not so much as tolerable grass within two mile of them. From hence two or three miles brings you to the end of the mountains, and then you enter into a pleasant enclosed corn country which in five or six miles brings you through very new made roads to Armagh.[3]

The danger to travellers from robbers on this road is emphasised by the reference to the 'Black Ditch' military barracks. These barracks had been built on land leased by the Crown in 1700 and by 1705 four fairs were listed in an almanac. Perched almost a thousand feet above sea level on a pass through the hills, it was not designed to attract settlement but to act as a place of refuge for wayfarers. It fell into decay after the construction of the Fews Barracks at Camly in the 1730s, midway between Dundalk and Armagh. Close by the Fews Barracks was Johnston's Bridge, a small settlement founded in 1714 by John Johnston. His son John, who took out a patent in 1731 for a weekly market and four fairs at Johnston's Bridge, held the appointment of barrack-master and gained a reputation for having 'cleared the roads to Armagh and all the neighbouring counties so well of the rogues that used to infest the country that he has rendered them passable'.[4]

Although this evidence confirms that the Dublin government did carry out its responsibility to make the roads safe for travellers, the government could not claim credit for the great and rapid expansion of the commerce that passed through these mountains. That was due rather to important economic changes in the regions adjoining the borderlands. To the north, linen, the product of a cottage industry based on processing the flax crop, was being finished for overseas customers and carried to Dublin, the commercial capital, where a Linen Hall had been erected in 1728. In Ulster the financial returns from this industry were inducing so many people to take up spinning and weaving that the linen-producing districts could not grow enough to feed themselves and had to import grain from the regions to the south and west. The extent of the dependence of linen workers on imports of oatmeal (and linen yarn) was explained by a County Armagh clergyman writing in 1751

> When food is dear, goods come cheap to market and the sale is quick and the profit upon each parcel reasonable; when food is cheap our goods are scarce and being bought dear in the country markets they lie upon the factor's hand in Dublin and London. . . .
>
> The weaver and spinster for the most part depend upon weekly markets for provisions for their family and it is a grievance to them to be obliged to pay sometimes a fourth penny more for the same quantity of food than they paid the week past; and this is perhaps owing to the artifice of mean dealers called hucksters.[5]

The scale of the trade between Leinster and Ulster in grain may be gauged from the comments of a pamphlet published in 1740, two years before the opening of the Newry Canal which was destined to provide cheaper transport for grain throughout the Lough Neagh basin:

> . . . generally in these hard years a great quantity of meal has been bought at Newry and carried to parts more northerly, even some as far as about Coleraine. . . . yet this year hath been the most extraordinary in that way of dealing. The number of horses that go to Newry three days in the week, and the quantity of meal brought from it is surprising: . . . A small quantity only of that meal could be the produce of the country next adjacent to Newry; but most of it came (and some at a considerable distance) from the counties to the southward of Newry, on finding a ready market for it there, and a high price, occasioned by the scarcity in the northern counties.[6]

This great demand from Ulster for grain had stimulated agricultural improvement on such a considerable scale that contemporaries talked about a revolution in agriculture. For the project that gave birth to the Physico-Historical Society with its ambition to publish up-to-date surveys of Irish counties, an account of Monaghan in 1740 explained the nature of the revolution

> This county which was naturally rough and barren, is greatly reclaimed by the labour of the husbandman. . . . Before the late happy revolution the greater part of it was under herds of black cattle, by which the inhabitants mostly lived and paid their rents being strangers (in a great measure) to tillage and manufactures. The hills that were then deemed barren are now under proper husbandry, being cleared from brush, wood and heath, produce a plentiful subsistence to the occupier, and the bottoms that were lost under water and flow bogs are by draining made good pasture and meadows.
>
> The grain this country produces is wheat, bere, barley, rye, oats – there is also plenty of potatoes – not only sufficient to support the inhabitants but likewise to supply some of the neighbouring counties with bere, barley and oatmeal. The redundancy is owing to the great improvement of late made in husbandry and to the qualities of marl found even in the coarsest and worst lands. . . .
>
> This county formerly bred good horses but the tillage with the inhabitants are so increased, and the farms are so little – being generally from ten to thirty acres – that there is no pasture for studs or breeding of cattle of any sort more than what is necessary for the immediate service of the farmer. The lands for the greater part are productive of flax and the linen manufacture has made great progress in this county . . .[7]

It was to undertake similar pioneering work in the neighbouring parish of Creggan in south Armagh that five landed proprietors in 1733 invited Presbyterians to settle on their estate and to encourage them they underwrote the stipend of a Presbyterian minister to take charge of the Creggan congregation. The success of this policy was considerable. Information collected in the 1830s by one of their descendants lists more than sixty individual surnames shared by those who colonised more than a dozen townlands in south-west Armagh. The majority of them were of Scots descent and came from County Down. Whereas some of them had settled previously throughout Monaghan and south Armagh, they were attracted to this nucleus.[8] An advertisement in the *Belfast News-Letter* dated 30 October 1747 spelled out the attractions of one of the townlands in the district:

To be let, at a reasonable rent, for lives renewable for ever, from the first day of May next, several convenient farms, in all about 1000 acres of good land, part of Tullyvallen in the barony of Fews and county of Armagh, lying on the great road leading from Armagh to Dublin by Dundalk, the estate of Alexander Hamilton, Esq., within 8 miles of Armagh, 11 of Dundalk, and 4 of Castleblayney, all good market towns, and on which lands of Tullyvallen is held a market every Saturday. On each of said farms there is plenty of good meadow and turf; a large river runs through the middle of said lands that never wants water sufficient to turn many mills, with many places very proper for bleaching greens, and a fall of 180 feet in less than two miles, and places where mill ponds may be easily made. By the great plenty of turf, water, bog, timber for building and meadow, the linen manufacture may be carried on as cheap as in any part of Ireland. Mr Hamilton's servant at his house on the lands, will shew the ground; and those who have a mind to take any part of it, may send their proposals to Mr Hamilton at his house in Henry Street, Dublin, or give the same to Mr John Gordon, merchant in Belfast.

Of especial interest in this advertisement are the references to the linen industry for which, it was inferred, Tullyvallen would prove such a suitable location. They take account of recent major technical developments in the industry. The successful adaptation of the technology used to finish woollen cloth in water-powered tuck-mills so that it could be employed in bleach mills to buck (wash) and beetle (finish) linen cloth, enabled bleachers to process greater quantities of cloth more cheaply than anywhere else in western Europe without spoiling the cloth.[9] Profits were to be made by those who could lay out bleachyards provided with plenty of water during the summer bleaching season. In south Armagh the major river was the Callan. Although the first bleachyard was opened there as late as 1743, by 1771 it was reckoned that with its tributaries it powered thirty-six bleachyards to finish annually 108,500 pieces of yard wide linens, each piece measuring twenty-five yards, totalling 2,712,500 yards.

The relationship between the expansion of the linen industry and land reclamation was described in 1795

and the manufacture gaining strength, about fifty years ago they began to push their improvements into the mountains which separate the low country from Louth, and by the assistance of turf fuel being convenient and good constant rivers for feeding bleachyards and working machinery, they were enabled to extend their improvements in the mountains. And many wealthy farmers and manufacturers were induced by the low price of them – about a shilling to half a crown an acre to take farms, lime and burn them although the limestone quarries were distant from the centre of the mountains measuring from the quarries at Armagh or those on the south side towards Dundalk at least eight or nine miles either way but their spirited industry has surmounted all difficulties. And within these forty years Newtown Hamilton, a considerable town, has been erected in the centre and a weekly linen market, well supplied, established. A strong yeomanry and many excellent houses and roads running through the country in all directions have been made here, formerly a perfectly black mountain. This is an example worthy the attention of the landed interest and landholders of Ireland, as these mountains were lofty without any internal manures, and generally very wet and bad stuff to work on, and yet it is no exaggeration to say those inhabitants have reduced more mountain to profitable and excellent tillage ground than any other county in Ireland can boast of. The small pot kiln is what they mostly all use to burn their lime.

The business of carrying limestone into all the recesses of the mountains is incessantly practised and in return bringing turf down to the bleachyards and the city of Armagh so that as long as a tuft of heath is to be seen in those mountains their profitable industry will

> not cease, and in place of its being a region where neither man or beast could subsist fifty years ago, this country is become the granary of the county in a great measure for oats and barley.[10]

In this description of County Armagh in 1795 Robert Stevenson catches the contemporary mood of optimism that by dint of hard work and shrewd investment men could improve their environment. Tenants who were prepared to carry turf to the bleachgreens and return with loads of limestone to manure their holdings were regarded as industrious and worthy of encouragement. They and their cottiers deserve the credit of converting tracts of mountain into enclosed farms. It is the cumulative achievement of men labouring year in year out that is so impressive.

As a clergyman pointed out in 1816

> Reclaiming ground here is attended with vast labour and expense. The land will not produce crops without lime, and it is naturally so wet, that it must be drained before lime is put on it. . . . On a fair and full calculation, the expense of reclaiming an acre, may be estimated at twenty pounds. Nevertheless the reclamation of land continued with each succeeding generation.[11]

Yet it is essential also to appreciate the scale of investment in fixed capital made by those who created bleachgreens and corn mills. Such a concern was advertised for sale in the *Belfast News-Letter*.

> To be set for any term of years, or sold for ever, as may be agreed on, and entered upon immediately, a convenient large bleach green, with all necessary utensils for bleaching, with a large turf stack. The head stock and green are supplied with a sufficient quantity of spring-water. An excellent mill, and all other conveniences thereto belonging, with three pair of rub-boards, drawing engine, wash-mill, beetling engine, traversing-engine, drying loft to dry one hundred pieces of linen at once, a large slated house and boiling house, with a convenient fall for another mill, all newly built by James Lowry, millwright, with thirteen acres of land, and two houses for bleachers on said land, and turf bog: Also, a corn-mill, with ten acres of land, and turf bog, for three lives, adjoining said bleachgreen, situated on the River of Jonesborough and County of Louth, adjoining the Bridge of Jonesborough, four miles from Newry. Any person who inclines to treat for the same, may apply to Messrs William and James Twibill in Jonesborough, who will show the premises, and receive proposals for the same. Dated this 19th October, 1764.

This must be the green mentioned by Robert Stephenson in his tour of 1761.[12] Although further details of the sale are missing, figures survive for a County Tyrone green capable of finishing annually seven or eight thousand pieces of linen: it was estimated at £838 in 1768 and sold in 1805 for £1,425.[13]

The linen bleached in Twybell's green, like that in the larger neighbouring green in Ravensdale owned by the Ogle brothers of Newry, was purchased in the counties of Down and Armagh. The weaving of linen had not spread south from County Armagh into County Louth and so north Louth continued its role as a spinning district. As Robert Stephenson had noted in his report of 1760: 'In the neighbourhood of Dundalk and towards Carlingford the yarn is made from two to four dozen [cuts] in the pound [i.e. a medium quality yarn], and mostly exported; their flax is but indifferent except about Dundalk. They have but few weavers and the small quantity of linen made by them is mostly coarse yard-wides and sold in Newry market.'[14] In effect, therefore, the linen industry was then concentrated on the northern side of the watershed of the south Armagh mountains, except for the outliers in Ravensdale alongside the main road from Newry to Dublin. Indeed, even within the following half century the industry made little penetration into the parishes of Creggan, Faughart, and Ballymascanlon, lying along the Armagh–Louth border.[15]

Associated with the opening up of the countryside was the development of the road network and the creation of new market towns. These phenomena were interrelated and depended to a considerable extent on the initiative and energy of the landlord class. They were well aware of the value of roads in the reclamation of tracts of marginal land. They knew that roads enabled wheel cars to fetch limestone from the distant quarries or transport turf and manure. A wheel car could carry five or six hundredweights whereas a pack animal was well laden with two hundredweights: a single driver could manage several cars as easily as he could control a string of pack-horses. Landlords also appreciated the opportunity that new roads often provided for reshaping holdings so that they would provide easy access from the new roads. They knew that they could attract a better class of tenant to estates serviced by good roads and that such tenants would enhance the value of the property by hedging, ditching and building farmsteads. In short, the construction of roads through an estate could multiply its rental within a generation or two.[16]

To initiate this process the first step for a landlord was to travel to Dublin where he would sue out and pay for a royal patent granting him the right to establish and administer a weekly market and several annual fairs. He would then announce in the local newspaper his intention to create a market town and invite tradesmen and shop-keepers to settle there. Since the law stipulated that major roads might be laid out between market towns only, the construction of roads linking the new market town to its older neighbours became the responsibility of the grand jury of the county. After the 1765 road act permitted the county grand juries to impose a county cess, or rate charge per acre, to finance the building of these roads, many more miles of road were laid and bridges constructed at the expense of the county rather than the landlord. This process was encouraged by a further 'Act for the making of narrow roads through the mountainous unimproved parts of this kingdom' (11 & 12 George III c.20) that permitted the grand juries to raise money for that purpose. There is often, therefore, a direct relationship between the creation of new market towns and the construction of roads by the grand jury. It is probable, for example, that the decisions first of Richard Jackson in 1762 to take out a patent for markets and fairs in Forkhill, and then of Sir Archibald Acheson in 1767 to do the same for

Table 1 Eighteenth century grants of markets and fairs

1731	John Johnston's patent for a Thursday market in JOHNSTON'S BRIDGE and fairs on 14 May, 14 July, 14 October and 14 November.
1743	Robert Nedham's patent for a Thursday market in BALLYBOUGHT (SOUTHWARK, that part of Newry in County Armagh) and four two-day fairs on the second Tuesday in each of the months of March, June, September, November.
1746	Alexander Hamilton's patent for a Saturday market in NEWTOWNHAMILTON (TULLYVALLEN) and two two-day fairs commencing on 26 April and 26 October respectively.
1754	James McCullagh's patent for a Friday market in CULLOVILLE and two two-day fairs commencing on 26 April and 26 October respectively.
1759	Provost's [of Trinity College Dublin] patent for a Friday market in KEADY and fairs on 4 April, 4 June, 14 August and 14 October. In 1815 a further patent provided fairs on the second Friday in every month.
1762	Richard Jackson's patent for a Wednesday market in FORKHILL and fairs on 1 May and 29 September.
1764	Thomas Fortescue's patent for a Friday market in RAVENSDALE and fairs on the Friday after Easter Sunday, the second Friday in July, the first Friday in October and the second Friday in November.
1766	George Nedham's patent for a Friday market in KILKEEL.
1767	Sir Archibald Acheson's patent for a Monday market in BELLEEK and fairs on 3 February, 3 May, 3 August and 3 November.
1769	Robert Ross's patent for a Tuesday market in ROSTREVOR and fairs on the Tuesday in Whit week, 1 August, 19 September and 1 November.
1771	Robert Sibthorpe's patent for a Thursday market in ROCHEDALE (AGHNEVACHY) and fairs on 20 June and 20 October.
1776	Roger Hall's patent for a Friday market in WARRENPOINT and fairs on 24 June and 30 November.
1813	Although a patent for a Wednesday market had been taken out for CROSSMAGLEN (CROSSMAGHENOGE) by Thomas Ball in 1674 with four two-day fairs commencing 15 May, 25 July, 24 August and 15 December respectively, they do not appear in the almanacs. In 1813 another Thomas Ball took out a patent for a Tuesday market and fairs on the first Friday after Candlemas, the first Friday after 17 March, Friday before Michaelmas and first Friday in November.
1813	Although a patent for a Tuesday market had been taken out for CULLYHANNA by Thomas Ball in 1674 with fairs on 9 May, 9 July, 9 October and 9 December, they do not appear in the almanacs. In 1813 another Thomas Ball took out a patent for the renewal of the Tuesday market with fairs on the second Tuesday in January, the second Tuesday in April, the second Tuesday before Midsummer Day and the second Tuesday in October.
1829	The earl of Charlemont took out a patent for CAMLOUGH with fairs on the third Monday in each month.

Source: *Report to the lord lieutenant of the commissioners appointed to enquire into the state of the fairs and markets in Ireland.* H.C. 1852–3 (1674) xli, appendix

Belleek, were related to the construction of the new road linking Dundalk with Markethill, the chief town on Acheson's estate.

Once a market town had been established, the major problem for its landlord was to attract people to attend his weekly market. During the middle decades of the eighteenth century there was great competition among landlords to institute markets for the sale of linen yarn and cloth by those engaged in the industry as well as the purchase of oatmeal for food and candles for light: many landlords advertised premiums for those prepared to buy and sell in the market. To attract linen-drapers it was necessary to provide a market house to shelter them from inclement weather and inns to sustain them and accommodate their business transactions. Without the attendance of linendrapers there was little prospect of success for markets. In many small market towns, therefore, it soon became difficult to sustain a weekly market or even a fortnightly market and by the close of the century such places rated as no more than villages. According to Sir Charles Coote's *Statistical Survey of the County of Armagh* (Dublin, 1804) Johnston's Bridge, Newtownhamilton, Culloville, Keady, Forkhill and Belleek no longer held markets. In Louth the market town of Rochedale, halfway between Dundalk and Castleblayney, disappeared, if it had ever existed, while Ravensdale lost any urban character.

It is clear that it was one thing to talk about creating new market towns but it was another problem to sustain them. The major purpose of a weekly market was to supply the inhabitants of the town where it was held with agricultural produce such as oatmeal, candles, meat and butter: it presupposed that the town was a centre for industries and services where people earned money in order to buy from the farmers. Ulster, however, had no major industries except the domestic linen industry and the majority of Ulster weavers preferred to live in the countryside working small-holdings as an adjunct to weaving. The inland towns of Ulster, therefore, were much smaller than the port towns. Yet many of the inland towns had important roles as collecting points for local agricultural surpluses for they could be regularly visited by merchants from the ports or their commission agents. As late as the 1820s the linen industry continued to be conducted on these lines by linen-drapers and agents sent out by the bleachgreens: weekly markets were held in some towns but monthly markets only in the smaller towns.[17] In the later decades of the eighteenth century the market for cattle and pigs increased rapidly with demand from Britain and so there was a need for more frequent fairs. Although many places had been authorised by their patents to hold either two or four fairs annually, some of them such as Newtownhamilton, now began to hold monthly fairs, usually on a fixed date in each month such as the 16th, or the third Thursday in order to coincide with the local market day. The owners of Keady, Trinity College Dublin, formalised the arrangement by securing a new patent in 1815 for monthly fairs but in this region no other landlords took the trouble. It is significant, however, that the landlord of the neighbouring villages of Crossmaglen and Cullyhanna, whose markets and fairs patents dating from 1674 had long fallen into disuse, took out new patents for markets and quarterly fairs in 1813: one form of urban renaissance. Indeed within a short time Crossmaglen had a Friday market for provisions and a fair on the first Friday in every month for farming stock.

The reappearance of the fairs of Crossmaglen and Cullyhanna in 1813 may be no more than a minor indication of the tremendous boost given to Irish agriculture by the French Wars. Yet it has been well said that those 'years from 1793 to 1815 were the culminating phase of a long wave of expansion going back to the 1740s'.[18] So far this essay has analysed and illustrated three major factors in that expansion as they affected the borderlands: communications, agriculture and the linen industry. To understand the fourth factor it is necessary to consider the borderlands as the hinterland of the two rising ports of Dundalk and Newry that define their southern and northern boundaries respectively.

Both Dundalk and Newry began to show obvious signs of development by the 1730s. Whereas Newry had been burned by the Jacobites during their retreat from Ulster in 1689, Dundalk with its much older townscape had escaped destruction. During the 1720s, however, Viscount Limerick who owned more than 7,000 acres, including the greater part of the town, turned out to be an enthusiastic improver. In return for the surrender by the corporation of any legal claims to its former Commons, Limerick founded a Free School in the town in 1725 and by 1740 he had provided a harbour by constructing into the river a pier that could accommodate vessels of up to 130 tons. This was the basis of further quay extensions later in the century by the corporation which were to prove essential to the future of the town and its hinterland. Lord Limerick was also concerned in the passing of an act in 1733 that permitted a body of eighty-five gentry and clergy to establish a turnpike trust to reconstruct and maintain the road north from Dundalk as far as Banbridge. Locally, in 1740 he contributed £600 towards the building of a new session house, supervised the demolition of the town walls and fortifications as well as the ruinous remains of eighteen or nineteen tower houses, such as survive in Carlingford, and used the stone to build a rampart for reclaiming some 800 acres of salt marsh.[19]

Lord Limerick's most impressive achievement in the eyes of his contemporaries was his success in attracting the De Joncourt linen enterprise to his town. About 1730 a Rev William Woolsey had set up a damask factory in Dundalk with twelve weavers brought from Portadown.[20] This scheme attracted the interest of Primate Boulter and he was the prime mover in encouraging the De Joncourt brothers to come to Ireland to set up a factory for weaving the variety of fine linens known as cambrics: he negotiated with the Dublin government and the Linen Board on their behalf and assisted in raising a subscription of £30,000 for the project. Lord Limerick's offer to provide houses for the workmen, ground for the factory, and ten acres of land for growing flax, probably secured the enterprise for Dundalk. The De Joncourts were encouraged to go to France to bring back two flax-dressers, two spinning mistresses skilled in preparing the special yarns, and two weavers. They were able to train and employ the children of the Charity School (converted in 1738 into a Charter School to benefit from the 1733 act), the girls to spin and the boys to serve in the bleachgreen. The houses for the weavers were specially constructed with looms placed in well-lit, underground vaults to keep the air damp and prevent the yarns on the loom from breaking in a dry atmosphere. The company purchased all the cloth woven and had their own bleacher who retained the Dutch style of bleaching for these fine cloths.[21]

The project met with considerable success. By 1757 it was claimed that the company had manufactured cambrics and lawns to the value of more than £40,000.[22] Even Robert Stephenson, the arch critic of the industry, admitted after his visit in 1755:

> it certainly has effected this general good to the public, that a proper knowledge of this branch in handling the yarn, sleaing and weaving cambrics, is now diffused all over the kingdom, and there is scarce a factory but there are some of the looms employed on thick or clear cambric for the use of the neighbourhood.
>
> . . . there were great quantities of cambrics in hands, some finished and they appeared as good as any foreign in respect of the manufacturing and colours.[23]

In 1764, however, Stephenson reported that the Cambric Company had 'in a great measure dissolved themselves' and were having 'to new form their scheme'. In the following year he noted that a John Christy was employing 120 looms at the Cambric Manufacture.[24] Some explanation of this state of affairs is provided by the comments of an American tourist, Samuel Rowland Fisher, when he visited the Manufacture in 1768. Although the scheme had been financed by subscriptions from merchants and the Linen Board itself, the production cost of the cambrics was double comparable French cloths while the quality was not so good. Fisher, who stayed with Thomas Christie at his home at Moyallen (near Gilford in County Down) saw the Dundalk cambric being finished at Christie's bleachyard. Indeed he had met Christie at the Manufacture where he was the only person still paying rent to the landlord.[25] It is very probable therefore that John Christy and Thomas Christie were the same man. However, when Arthur Young visited Dundalk in 1776 he learned that 'a cambric manufacture was established here by Parliament, but failed; it was, however, the origin of that more to the north'.[26]

The disappearance of the Cambric Manufacture had little lasting effect on Dundalk because prosperity was based on the agricultural products of its hinterland. By the final quarter of the eighteenth century Dundalk was sending large quantities of barley to Dublin by sea as well as exporting oats to ports around the Irish Sea and to London itself,[27] but it was still able to maintain several distilleries and breweries. The major grain growing districts were the barony of Farney in Monaghan and the county of Louth. This activity was responsible for the erection of corn-mills in the foothills of the mountains at such places as Forkhill and Ball's Mills where three annual fairs were held. Dundalk was able to support nine tanneries. Carrickmacross was the major market for grain, pigs and butter while the tiny village of Mullacrew had long been famous for its great fairs for sheep as well as cattle and pigs.

Hearth tax returns for 1800 record that among the boroughs returning members to the Irish parliament Dundalk ranked eighteenth out of forty. To pay its tax return of £174 only 238 houses, or twenty two per cent of its housing stock, contributed. The average of £30.73 per house suggests that the quality of these houses was good and compared well with its neighbour, Drogheda. The remaining 845 houses were exempt because they did not exceed the standard of artisan housing. The population of all the 1,083 houses is unlikely to have been much more than 7,500. By 1813 the population had reached 8,600, then 9,256 by 1821 and 10,078 by 1831. In comparison Newry's tax return was £361 paid by 542 houses (£30.66 per house) or thirty-six per cent of the housing stock. This pattern more closely resembles those of Belfast and Londonderry. Newry's population reached 10,013 by 1821 and rose to 13,065 by 1831.[28]

It is probable that Newry would have grown into a considerable port-town without the construction of the Newry to Lough Neagh canal in 1742, the earliest in the British Isles. In 1726, for instance, the custom-house for the district had been transferred to Newry from Carlingford. Yet the canal had a tremendous impact on the economic development of mid-Ulster and as late as 1768 it was said in north-west Ulster that 'most of the inhabitants above [south of] Omagh go to Newry for their goods'. The completion of the canal in 1742 gave Newry commercial dominance of the Lough Neagh basin for the next half century and a monopoly of supplying the major bleachgreens on the rivers Bann and Callan. In 1761 it was reckoned that 12,000 tons of merchandise annually passed through the canal as well as Tyrone coal, Carlingford limestone, and linen cloth, all of which paid no navigation tolls. It is a measure of the perception of contemporaries that in 1782 the majority of linen drapers in mid-Ulster supported the case for the erection of a white linen hall in Newry rather than Belfast: during the 1770s Newry had exported rather more linen than Belfast to Britain. The linen-drapers did not foresee that in the 1780s and 1790s Belfast would outpace Newry.[29] Yet Newry continued to prosper as a port. It conducted its own trade with the Baltic, the West Indies and the United States. Its reputation for shipping butter, pork, beef, hides for tanning, and (from the 1770s) live cattle and pigs, made it the major port for the counties of Cavan, Fermanagh and Monaghan as well as Armagh and west Down: butter was sometimes sent from as far away as Sligo. Like Dundalk, Newry had industries to process agricultural products such as distilleries, malthouses and breweries, soap and candle manufactories, tanneries, and mills for both flour and oatmeal. It also had mills for plating, rolling and slitting iron to make spades, shovels and scythes, as well as a foundry and ropeworks. For a time in the 1790s it had a pottery for blackwares, a tobacco-pipe manufactory and a flint glass manufactory.[30]

The major contrast between Dundalk and Newry lay in the character of their respective hinterlands. While Dundalk organised the agricultural economy of the wide plain of north Louth, Newry controlled the head of the long sea lough of Carlingford and the canal that linked it with the Lough Neagh basin. The most significant settlements on Carlingford Lough had been the ancient borough of Carlingford and the crossing place at Narrow-water where ferries operated and the larger ships transferred their cargoes to gabbards for the upstream journey to Newry. The urban functions of Carlingford had withered although its inhabitants were noted fishermen and purveyors of oysters to Dublin and other Irish Sea ports. They profited also by supplying lime for building the new streets and docks of Newry.[31] Narrow-water, which held three fairs in the year, was known for its salt-works. Its importance declined with the development by its landlord, Roger Hall, in the 1770s and 1780s of the new town of Warrenpoint where a dock and piers had been built for transhipping cargoes: Warrenpoint soon developed into a considerable town with a large distillery driven by a tall windmill. It became a seaside resort like its neighbour, Rostrevor, which had developed around a saltworks, a pottery and a quay that provided a refuge for shipping just inside the bar of Carlingford.[32] Yet the most remarkable illustration of change was to be found in the hills that lie to the north-west of Newry. From the ninety-acre lake of Camlough flowed for two miles into the river at Newry a stream that supplied power to drive mills for grinding corn, boulting flour, scutching flax and bleaching linens.[33] It should not be overlooked, however, that the mountainous character of the hinterland that provided Newry with some of its most profitable enterprises, also posed a threat to its economic future. The major road that ran west from Newry through Camlough, Belleek and Newtownhamilton to Castleblayney was reckoned to be

> a great thoroughfare on which is brought the whole trade of Cavan and Monaghan counties for the Newry market, but it is always in the most wretched state; the distance between these towns is but seventeen miles and, though so short is the distance, it is yet a good journey to accomplish it in one day; the traveller must not only risk the failure of the best appointed chaise and horses, but must also run no small danger of having his bones broken in the attempt.

Not surprisingly, the same author called attention to a scheme to link Castleblayney with Dundalk either by a canal or an 'iron road' which would leave Newry to mourn its loss.[34]

The condition of the Newry–Castleblayney road was not the result of neglect. The solution of the problem was not within the ability of contemporaries with such limited resources. The same might be said about the whole of the borderlands. No amount of activity could have converted it into fertile countryside. Here and there patches of land responded to spade cultivation and lime manure to give good crops. Throughout the region, however, many people had to be content with the returns of subsistence agriculture supplemented during this century by the potato, known then as 'the winter food of the poor'. Like much of upland and bogland Ireland this region might be classed as 'the best poor man's country': with potatoes for food and turf for warmth people were unlikely to die from hypothermia even when living in the ramshackle dwellings such as one traveller described in this region: 'The cabins one sees on the sides of the hills are the most miserable huts I ever saw, built with sods and turf, no chimney, the door made of a hurdle, the smoke goes all out of the door, the cocks and hens, pigs, goats and if perchance they have a cow, inhabit the same dwelling.'[35] In bad years such as 1783 there was serious hardship that had to be relieved by the local landowners but the causes of rural poverty were beyond their capacity to remedy.[36] It was the poor, however, who provided cheap and inexhaustible supplies of labour for those farmers who could take advantage of the spreading commercialism of fairs and markets. They were the people too who devised other ways of making a living. As a parish priest of Creggan told the Devon Commission in 1844

> It is not by farming the people live but by dealing; they look upon their holdings, or little farms, as rather a lodging and resting place; and they pay rent chiefly by dealing. They go to England to labour; and many of them purchase various articles, and go through the country with them, such as oranges and lemons, etc; others buy pigs, cattle, etc., and exchange goods in various ways.[37]

By 1800 therefore, the borderlands displayed wide contrasts between the fine new buildings in the towns and the ramshackle cottages inhabited by the poor on the hillsides. They reflected the widening gap between rich and poor. Many of its children therefore had to find a variety of ways to supplement their incomes while others left the region for good. Around the major towns with their busy markets and commerce clustered new industrial enterprises. The countryside, too, had been transformed from the desolate wilderness through which Molyneux had travelled in 1708, into a patchwork of small stone-fenced fields criss-crossed by a multitude of roads. This great change had been wrought by many hands determined to create farms for their families out of the boggy uplands. This land, however, was neither extensive nor fertile enough to provide more than a poor living for large numbers of people. It was not able to carry a large stock of either cattle or people.

Plate 1: *Newry from Trevor Hill, Co. Down, from* Ireland illustrated *(London, 1829) by G. N. Wright.*

8 Dietary Considerations in Pre-Famine Louth and its Environs

E. MARGARET CRAWFORD

The north Louth-south Ulster region has long been noted as a frontier zone. Several different types of frontier, for instance, cultural, political, social, county and provincial boundaries, have existed at various times within the area. Nevertheless, certain features in common with Ulster have also been observed. The geographer T. W. Freeman remarked that 'County Louth, though part of Leinster province, is in many ways transitional and possesses qualities of the Ulster landscape'.[1] J. A. Edwards, in a study of County Louth landless labourers, suggests that the survival of the county's linen industry into the nineteenth century 'may well be an index of its affinity to Ulster'.[2] L. M. Cullen has identified the existence of a dietary frontier during the first half of the eighteenth century between the cereal-pulse region of north Meath and the poorer lands of County Monaghan.[3] Thus, in dietary terms as in geography the north Louth-south-east Ulster region may have been one of uniformity rather than diversity, contrasting with more southerly and northerly frontiers. The intention of this essay is to put this area of north Louth, south Down, south Armagh, and east Monaghan under the microscope, to discover precisely what the dietary patterns of the region were. The essay will also compare the region with its surrounding districts of south Louth, north Meath, east Cavan and portions of central Monaghan and Armagh.

Earlier research on dietary patterns of the labouring classes in Ireland during the nineteenth century indicates an overwhelming homogeneity in the diet as well as a marked monotony of fare.[4] Notwithstanding this, some regional variations have been located and also certain well-defined pockets of particularly acute dietary deprivation identified. One such pocket was a narrow corridor extending east-west from County Louth, through County Cavan, leading to the western counties of Longford and Roscommon. This present investigation, therefore, allows a more precise identification of the geographical extent of this exceptionally poor dietary area, and asks why such an agriculturally productive region failed to provide the majority of its population with a richer diet.

I

Dietary evidence of sufficient detail for a relatively small area, and for different points in time is difficult to come by. The only available information we have of the diets covering most of the area of study comes from the Poor Inquiry of 1836.[5] This inquiry was instigated to assess the social conditions of the labouring classes in Ireland before the setting up of a national poor law system. A lengthy questionnaire was dispatched to prominent local residents, such as churchmen, magistrates, industrialists, and the 'gentry', of the 2,500 or so parishes in Ireland, seeking information on many aspects of labouring class life. As well as dietary facts, information was sought on the number of labourers in the parish, employment opportunities, patterns of work (such as seasonal or constant), the quality and rent of housing, number of families living in each cabin, quality of dress, conacre rents, wages, methods of wage payments, additional family income, thrift facilities, and labour hiring arrangements to name but some of the subjects examined. The results were presented in massive appendices to the Poor Inquiry which, to quote George O'Brien, are 'models of erudition and orderly arrangement'.[6] These large tomes now provide historians with an excellent tool for surveying the social conditions of the labouring class just before the Great Famine of 1845–9.

1,569 usable dietary responses were received from the whole of Ireland to the question 'what is the ordinary diet, . . . of the labouring classes in your parish?'[7] For a number of parishes no response was received though, to counterbalance these omissions, for others there were two, three, four and even five responses submitted. Because of the smallness of the Louth and surrounding region unrecorded parishes have severely reduced the sample size, and consequently left some parts of the region unrepresented or sparsely represented. For instance, County Louth contained sixty-five civil parishes, but responses were received from only thirty-five (53.8 per cent). In a few cases several parishes had been amalgamated giving just one set of answers for two, three and even four parishes. The methodological problems relating to the use of this material are explained in detail elsewhere, and so will not be dealt with here.[8] Nevertheless, despite the paucity of data and the methodological problems, it is possible to paint a general picture of the food consumption pattern of the Irish labouring classes during the early 1830s, and even find out if different regional patterns existed.

To this end the area under study will be subdivided into smaller units, corresponding to the Poor Law unions. They not only fit neatly into the geographical boundaries, but also are the basis of 'impeccable' data on

Table 1 Poor Law Unions & no. of samples of inquiry

Poor Law union NORTH LOUTH/ SOUTH-EAST ULSTER REGION	Sample No.	Poor Law union PERIPHERY REGION	Sample No.
Dundalk	15	Ardee	11
Newry	25	Drogheda	13
Kilkeel	9	Bailieborough	9
Castleblayney & Carrickmacross	8	Cootehill	14
		Navan & Kells	21
		Armagh	15
		Monaghan	14
	57		97
Total samples = 154			

statute acreage, holding size and population statistics in the Devon Commission of 1844.[9] The north Louth/south-east Ulster region is represented by the unions of Dundalk, Kilkeel, Newry, Castleblayney and Carrickmacross. For comparison we examine the surrounding area of west Monaghan, east Cavan, south Louth, north Meath and part of Armagh, using the diet in the unions of Cootehill, Bailieborough, Ardee, Drogheda, Navan, Kells, Armagh and Monaghan. This area will be called the periphery region. These regions are shown in map 1.

Early nineteenth century travellers to Ireland were uninhibited in their comments on the diet of the labouring classes. Sir John Carr touring the island in 1805 described the peasant's diet of potatoes and buttermilk as 'a degrading repast . . . a little oatmeal [was] a delicacy; a Sunday bit of pork, a great and rare luxury'.[10] Mr and Mrs S. C. Hall, travelling around Ireland in 1840, observed that 'for above a century and a half, the potato has been almost the only food of the peasantry of Ireland'.[11] Local residents too commented on the spartan fare of the labouring classes. In 1835 the Rev T. Brady, a parish priest in the barony of Loughtee, County Cavan remarked on the very slender meals of the labourers in his district, which were often composed of only potatoes.[12] At the bottom end of the dietary spectrum, the very poorest had nothing but potatoes to eat so long as the season lasted. During the gap between potato crops, in June, July, and August, many went hungry, depending on begging and what they could scavenge. Others acquired small rations of oatmeal or potatoes on credit from their landlords. Yet others again, particularly those near the coast had the benefit of fish, primarily herrings; the herring season coinciding with the potato gap. Thus the summer months were very lean times indeed. 'During . . . July and August the majority used a little oatmeal, but far from a sufficient supply', wrote the Presbyterian minister from Aughnamullen, in east Monaghan.[13] A similar dietary regime was reported from many parts of Ireland. It was only the better-off labourers, who regularly

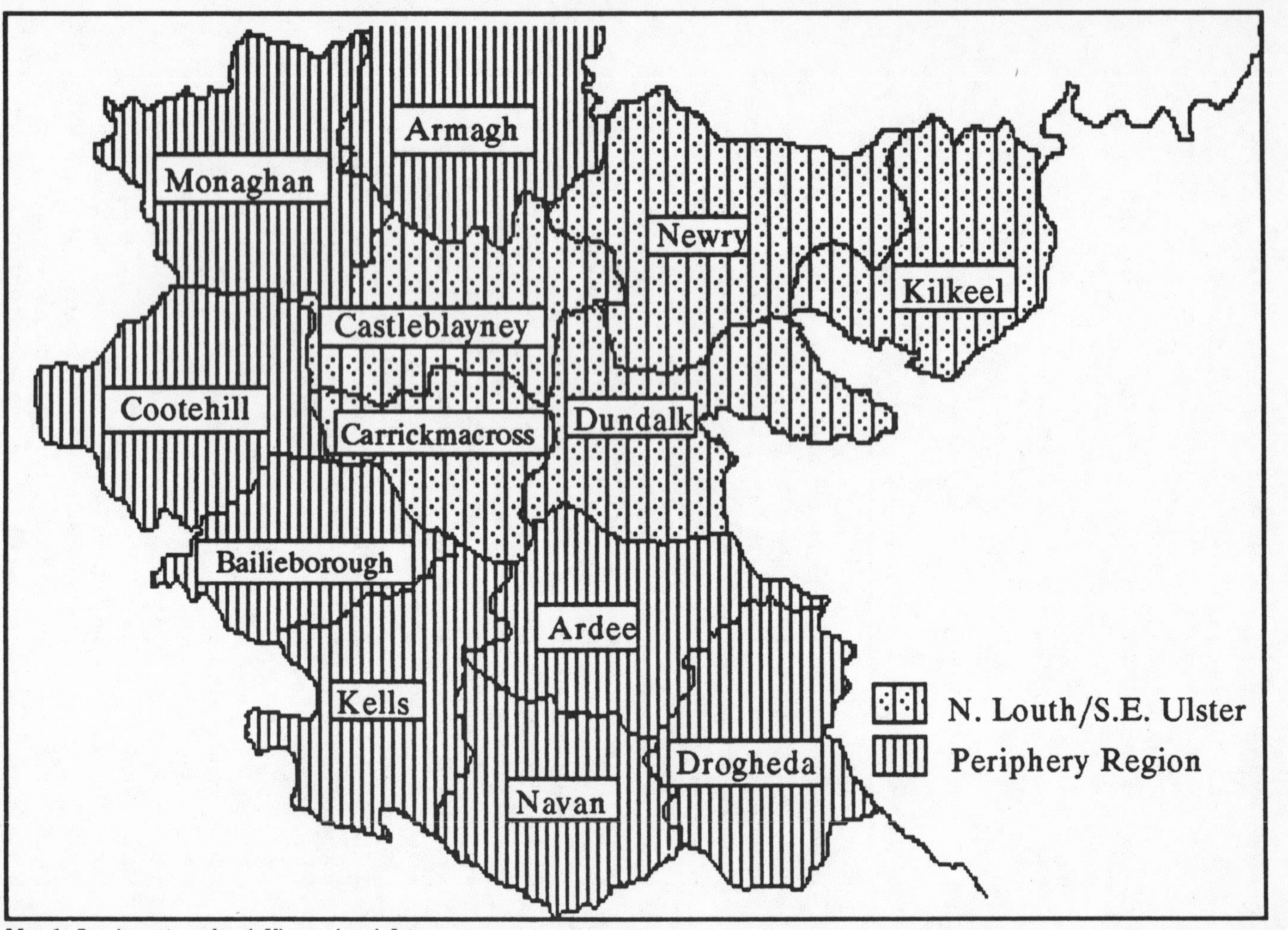

Map 1: *Poor law unions of south Ulster and north Leinster.*

supplemented their diet with milk, buttermilk, oatmeal stirabout, oaten bread and butter, and occasionally had eggs or bacon. The 'ordinary diet for the greater part of the year is potatoes and milk', reported a witness about the diet in the parishes of Stamullen, Moorchurch and Julianstown in County Meath, to the Poor Inquiry, adding that there is 'occasionally butter; in summer, and part of harvest time, when potatoes are scarce, they have stirabout, oat bread . . . [and those] who are cottiers to *some* of the resident gentry, live more comfortably, and a few who have cows, if not improvident, have butter, milk, and bread for a greater part of the year'.[14]

In order to establish if indeed dietary differences existed some means is needed by which the two areas, of north Louth-south-east Ulster and the periphery region can be compared. This has been done by creating three indices to measure the quality of the labouring classes' diet. The first monitors the *frequency* with which an individual food was mentioned in the Poor Inquiry. The second, an *intensity* index, records the regularity with which a particular food was eaten, for example, daily, weekly, seasonally etc. The third is the sum of the *intensity* scores for each union, which provides a *variety* index.[15]

The *frequency* index is a simple technique of scoring one every time a food was mentioned as being consumed by the labouring population. Table 2 therefore provides us with an indication in percentage terms of the number of items eaten. For example, 100 per cent of the parishes in the union of Dundalk mentioned potatoes, 27 per cent mentioned oatmeal, 80 per cent milk, 27 per cent fish, and 7 per cent each butter and meat.

Table 2 Percentage frequency of foods mentioned in Poor Inquiry

Poor Law union	Potatoes	Oats	Milk	Fish	Bread	Butter	Meat	Eggs	Tea
NORTH LOUTH-SOUTH-EAST ULSTER REGION									
Dundalk	100	27	80	27		7	7		
Newry	100	32	68	44	4		4		4
Kilkeel	100	22	66	44			11		
Castleblayney & Carrickmacross	100	25	50	25	13				
Mean value N = 57	100	28	68	37	4	2	5	0	2

Poor Law union	Potatoes	Oats	Milk	Fish	Bread	Butter	Meat	Eggs	Tea	Veg
PERIPHERY REGION										
Bailieborough	100	56	56	11						
Cootehill	100	64	64	7		7	21	7		
Ardee	100	45	64	45			9	9		
Drogheda	100	38	62	8	15	15	8			
Navan & Kells	100	57	67	5	5	5	5			
Armagh	100	80	73	7	7	7	27	8		7
Monaghan	100	23	92	15		7	23	15		
Mean value N = 97	100	53	69	12	4	6	14	5	0	1

The *frequency* index confirms the general impression that potatoes were the staple food everywhere. Fish, oatmeal and milk were seasonal extras, often plugging the gap between potato crops. By any standards, the menus displayed by the above table were very limited in both the north Louth-south-east Ulster and periphery regions. Indeed at this level the differences in the dietary patterns of the two regions were small, and in certain foods more a function of topographical features rather than of social or economic conditions. For example, the frequency of fish consumption in the north Louth-south-east Ulster region was three times greater than in the periphery unions undoubtedly because three of its five unions are coastal. Herrings were cheap and so the most popular; being reported in the diets of Clonallan, Forkhill, Killevy all in the union of Newry as well as Newry town, Maghera (Kilkeel union) and Kilkeel. They were generally a spring-summer food, although sometimes smoked or dried and eaten in winter. Such food processing was reported from Kilkeel and Newry.[16] At Kilbroney, also in the union of Kilkeel one of the witnesses noted particularly the eating of 'shell-fish, to serve as kitchen, as it is termed'.[17] Only two of the eight periphery unions had a coastal boundary, Ardee and Drogheda, and of these only Ardee exhibited sizeable fish consumption. Here too herring was favoured, suggesting that it was both plentiful and cheap. Shell-fish was generally held in low regard as a food, a point illustrated by John McClintock Esq, J.P. of Drumcar, in Ardee Union, when he described it as 'inferior fish'.[18]

An examination of the individual answers to the Poor Inquiry's dietary question confirms this impression of a uniformly monotonous food consumption pattern throughout both regions. For example, in the adjoining districts of Ballymascanlon and Carlingford, in the Poor Law union of Dundalk, the respondents, the Rev Owen Ormsby and William Moore Esq both made short staccato statements naming potatoes as the sole food of the labouring classes.[19] From the periphery region the same responses can also be found. 'Their entire diet is potatoes, with the additional luxury at supper times of dipping them in salt and water', submitted the parish priest about Moymet and Churchtown, in the union of Navan, in County Meath.[20] There were other cases of respondents reporting a diet of one food only: the potato. Nevertheless, some districts from both regions recorded more varied menus. From the Clougill district, in Navan union, in the periphery region, A. H. C. Pollock stated that the diet of the labouring classes was varied, consisting of 'potatoes, meal, milk, butter, and occasionally (but seldom) bacon or herrings'.[21] And similarly, from the north Louth-south-east Ulster area, in Killevy and Camlough, south Armagh, the diet had some variety being composed of 'potatoes chiefly, [with] a small portion of oatmeal, and occasionally buttermilk or herrings'.[22] Overall however, where the periphery region scored more highly, was in the 'luxury' foods – butter, meat and eggs – displaying a marginally more varied diet.

Table 3 Regularity of consumption scores

Daily	5
Weekly	4
Monthly	3
Sometimes, seldom, occasionally	2
Seasonal, festivals, etc.	1

The next task is a further refinement of the data to see if more subtle differences can be identified in the diets of the two regions. To do this the frequency of observation is combined with regularity of consumption – daily, weekly, monthly, seasonally or rarely – to produce the *intensity* index. Here the score is as follows:
A food which was eaten daily thus would score five on the regularity index, and when combined with the *frequency* index it produces an *intensity* value which ranges from 500 to 0.

The results from this scoring technique are presented in Table 4.

Leaving aside potatoes, which in both regions score a maximum of 500, the north Louth-south-east Ulster region scored less well in all foods except fish and tea. This *intensity* index makes more pronounced the better scoring of the periphery region in the 'luxury' foods, and emphasises the overall better diet of many unions there. However not all unions in the periphery region displayed a varied diet. Indeed both Tables 2 and 4 highlight the exceptionally narrow range of foods eaten by the labourers in the peripheral

Table 4 Intensity index by Poor Law unions

Poor Law union	Potatoes	Oats	Milk	Fish	Bread	Butter	Meat	Eggs	Tea
NORTH LOUTH/ SOUTH-EAST ULSTER									
Dundalk	500	80	180	40		7	14		
Newry	500	108	184	76	4		16		8
Kilkeel	500	78	122	111			22		
Castleblayney & Carrickmacross	500	38	175	38	25				
Mean value N = 57	500	86	171	67	5	2	14	0	4

Poor Law union	Potatoes	Oats	Milk	Fish	Bread	Butter	Meat	Eggs	Tea	Veg
PERIPHERY REGION										
Bailieborough	500	200	233	22						
Cootehill	500	171	179	14		14	43	36		
Ardee	500	64	209	191			18	45		
Drogheda	500	108	262	38	23	54	8			
Navan & Kells	500	176	286	10	20	24	10			
Armagh	500	307	213	13	13	13	60	7		13
Monaghan	500	57	264	50		14	36	50		
Mean value N = 97	500	159	239	42	9	18	26	18	0	2
Ireland	496	104	242	82	28	37	33	23	8	

Table 5 Variety index by Poor Law unions

Poor Law Unions		Index
1.	Castleblayney & Carrickmacross	776
2.	Dundalk	821
3.	Kilkeel	833
4.	Newry	896
5.	Bailieborough	955
6.	Cootehill	957
7.	Monaghan	971
8.	Drogheda	993
9.	Navan & Kells	1026
10.	Ardee	1027
11.	Armagh	1139
	Ireland	1053

union of Bailieborough, although the frequency and intensity scores are high enough to be more akin to the other peripheral unions in its surrounding area. By totalling the *intensity* values of the individual foods for each union we arrive at a *variety* index. In Table 5 the unions are ranked by *variety* index giving a better impression of the relative qualities of the diets.

Viewed in this way it is apparent that the labourers in the unions of north Louth-south-east Ulster endured a particularly monotonous diet, compared with their neighbouring unions. The *variety* index of the combined Castleblayney and Carrickmacross unions was exceptionally low, with Dundalk, Kilkeel and Newry not much higher. Bailieborough, although outside the north Louth-south-east Ulster region, yet adjacent to it, scored poorly too, as did Cootehill and Monaghan also. The best scores came from the southern unions of the periphery region and Armagh, though only one of these, Armagh, surpassed the national average of 1,053 with Ardee, Navan and Kells not far short. The better diet enjoyed by Armagh labourers was not unique to the 1830s. In 1804 Charles Coote observed in his survey of County Armagh that 'the food of the lower rank [is] potatoes, stirabout, oaten bread, garden vegetables, bacon in summer, and beef in winter: there is no part of Ireland, where the peasantry consume so much flesh meat'.[23]

The eleven unions readily divide into three groups. Those of north Louth-south-east Ulster have the lowest *variety* index. Bailieborough, Cootehill, and Monaghan a middle band; and Drogheda, Ardee, Navan & Kells and Armagh the highest. Geographically the middle range is a western extension of the poorest area. An alternative approach reinforces this north–south divide. If we calculate the mid-point *variety* index of the range 776 to 1139 we find it corresponds to that of Cootehill union at 957. Unions with a *variety* index below this figure can be regarded as of exceptionally poor quality, and those above rather better. Map 2 relates these figures to regional variations. The pattern which emerges further

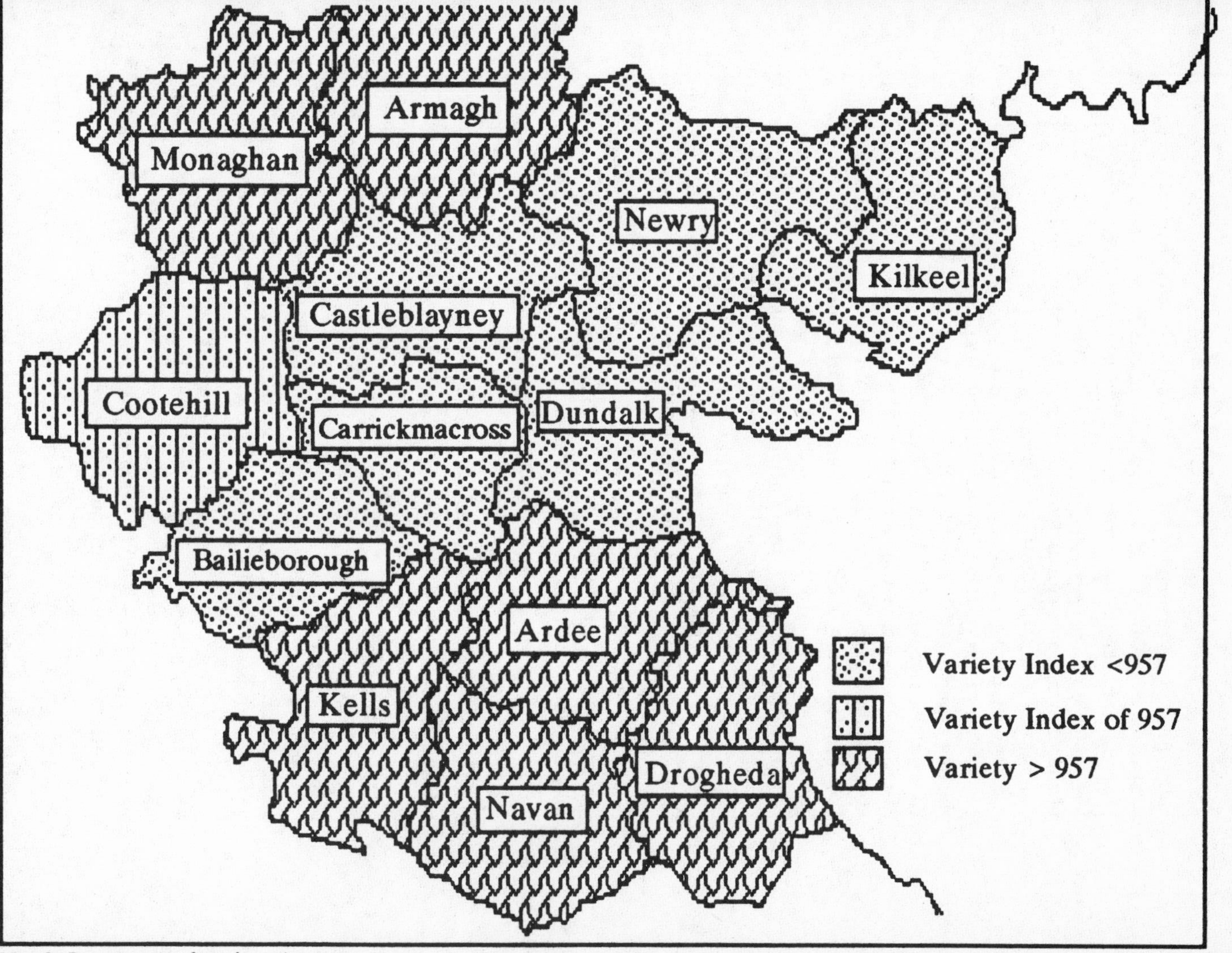

Map 2: *Dietary pattern of poor law unions.*

substantiates the existence of a corridor of dietary deprivation extending westwards from County Louth. In addition, this more detailed study also pinpoints smaller pockets of exceptionally poor diets. For example, the Castleblayney and Carrickmacross unions produce a score lower than any of the county scores calculated in earlier research, in which the bottom score was 806 for the county of Roscommon.[24]

Examined in an even wider context the poverty of the north Louth-south-east Ulster diet is further demonstrated by comparing the Irish fare with the diet of the Scottish labouring classes. The potato was also extensively eaten along the western coast of Scotland, and in some of the poorer districts consumption was very high. This area, therefore, provides an appropriate region for comparison. Scotland reformed its existing Poor Law in 1845, seven years after the implementation of the Irish Poor Law, and as was the case with Ireland a social survey was carried out to assess the condition of its labouring classes prior to the passing of the new Act. One of the questions sought information about the food eaten by the labouring families.[25] The format of the dietary answers is very similar to the Irish, and consequently it is possible to apply the same techniques of analysis to the Scottish data. The exercise has been confined to the potato-eating area of the south-west, the counties of Wigtownshire, Dumfrieshire, Kirkcudbrightshire, and Argyll. The data were presented in synods, subdivided into presbyteries, and further divided into parishes. Thirteen presbyteries were analysed and their *variety* indices are presented in Table 6.

Table 6 Variety index by Scottish Presbytery

Synod	Presbytery	No. of parishes	Index	Synod	Presbytery	No. of parishes	Index
Dumfries:	Annan	7	1556	Argyll:	Inverary	8	1725
	Dumfries	17	1565		Dunoon	8	2013
	Langholm	7	1872		Kintyre	10	1670
	Lochmaben	13	1546		Isla & Jura	7	1357
	Penpoint	9	1265		Mull	8	1675
Galloway:	Kirkcudbright	15	1498				
	Stranraer	9	1721				
	Wigtown	9	1977				

Source: Dietary data from which the variety index was calculated is in *Report from Commissioners. Poor Law Inquiry (Scotland)* H.C. 1844 [597] xxiii, Part IV, Appendix D.

These Scottish *variety* indices are far higher than even the highest Irish figure, further emphasing the very poor variety in the Irish diet. The very lowest Scottish figure is 20 per cent greater than the largest Irish *variety* index, and over 60 per cent above the lowest Irish figure.

II

What accounts for the great poverty of diet in the north Louth/south-east Ulster region? Were wages lower, rents higher, alternative sources of income fewer and farming practices different from elsewhere? The Poor Inquiry once again is the main provider of information on such matters, though care is required to adjust for seasonal and local variations in economic conditions. The format of the questions, however, reveals that the Poor Inquiry Commissioners were aware of problems which the respondents might have in providing accurate responses on these topics. Some respondents did indeed find the permutations too much for them to cope with, and so either left the question unanswered or made such general statements as to be useless for meaningful analysis.

On wages the respondents were asked to provide information on daily wages rates including diet and without diet, summer and winter.[26] In addition, the wage rates of women and children were also sought.[27] The information has been summarised in Table 7. The method used to derive a figure for each union is simple. The mid-point between the lowest wage rate quoted and the highest for those rates paid to labourers without diet has been taken.

The difference in wage rates between the two regions is negligible. Two south-east Ulster unions in fact scored higher than all but two of the periphery region, and one of the periphery region unions, Bailieborough, had the lowest score of all.

Another aspect of wage payments is that money was not the only medium used to remunerate labour. Sometimes wages were paid partly in money and partly in provisions and sometimes rent was first deducted, the remainder being given in cash. A combination of all three was not unknown. The Poor Inquiry Commissioners realised that remuneration for labour was not always a straightforward cash transaction, and therefore asked for information about the various ways a labourer was paid for his labour.[28] The answers to this query can be classified into three broad categories, money, provisions and net of rent for a conacre holding.[29] Drawing upon a technique utilized by Mokyr,[30] a table has been constructed to show the degree of monetisation which occurred in the two regions. The coding scheme is straightforward. When only one medium of payment

Table 7 Daily wage rates extracted from the Poor Inquiry

NORTH LOUTH/ SOUTH-EAST ULSTER		PERIPHERY REGION	
Poor Law union	Old pence	Poor Law union	Old pence
Dundalk	9.35	Bailieborough	9.31
Newry	9.98	Cootehill	9.68
Kilkeel	10.33	Ardee	9.75
Castleblayney & Carrickmacross	9.65	Drogheda	10.81
		Navan & Kells	9.83
		Armagh	10.63
		Monaghan	9.43
Total weighted mean	9.82	Total weighted mean	9.95

Source: *Poor Inquiry (Ireland),* H.C. 1836 (36) xxxi Appendix D.

was stated a maximum score of three was assigned to it. Hence if it was stated that wages were paid only in the form of money, cash scored three, and if remuneration was only in the form of food then provisions would score three. When payment was a combination of money and kind, a judgement had to be made as how to weight the categories. For example, if the respondent said that the labourers in his district were paid 'both in money and provisions, but generally in cash',[31] cash would score two and provisions one. From Table 8 we can then see what disposable cash was available for purchasing a wider variety of goods.

As before no significant differences emerged between the two regions. Low cash scores were recorded for the two unions with the poorest dietary *variety* indices, while those unions with high *variety* indices also had the highest cash scores. Individual unions do, however, display interesting variations. For example, Navan and Kells unions had a high *variety* but low monetisation score, and Newry union though low in *variety* indices had a higher level of monetarisation than several of the peripheral unions. The greater use of money among the labourers of Ardee, Armagh, and Drogheda unions does provide an explanation for their ability to enjoy a more varied diet, whereas in unions where cash renumeration was less common than other forms of payment dietary variety was more limited.

Alternative sources of income also influenced the ability of households to acquire a greater variety of foods. Women and children often earned additional income for the family budget. Older children entered into domestic service and older boys were hired out as farm servants for a limited period, often for one year. In areas where linen manufacture was

Table 8 Medium of wage payments

NORTH LOUTH/SOUTH-EAST ULSTER			
Poor Law union	Cash	Provisions	Rent
Dundalk	1.30	0.60	1.10
Newry	1.72	0.60	0.68
Kilkeel	1.61	0.83	0.56
Castleblayney & Carrickmacross	1.21	0.75	1.00
Mean value N = 57	1.53	0.66	0.81
PERIPHERY REGION			
Poor Law Union	Cash	Provisions	Rent
Bailieborough	1.39	0.56	1.06
Cootehill	1.70	0.65	0.65
Ardee	2.05	0.23	0.73
Drogheda	1.92	0.54	0.54
Navan & Kells	1.45	0.69	0.86
Armagh	2.03	0.52	0.45
Monaghan	1.79	0.41	0.80
Mean value N = 97	1.75	0.53	0.73

Source: *Poor Inquiry (Ireland)*, H.C. 1836 (36) xxxi Appendix D.

still flourishing women were employed in spinning and children in reeling. At Grange, County Armagh, for instance, where 'linen cloths, unions and calico [were] made . . . women and children [had] constant employment; . . . [and] therefore, . . . could make from £10 to £12' a year.[32] The agricultural sector also employed both women and children primarily on a seasonal basis, and thus potential earnings were lower. The Poor Inquiry sought information on the total family income too. Some respondents, however, realized that additional income depended on many circumstances. A clergyman from Newtownhamilton, in County Armagh reported as much, stating: 'I cannot form any idea, nor have I been able to ascertain by inquiry'.[33] Many of the answers to this question were incomplete, and so the results in Table 9 are from a very small sample.

In the unions of Kilkeel, and Castleblayney and Carrickmacross annual average incomes earned by family members (other than the labourers themselves) were very much lower than the other unions. Of the north Louth-south-east Ulster region, only the Dundalk union labouring families appeared to have significant additional income, which was not reflected in their dietary pattern. Ardee and Drogheda labourers on the other hand enjoyed the benefits of a more varied diet because of quite considerable family earnings. The responses for the Navan and Kells unions were very wide ranging from £30 down to £1.15*s* per annum, though over half of the cases reported values in excess of £10.

By 1835 the decline of the domestic linen industry had made a great dent in the supplementary income of labourers' households. Many respondents from both regions referred to the loss of earnings as a consequence of a reduction in the spinning of linen yarn. From Drumcar in the union of Ardee the position of many was summed up by one labourer: 'since the failure of the linen trade *the wife* had lost the advantage of spinning, and the children the reeling; little occupation for them except in harvest'.[34] Those households still spinning were doing so at a very much reduced rate. In

Table 9 Additional family income extracted from Poor Inquiry

NORTH LOUTH/ SOUTH-EAST ULSTER REGION			PERIPHERY REGION		
Poor Law union	N	£	Poor Law union	N	£
Dundalk	7	10.78	Bailieborough	6	9.00
Newry	15	7.00	Cootehill	11	8.88
Kilkeel	6	6.30	Ardee	8	15.70
Castleblayney & Carrickmacross	4	4.75	Drogheda	13	16.65
			Navan & Kells	13	9.85
			Armagh	7	8.00
			Monaghan	8	7.80
N = 32			N = 66		
Total weighted mean		7.41	Total weighted mean		11.21

Source *Poor Inquiry (Ireland)*, H.C. 1836 (36) xxxi Appendix D.

1835 C. G. Otway, who examined the industry for a government report, stated that earnings from hand-spinning had fallen from 6*d* per-day to 2*d* or 1*d*.[35] Rates quoted in the Poor Inquiry confirm this statement. In Clonallon, county Down a labourer's wife could earn no more than 1/2*d* per day from spinning.

Conacre rent was a major claim on household expenses. Vital to survival this commitment had to be met. The Poor Inquiry asked several questions about rentals, but the following test is based upon that which asked: 'name the highest and lowest rent normally paid for con acres?'[36] Once again there were many permutations in local practice. Rents differed according to the crop being planted, whether the land had been manured or not, ashed or not, and whether it was a first or subsequent letting. In an effort to overcome so many variations a mid-value between the lowest and highest rent quoted has been used.

Table 10 Annual rental of conacre land

NORTH LOUTH/ SOUTH-EAST ULSTER REGION		PERIPHERY REGION	
Poor Law union	Shillings	Poor Law union	Shillings
Dundalk	138.31	Bailieborough	140.22
Newry	172.02	Cootehill	167.67
Kilkeel	168.71	Ardee	143.40
Castleblayney & Carrickmacross	158.57	Drogheda	153.55
		Navan & Kells	139.70
		Armagh	129.67
		Monaghan	167.46
N = 57		N = 97	
Total weighted mean	161.13	Total weighted mean	149.39

Source: *Poor Inquiry (Ireland)* H.C. 1836(38) xxxiii, Appendix F.

Here a sizeable difference emerges. Labourers taking land in the periphery region had to pay less rent for their conacre land than their counterparts in the north Louth/south-east Ulster region. The difference between the weighted mean of the two regions was almost twelve shillings (11*s*. 9*d*.), which in a very poor household made a considerable difference to the amount of disposable income available for the other necessities of life.

Another question to be considered is whether numbers of people scraping a livelihood from the land influenced food consumption patterns. Was dietary fare worse in areas where pressure of population numbers was greater? We can calculate the number of people per acre of cultivatable land using the agricultural statistics, and the results are shown in Table 11.

All the north Louth-south-east Ulster unions as well as Bailieborough, Cootehill, Armagh and Monaghan had a higher density of population than those unions to the south of the region. It was in these southern unions of Ardee, Drogheda, Navan and Kells, where density of population was lower,

Table 11 Population density

NORTH LOUTH/ SOUTH-EAST ULSTER REGION		PERIPHERY REGION	
Poor Law union	Population/acre of cultivatable land	Poor Law union	Population/acre of cultivatable land
Dundalk	0.77	Bailieborough	0.85
Newry	0.83	Cootehill	0.69
Kilkeel	0.65	Ardee	0.48
Castleblayney	0.70	Drogheda	0.56
Carrickmacross	0.71	Navan	0.39
		Kells	0.44
		Armagh	0.78
		Monaghan	0.68

Sources: Population figures for the Poor Law unions are taken from *Report from Her Majesty's Commissioners of Inquiry into the State of the Law and Practice in Relation to the Occupation of Land in Ireland (The Devon Commission)*, H.C. 1845 [672] xxii, Part IV Appendix 94. Cultivatable land acreage provided by the *Returns of Agricultural Produce in 1851*. H.C. 1852–3 [1589] xciii.

that high dietary variety scores are to be found. Nevertheless, one of the most densely populated unions, Armagh, had also the highest variety dietary score. It would appear, therefore, that the numbers of people supported on the land did not necessarily have a direct relationship to the variety of diet. Mokyr and Ó Gráda examining population density as a proxy for poverty also failed to find any relationship.[37]

Differences in natural environment accounted for the varying land use patterns, which in turn dictated the demand for labour. The fertile rich land of County Meath and all but the northern tip of County Louth were suitable for both arable and pastoral farming. In Louth, except for the uncultivated rough pastures on the mountains of the Carlingford peninsula, small farms proliferated and only eight per cent of its farms were above 30 acres in size in 1841. By contrast in County Meath 20 per cent of holdings were above 30 acres. Between the Napoleonic Wars and the Famine there was a move to change large tracts of land in Meath from tillage to grazing. 'Much tillage land has, of late years, been converted to grass', observed a witness to the Poor Inquiry, explaining that 'the effect has been the throwing [of] nine-tenths of the labourers upon such land out of employment'.[38] Pastoral farming had a low demand for labour which was reflected in the lower population density in the unions of Navan, Kells, Ardee and Drogheda as compared with the more populous tillage and marginal lands of north Louth-south-east Ulster. Furthermore, in pastoral farming the labour requirement was not seasonal, but continuous throughout the year. Labourers thus employed had a steady income, enabling them to supplement their basic diet with some extras. This pattern has been demonstrated in the research of Edwards who observed that, 'in terms of material welfare, . . . the labourer with an annual contract, . . . was somewhat better'.[39] A Kells respondent explained that 'potatoes form the chief food of the labourers; oatmeal is only used in summer (when potatoes are bad) by men

Table 12 Percentage of land holders with 10 acres or less and more than 50 acres

NORTH LOUTH/ SOUTH-EAST ULSTER REGION			PERIPHERY REGION		
	Percentage			Percentage	
Poor Law union	10 acres & less	more than 50 acres	Poor Law union	10 acres and less	more than 50 acres
Dundalk	63	5	Bailieborough	57	2
Newry	70	1	Cootehill	54	1
Kilkeel	68	2	Ardee	46	12
Castleblayney	66	0.8	Drogheda	52	14
Carrickmacross	67	1	Navan	57	13
			Kells	53	11
			Armagh	66	2
			Monaghan	61	1

Source: *Report from Her Majesty's Commissioners of Inquiry into the the State of the Law and Practice in Relation to the Occupation of Land in Ireland (The Devon Commission)*. H.C. 1845 [672] xxii, Part IV Appendix 94.

in good employment on some particular occasions, and on those only labourers may have a morsel of bacon, a herring, or an egg, as a treat'.[40] Table 12 clearly demonstrates the division between the north and south of the area. The percentage of landholders with ten acres or less was remarkably high where tillage continued and the pressure of population forced the labourers to take small plots at ever increasing rents. By contrast, in the south, pastoral unions had a considerably greater number of holders with more than fifty acres.

It was somewhat ironic that such a productive area as Louth and its environs which both produced sizeable quantities of food and had large consignments of various food commodities transported across the county, provided such poor fare for its labouring classes. The corn trade of Dundalk was very extensive, catering for two breweries, one distillery and a corn mill. Furthermore, Dundalk was one of Ireland's major ports ranking sixth (exceeding Drogheda and Newry) in terms of grain exports by volume, moving 30,216 tons of corn, meal and flour for the year 1835.[41] In monetary value the port ranked eighth, exporting £452,813 worth of flour, meal, malt, butter, beef, pork, cattle, sheep, pigs, linen, flax, eggs and poultry in 1836.[42] Virtually all Dundalk's exports were agricultural products from its immediate hinterland and beyond, grain being brought in from the surrounding area and adjoining counties to be exported. A large portion of the exported grain was the produce of Louth, Cavan and Monaghan. Wheat and barley supplies were grown in Louth and Monaghan, while the suppliers of oats were principally from further afield in the counties of Cavan, Monaghan and Fermanagh; the quantity grown in Louth being only sufficient for local consumption.[43] In addition, flour was supplied by Dundalk millers to many towns in the north of Ireland. A large quantity was sent to Newry in carts, and thence forwarded by boat on the canal for consumption in Tyrone.

Exports were not confined to grain. Butter was brought in from counties Monaghan and Cavan, and the northern part of Longford, all sent ready coopered for shipment. The quantity was about 550 tons in the season. The eggs sent in were collected principally in the same counties; the local supply being much lower than the quantity exported. Despite such trading activity, by both contemporary and modern evaluations County Louth was one of the most impoverished regions in Ireland. In the words of Henry Inglis, who toured Ireland in 1834: 'the traveller . . . will not have travelled many miles from the boundary line of the province of Ulster, before he recognises the genuine Irish cabin . . . Dundalk is a short interruption to the spectacle of poverty, which all through the county of Louth stares one in the face'.[44]

This survey of wages, additional income, and rents as well as the population density and land holding size, generally indicates that only two of these variables – rental value and supplementary income – had even tenuous links with quality of dietary variety. Of greater impact on dietary patterns was the type of agriculture practiced in the area. Where pastoral farming occurred, more labourers were in regular employment, and consequently had a regular income. It was that group who were able to enjoy relatively better variety of fare when compared with their counterparts working intermittently on tillage farms. Furthermore, labourers on pastoral farms sometimes were fed by their employer, in some cases one meal a day, in the case of living-in labourers all meals. Such employees generally enjoyed a better diet than those feeding themselves. The one exceptional union was Armagh. It had a high population density, a high percentage of small holdings and low percentage of large farms, yet its labourers enjoyed the greatest variety of dietary fare.

III

Having established that the labourers of north Louth and its environs consumed a less varied diet than the surrounding area is it possible to ascertain if their nutritional status was also poor? The Poor Inquiry did not systematically set out information on the quantities of food consumed, but something can be gleaned from the oral examination taken from witnesses invited to give evidence to the commissioners, and published in appendix E of the Inquiry.[45] The investigating commissioners were fascinated by the large quantities of potatoes consumed by the labouring classes, and repeatedly asked for estimates of consumption from the witnesses. The dietary historian is, therefore, provided with a valuable legacy, since from this quantitative material we can establish the daily consumption of potatoes by a labouring family.

The quantitative data are not available at the townland or parish level but according to the barony. In the case of County Louth we know the

Table 13 Daily quantities of potatoes eaten by labourers' family as recorded in the Poor Inquiry

NORTH LOUTH/SOUTH EAST ULSTER REGION.			
Louth	Upper Dundalk	4 stones (56 lbs)	potatoes per day per family
PERIPHERY REGION			
Meath	Kells	3 stones (42 lbs)	" " " " "
Armagh	Lower Fews	3 stones (42 lbs)	" " " " "
Cavan	Loughtee	2½–3 stones (35–42 lbs)	" " " " "
Monaghan	Monaghan	3 stones (42 lbs)	" " " " "

locality of some of the witnesses, and so it is possible to pinpoint more accurately from where in the county the information came. The one estimate we have for potato consumption in County Louth was supplied by a labourer, Mr Robinson who lived in Faughart, which falls within the boundary of the Dundalk Poor Law union. He reckoned that 'a labouring man, his wife and three or four children, using the quantity sufficient to keep them in health and strength, would consume four stones of potatoes per day.'[46] For the periphery region there are more estimates, ranging from 2½ to 3 stones (35–42 lbs.) daily per family as shown in Table 13.[47]

Dividing the whole area into the two regions is not helpful, because of the way the data have been presented. Instead, we will compare the nutritional content of the diet containing the largest potato ration with that of the smallest. In order to establish the quantity of potatoes eaten by a labouring man it is necessary to attach some kind of weighting system to the family ration, to take account of the uneven distribution of food within families. Atwater, an American food scientist, pioneering the skills of nutritional analysis in the 1890s, developed such a scheme, though to carry it out properly one needs to know the ages of all the children.[48] In the absence of this information a simplified version will be used in which it is assumed that a woman ate 80 per cent of a man's ration and a child 50 per cent.[49] Thus a man would be rated as 1, a woman as 0.8 and a child as 0.5. A family composed of a man, his wife and four children would have therefore a total weighting of 3.8. If we then assume an average daily family consumption of about 3 stones (42 lbs.) of potatoes, the man's ration would be just over 11 lbs. with a maximum of 14.7 lbs. calculating for the higher figure of 4 stones (56 lbs.), and a minimum of 9.2 lbs. based on the family consumption of 2½ stones (35 lbs.) daily.

With the aid of food composition tables we are now able to calculate the nutritional adequacy of a north Louth-south-east Ulster labouring man's daily diet. Table 14 shows the protein, fat, carbohydrate, and energy value, calcium, iron and vitamins A, D and C levels of a daily diet consisting of 14.7 lbs of potatoes, the highest ration quoted.

By to-day's standards this diet was more than adequate in protein, energy value, minerals and vitamin C. Although not included in the table

Table 14 Nutritional analysis of the daily diet of a County Louth labouring man (4 stones potatoes per family/day)

	Quantity g./ml.	Protein g.	Fat g.	Carbo-hydrate g.	Energy value kcal.	Ca mg.	Fe mg.	Vit A R.E.[2] μg.	Vit D μg.	Vit C[1] mg.
Potatoes[3]	5845	81.8		1152.0	4676	251	28.4	–	–	683
B'milk	600	20.4	0.56	28.9	204	687	Tr.	–	–	6
		102.2	0.56	1180.9	4880	938	28.4	–	–	689
R.D.I.[4]		84.00			3350	500	10.0	750		30

[1] Vitamin C is a very unstable vitamin, losses are incurred through storage, and cooking. The calculation has been made on the main crop value using only 70 per cent of the mean raw value to allow for storage losses, plus additional deduction to account for cooking losses.
[2] Retinol Equivalents.
[3] Potatoes 235.2 oz less 29.4 oz lost in cooking = 5844.7 g.(5845 g.)
[4] R.D.I. *Recommended Dietary Amounts of Food Energy and Nutrients for groups of people in the United Kingdom*, Report on Health and Social Subjects No. 15, HMSO, 1979.
Nutrient values calculated from *The Composition of Foods*, Special Report Series No.297, Medical Research Council, HMSO, London, 1960.

above all the vitamins of the B complex group were well above requirements as also was vitamin C. The nutrients which failed to meet acceptable levels were vitamins A & D. If, however, whole milk was substituted for buttermilk this defect was considerably remedied. Even when potatoes only were consumed, plenty of energy was provided for a day of hard physical labour. Modern assessments for the nutrient requirements of a man doing 'very active' work regard a calorific value of 3,350 kcal and protein level of 84 g. as sufficient. Our County Louth labourer, therefore, had both protein and energy to spare. Indeed, bearing in mind that labouring activity was seasonal, it would appear that during the winter months when the potato supply was good and work very intermittent nutrient supplies were in excess of requirements. Even at seasons of intensive labouring activity, when energy expenditure was much higher than allowed for by modern estimates, adequate nourishment was provided.

Not all labourers enjoyed such a large daily ration of potatoes. The poorest diet recorded in the Poor Inquiry for the area under investigation related to the district of Loughtee, in County Cavan, part of which is in the union of Bailieborough. There a family of six people lived on a ration of 2½ stones (35 lbs) of potatoes a day. The nutritional analysis of this diet is shown in Table 15.

It is immediately apparent from the above analysis that the recommended protein and energy values were not achieved in this diet. Not even the addition of a pint of buttermilk brought the nutrient levels up to the recommended dietary intakes and certainly were inadequate for a labouring man to carry out efficiently a heavy day's labour. During the leanest time of the year, from June to August, the nutritional value of the diet must have been even worse and thus seriously defective, but, as we have no

Table 15 Nutritional analysis of the daily diet of a County Armagh labouring man (2½ stones potatoes per family/day)

	Quantity g./ml.	Protein g.	Fat g.	Carbo-hydrate g.	Energy value kcal.	Ca mg.	Fe mg.	Vit A R.E.[2] μg.	Vit D μg.	Vit C[1] mg.
Potatoes[3]	3669	51.37		723.1	2935	157	17.6	–	–	428
B'milk	600	20.44	0.56	28.9	204	687	Tr.	–	–	6
		71.81	0.56	752.03	3139	844	17.6	–	–	434
R.D.I.[4]		84.00			3350	500	10.0	750		30

[1] As in Table 14, this calculation is based on the main crop value using only 70 per cent of the mean raw value to allow for storage losses, plus additional deduction to account for cooking losses.
[2] Retinol Equivalents.
[3] Potatoes 147.4 oz. less 18.4 oz. loss wt in cooking = 3669 g.
[4] R.D.I. *Recommended Dietary Amounts of Food Energy and Nutrients for groups of people in the United Kingdom*, (1979).
Nutrient values calculated from *The Composition of Foods*.

quantitative data of food eaten during these months it is impossible to estimate the nutritive value of the summer diet. Basing the calculation solely on the potato, it was necessary to eat at least 10½ lbs. per day, in order to meet the energy requirement recommended for a day of heavy labouring work. Thus labourers who failed to consume this amount certainly failed to reach full energy potential. The lassitude of Irish labourers, so often referred to by contemporary observers, was probably the result of insufficient potatoes in their daily diet, and not laziness of which they were so often accused.

An important point to note is that variety of fare did not guarantee a nutritious diet. Given the Irish proclivity to eat potatoes in large quantities, this exercise has demonstrated that it was perfectly possible for the Irish labourer to acquire a good nutritious diet if sufficient potatoes were consumed with the addition of whole milk. But as other work has shown, once the Irish labourer acquired a taste for the luxury foods, which in his terms were bread, sugar and tea, the nutritional quality of his diet considerably deteriorated.[50]

Since an Irish labourer when eating a daily ration of 10½ lbs. potatoes for at least eight to nine months of the year was receiving nutritious meals, is it possible to find some reflection of this good diet in his health? Our knowledge about the disease patterns in pre-Famine Ireland is very fragmentary. It is unfortunate that registration of deaths and their cause did not commence in Ireland until 1864. Information comes therefore chiefly from a number of dispensary minute books which have survived in widely dispersed locations and for different points in time, and from articles in Irish medical journals. One Doctor, John Brown wrote a short article on fever in the locality of Dundalk. His observations covered a two year period commencing April 1835, and were published as a 'Medical Report of the

Dundalk 'Destitute Sick Society', together with . . . the Medical Topography and Statistics of the Town and Parish'.[51] In addition to his observations on feverish (febrile) disorders he also recorded the number of cases of each disease treated in the local dispensary and Destitute Sick Society. Dysentery, dyspepsia, flatulence and fluxes and chest afflictions seem to have been common in Ireland, and Dr Brown's report indicates that the Dundalk region had its fair share of these complaints. He attributed a marked reduction in fever patients, particularly in cases of intermittent fever, to improvements in the town's drainage, and certainly that was an important factor. Nevertheless, one must wonder to what extent the diet of potatoes and milk was also responsible. Judging by recent research on the effect of nutritional status on infection,[52] the indications are that when harvests were good, and potatoes plentiful this highly nutritious fare made a major contribution to reducing vulnerability to infection.

IV

What is the conclusion of this study? Whatever distinctive qualities some historians and geographers may claim for the north Louth-south-east Ulster region, in dietary terms the labouring classes had much in common with their fellows in the rest of Ireland. The staple food was potatoes, with oatmeal, milk and fish seasonal extras. Where subtle differences did emerge was in the consumption of the less commonly eaten foods such as bread, butter, tea and bacon. Labourers living in the unions of Kells, Navan, Ardee and Armagh, all in the periphery region, enjoyed a more varied menu of the 'luxury' foods from time to time, unlike those in north Louth and south-east Ulster. Furthermore the food pattern analysis revealed the existence of a corridor of marked dietary deprivation, extending westwards from County Louth. In addition, pockets of extremely poor dietary fare were identified in Castleblayney, Carrickmacross, Kilkeel and Newry. An examination of labourers' income and expenditure gave clues to an explanation for the dietary differences. Labourers in north Louth and its hinterland existed on lower wages, and considerably less additional supplementary income from the earnings of wives and children, yet had to pay more for rent, leaving them with less disposal income for purchasing the 'luxury foods'. The type of agriculture practiced also appears to have had an impact on the quality of diet eaten. In areas of pastoral farming where labouring employment and wages were regular, diet was better, albeit to a limited degree. Thus those in north Louth-south-east Ulster suffered a greater degree of poverty, though it should be emphasised that their suffering was one of degree not kind.

Plate 1: *Charles Russell, unsuccessful Liberal candidate at Dundalk election 1868 and 1874, and Liberal M.P. for the borough 1880–5; later appointed Lord Chief Justice for England and created Lord Russell of Killowen. From the Life of Lord Russell of Killowen (London, 1901), by R. Barry O'Brien.*

9 'The Advance on the North'

The difficulties of the home rule movement in south-east Ulster, 1870–1883

GERARD MORAN

In examining political developments in Ulster in the decade which followed W. E. Gladstone's election as prime minister in 1868 the fact that the province had always proved difficult to influence from outside or to win over to new ideas should not be forgotten. In the 1870s repeated attempts were made to introduce home rule as a viable political ideology into south-east Ulster and all failed. While the rest of the country quickly involved itself in the constitutional nationalism of the home rule movement of the 1870s Ulster was unenthusiastic about the movement despite numerous efforts to bring it into line with the rest of the country. The problems which impeded the movement's advancement in the 1870s occurred on two fronts: the difficulties which beset the movement generally at a national level and those which were entirely of a local nature. However, the problems of the borderland region were not experienced by the movement elsewhere and were to hinder its advancement. The history of elections over the period 1870 to 1883 provides a framework for understanding these problems.

Between 1801 and 1885 a total of ten parliamentary representatives were elected by the different constituencies in the south-east Ulster region. Each of the counties Louth, Monaghan, Down and Armagh, elected two M.P.s each, while each of the boroughs, Dundalk and Newry, sent one representative each. (As the three other boroughs in the region: Drogheda, Downpatrick and Armagh, are on the periphery of this region they have not been examined in this study). At the 1868 general election the representation of the region was divided between six Conservatives and four Liberals. The constituencies where Liberals were returned – Louth (two seats), Dundalk and Newry – were to become the main area of support for the home rule movement over the next fifteen years.

From the outset it was inevitable the home rule movement would encounter severe difficulties in its attempts to secure an electoral foothold in Ulster. The history of the tenant right movement in the 1850s and its failure to turn its support into parliamentary representation was one of the fundamental reasons for that movement's failure in the province. Nowhere were these difficulties more evident than in Monaghan, which was viewed by all nationalist movements in the nineteenth century as the gateway to the rest of the province. As seventy-four per cent of its population was Catholic it was felt to offer most possibilities to the nationalists. One of the most noteable features in the county was the polarisation which ensued as a result of the nationalists attempt to gain control. Organisations such as repeal, tenant right and fenianism had all helped to swell the ranks of the Orange Order in Monaghan. The singularity of Monaghan in a northern context is evident from the fact it was the only Ulster county which was contested at the 1868 general election. However, in this election, as in the other elections in the county in the 1850s and 1860s, Catholics did not participate in any major way in electoral affairs; their involvement being largely confined to supporting the landlords' nominees.

One of the movements which contributed to the growth of the new nationalism was the Amnesty Association, which was holding nationwide demonstrations in support of the release of the fenian prisoners from English jails. As in the rest of the country the upsurge in support for the amnesty movement was also evident in south-east Ulster. Dundalk was the central point attracting people from all over the region and acting as a testing ground for all nationalist movements such as amnesty. At the Dundalk demonstration in 1869 large numbers of people from the adjoining counties attended, highlighting the level of nationalist support for the issue. Nevertheless, one of the most noteable features of the region was that nationalist demonstrations, either in the form of amnesty meetings or as gatherings for the return of home rule candidates, were very slow to take root in Ulster. Amnesty only became an important feature in Ulster in October 1869 when the first meeting was convened in Newry, nearly two months after it had ignited the rest of the country. Still the holding of such demonstrations indicated the manner in which the amnesty issue had infected the region for it had not been involved to any great extent with the fenian movement in the 1860s.[1] At the same time it indicated that caution was essential for nationalist movements attempting to infiltrate the borderlands. As in other parts of the country which had not embraced fenianism, the activities of the Amnesty Association did stimulate the expansion of fenianism into the region.[2]

While the amnesty demonstrations heightened nationalist awareness they also sent shock waves through their opponents who responded more vigorously than their less numerous colleagues in the rest of the country. As the Amnesty Association was regarded as a Catholic based movement it was inevitable that their gatherings caused divisions between the two communities. The holding of the first amnesty demonstration in Ulster at Newry in October 1869 worried the local authorities who felt that rioting would ensue.[3] The failure of the movement to gain any foothold in Monaghan must be attributed to the actions of John Madden, the high sheriff for the county, who refused to allow such a demonstration convene in the county.[4]

Madden's action in refusing the nationalists the right to convene the amnesty demonstration was a return to the tactics which Orange groups had utilised in the same region against O'Connell's repeal movement in the 1830s.[5] Such actions indicate that while nationalists considered Monaghan to be a frontier county this view was also shared by their political opponents. Monaghan proved to be as important to the Orange groups for the preservation of the status quo as it was to the nationalists in extending their political philosophy. While O'Connell and Isaac Butt regarded control of it as the first step in securing control over the whole of Ulster their opponents viewed it as the barrier in checking this advance.

In this respect the perception of the political border in the nineteenth century existed well before 1885 when it became more pronounced with the rise of the home rule question. It was a perception that existed in the minds of both nationalists and unionists alike from at least as early as O'Connell's repeal movement. The unionists tolerated the spread of nationalist organisations in counties like Louth and Meath, but once they moved into Ulster they were resisted with all the venom that could be mustered. In this way Monaghan tended to be the frontier zone between nationalist Louth and Conservative Down.

Another factor which aided the formation of the home rule movement was the resurgence of the agrarian question onto the national scene due to Gladstone's proposed land legislation. Once more differences were evident in south-east Ulster compared to the rest of the country and the movement had to tread more cautiously than elsewhere. Ribbonism was a major force; this region being one of its principal strongholds in the country.[6] While Catholics in the region supported constitutional nationalist movements, such as Daniel O'Connell's, when they existed, they turned to ribbonism when such outlets ceased to operate. Ribbonism in the borderlands contrasted with that in other parts of the country in that its priorities were agrarian rather than nationalist. This brought divisions between ribbonmen and fenians in the region in 1869 with the latter breaking up tenant right meetings in Dundalk and Newry on the grounds that they were diverting attention away from the amnesty issue.[7] Such conflict was inevitable for both groups vied for public attention and since the mid-1860s had been in competition with each other as they both attempted to attract the same type of person into their organisation. However, by 1870 the divisions between the two groups waned because of Gladstone's failure to provide satisfactory solutions to both sets of grievances. The prime minister's partial release of fenian prisoners and his inadequate land legislation resulted in a merger between the two groups. The newly merged organisation on the Ulster-Leinster border never had the impact on political affairs that it had in other parts of the country. In Mayo and Galway, for example, it made a significant contribution in the electoral successes of home rule candidates.[8] Nevertheless the extent to which the fenian movement had come to absorb ribbonism can be seen in its acceptance of the agrarian question as an issue of major importance for Ireland, as at the fenian meeting at Scotstown, County Monaghan in 1878, when the 5,000 people assembled passed a resolution in favour of tenant right.

While the land question was harnessed to increase the support of the home rule movement it was clear there would be difficulties for the movement along the borderlands. While a large number of land demonstrations had been held throughout the country in the immediate months before the unveiling of the 1870 land legislation, no attempt was made to hold any such meetings in Ulster, except at Newry. Such a situation was not surprising given the general failure of the tenant right agitation of the 1850s and must be attributed to the more accommodating approach of the Ulster Conservative representatives towards land reform proposals than their colleagues in the rest of the country.

Gladstone's failure to deliver sufficiently on the land question in 1870 resulted in the formation of no less than three tenant movements in the south-east Ulster region over the next three years: the Farney Tenants' Defence Association in 1870, the Monaghan Tenants' Defence Association in 1875 and the Louth Tenants' Defence Association.[9] It was assumed that the formation of such associations would have helped the home rule movement in uniting south Ulster with the rest of the country and Isaac Butt did attempt to accommodate the northern farmers.[10] In the lead up to the 1874 general election agrarian proposals were part of the home rule programme, but the movement failed to secure the support of the farmer associations in areas like Monaghan. While the Farney Tenants' Defence Association held meetings protesting at the arbitrary powers of the landlords, they did not involve themselves with the home rule movement to redress these problems.[11] John Madden's defeat in Monaghan at the 1874 general election was attributed to the failure of the Farney farmers to support him and the fact that Shirley, his Conservative opponent, was prepared to make agrarian concessions to the Catholics of Monaghan. Meanwhile, in Newry the tenant right issue was not regarded as a priority in the area.[12]

The problems confronting the home rule party in south Ulster first became apparent at the 1871 by-election in Monaghan. It was the sixth contest for the party in its brief fifteen month history and nationally the movement was in a euphoric state having won the two previous contests in Galway county and in Westmeath. However, Monaghan presented a completely new situation, being in a part of the country where previous nationalist movements had difficulties in securing a foothold. At the same time it was the most likely of the Ulster constituencies where the party could hope for a win. A success would have a spin off effect in that it would encourage other areas of Ulster to express support for the nationalist cause and the failure to win the constituency in 1871, 1874 and 1880 proved a major handicap for the movement. Its progress in the province had thus been retarded until the 1880s, making it the last region of the country where inroads could be made. It was only after 1883 and Tim Healy's victory in Monaghan that the National League, the organising wing of the party at a local level, began to exert an influence in Derry, Fermanagh, Tyrone and Monaghan.[13]

The 1871 contest highlighted the high level of support which a group of former Orangemen were giving to the home rule movement. People such as Rev John Flanagan, the Church of Ireland rector of Killevan and a leading member of the Monaghan Orange Order, viewed the new movement as a means of curtailing the growth of Catholic power in Ireland.[14] At the same time similar attitudes were not to be found in south Down and south Armagh amongst the Orangemen. The conversion of Flanagan and John Madden of Hilton Park, Clones to home rule was thus unusual, given their former staunch unionist attitude, and provides an indication as to why some Protestant groups flirted with the home rule movement for a brief period. At the same time the participation of such men resulted in a confused attitude within Monaghan as to what home rule meant.

The failure of the home rule candidate, Isaac Butt, to win Monaghan in 1871 must be attributed to the failure of the Catholic bishop and clergy to support him while most Protestants viewed the movement as a nationalist/Catholic body and thus stayed away from it. The Catholic bishop and clergy tended to be cautious in accepting Protestant candidates who were waving the nationalist flag. Coupled with this was their continued acceptance of the Gladstone administration as being the only way of securing a redress of Ireland's major grievances.

These events pose the question why did it take so long for the nationalists' ideas to take root in Monaghan, considering the strong Catholic presence? One factor which proved crucial was that the Conservatives, aware of this threat, played the right card advocating, for example, tenant reform. Such a response was important as there were estates in Monaghan where the Ulster custom was not in existence. While Tim Healy claimed his success in 1883 was due to the disillusionment of the Farney people with their lot, they did not flock to the home rule cause in the 1870s.[15] The long term effect of failing to secure Monaghan had a strong psychological impact on the home rule movement in Ulster. There was little development of the organisation in the province overall.[16] It was felt there was little point in fighting such constituencies with large Conservative majorities, even from the point of building up a party framework within the region with a view to contesting future elections.

Only in 1880 with the defeat of the Conservatives, Leslie and Shirley, in Monaghan did the home rule breakthrough become apparent. It was the first part of the process which eventually led to the movement gaining control of the country and followed the trend that had taken place in the rest of Ireland in the late 1860s and 1870s. It was rare for counties to proceed from one political extreme to the other, from Conservatism to advanced nationalism. The usual trend was a progressive line from Conservatives to Liberals and then the nationalists. Thus the liberal victory of 1880 provided the first indication that the process was under way in Monaghan.

While the events at the 1871 Monaghan by-election highlighted the local problems in south-east Ulster that were fundamental and deep-rooted, by far the greatest difficulties which the movement encountered at national level concerned the securing of suitable candidates to contest elections and the perpetual shortage of money to fight effective campaigns. While such problems were evident in constituencies throughout the country they were most acute in the border region. By far the most daunting of these problems was the recruitment of suitable candidates who had the finance and political fervour to actually contest an election. This problem was as acute in 1880 as it had been in 1874, when the problem was resolved with the 'conversion' of Liberal representatives to the cause. While close on twenty Liberal M.P.s joined the movement at the national convention in November 1873, most of them did so to retain their seats. However, south Ulster was the one region, and in particular Louth, where the outgoing Liberal M.P.s did not consider their positions so threatened to have to seek refuge within the home rule association. The only representative in the region who joined the new movement was Philip Callan, the M.P. for Dundalk, who joined the party in 1870 riding high on local support. Nowhere did the importance of a strong candidate become so relevant as in Louth in 1874 when Callan was persuaded by Isaac Butt to oppose the leading Liberal representative in Ireland, Chichester Fortescue.[17]

It was relatively easy to secure Liberal candidates with the finances to contest elections to come forward for what can be regarded as relatively safe seats but more difficult to procure them for constituencies in south Ulster where the chances of victory on the home rule ticket were more remote. In this respect A. M. Sullivan was only added to the ticket in Louth in 1874 because he was able to guarantee £500 towards his election costs.[18] The inability of the local political power broker in the region, Philip Callan, to put forward any money had created this opening. At the same time the only hope the party had of securing the Monaghan seat in 1874 was a successful election petition to unseat the two successful Conservative candidates. In return they would guarantee the seat to an English political carpet-bagger if he was prepared to put up the finances to contest the petition.

Closely allied to the lack of suitable candidates was the embarrassment of being constantly short of funds, especially at election time. Electioneering costs were extremely high for candidates who had little financial backing: Viscount Castlereagh spent £14,000 to secure Down at the 1878 by-election, while one candidate at the 1869 Antrim by-election paid out £9,000.[19] Such expenditure was out of reach of most home rule representatives who at the 1874 Louth election had spent over £800 to have their two candidates returned. While the average sum required to return a home rule M.P. in 1880 was £414, a sum well out of reach of many of its candidates, Philip Callan fought and won the Louth election with £155.[20] Callan had severe financial difficulties following a number of legal actions in the 1870s. However, thanks to contributions provided by friends and the Dublin vintners association he was able to fight the 1880 Louth contest. He had only a few days earlier contested and lost his old seat in Dundalk, adding greatly to his difficulties.

This shortage of finance resulted in the movement neglecting the important function of registration of voters, which was particularly important in such areas as Monaghan. The significance of registration in Monaghan lay in the almost even split between the number of Catholic and Protestant voters. In such constituencies, where the political parties were equally divided, total attention had to be given every year to the registration of voters. The advent of the home rule movement, especially after 1874, resulted in the Conservative party taking a greater interest in registration.[21] This was achieved through the County Monaghan Constitutional Association whose activities were set out in a circular of 1879 from its secretary, Samuel Mitchell, to its members. This offered 2*s* 6*d* to land agents for each Catholic voter they helped get struck off the register, and the same amount for each additional Protestant voter that they added.[22] Only after 1884, when the Franchise Act greatly increased the Catholic proportion of voters, did this group's activities in Monaghan decline.

No such organisation existed for the home rule movement, a factor which clearly limited its political effectiveness, stirring little enthusiasm amongst its supporters at a local level. Little or no attention was paid to registration in the counties, a point very evident in Louth. It was a constituency which had been closely worked upon by the Liberal M.P. Chichester Fortescue, up to his defeat in 1874. The extent of the home rule party's inattentiveness can be seen in that there were 200 fewer voters on the Louth register for 1880 than in 1874.[23] Various reasons were responsible for people being disenfranchised, such as their failure to pay their rates on time, but by far the most important reason for the decline in numbers was the home rule party's failure to attend to the annual registration list hearings. Between September and October electoral revision courts were held to ensure that all those entitled to vote had a final opportunity to ensure their names were on the lists.[24] Much of the decline in the number of registered voters must be attributed to the ease with which objectors could have voters struck off the register. The problem of under registration was exacerbated by the demise of registration organisations, such as the Liberal party, to protect non-Conservative electors. The only group in counties such as Monaghan who could have successfully carried out this function were the Catholic clergy, but in the 1870s it clearly indicated that its support lay with the Liberal party. It was not until the mid-1880s that the National League took over the registration of voters for the home rule movement.[25]

The variation in proportion of electors to population and adult males in different constituencies, both counties and boroughs, was due to the activities of registration agents and also the payment of rates and local differences in valuation. Even after the 1885 election, when the franchise had been greatly increased, the role of the election agent remained important in ensuring that potential voters were registered. Their importance tended to be greater in the counties than in the boroughs.[26] In this way the role of the agents in Monaghan, Down and Armagh was much more evident, especially amongst the Conservatives, than in County Louth. In both 1871 and 1881 the number of electors as a percentage of adult males was lower, 15.1 and 15.0, than any of the other counties in the region: Monaghan 18.7 and 19.7, Down 17.6 and 21.8 and Armagh 17.3 and 18.7. It contrasts sharply with the situation in 1861 when 14.2 per cent of adult males were electors, a figure well above that of Armagh, at 12.7 per cent.[27] This highlights the manner in which the home rule movement neglected the function of registration in County Louth.

While issues such as registration, organisation and finances were important impediments in the advance of the home rule movement into Armagh and Down, by far the most important factor was the fact that both constituencies were perceived as strong bastions of Conservative party support. In County Down, no Liberal M.P. was returned between 1832 and 1885 except for James Sharman Crawford's brief spell as M.P. between 1874 and 1878. In the neighbouring county of Armagh the Liberals fared just as poorly, not having any representative between 1857 and 1880, when J. N. Richardson won a seat, mainly because of the intervention of a third Conservative candidate which split the vote. Indeed the problems of the Liberal party in both these constituencies were compounded by their failure to contest these seats in the 1860s and it was only at the 1874 general election that they decided to put forward candidates. Given the difficulties of the Liberal party in making any headway in these counties it was not surprising that the home rule movement did not exert itself in an attempt to gain a foothold there.

As in the rest of Ireland the home rule movement in the borderlands lacked a proper organisation at a local level. As early as 1871 the national leadership conceded the importance of establishing local associations to promote its ideals. Branches were established in Dundalk, Drogheda,

Newry, Ballybay and a number of other towns, but in the main these were not successful.[28] In some cases the local association that was established, as in Newry in June 1877, failed to promote the movement's activities. The Newry association was more interested in advancing the Liberal cause in the borough than the specified aims of home rule and its membership mainly comprised clerics and the commercial classes. It was more concerned in laying the foundations for the return of a non-Conservative, undoubtedly a Liberal, than in bringing about the election of a home rule candidate.[29] The moderate tone of this association was no doubt brought about by the opposition that had been previously witnessed in the town to anything nationalist.

In the immediate aftermath of the 1874 general election an attempt was made to establish some form of local organisation in Ulster. This was carried out through eight meetings in August in locations throughout the province, including Lurgan, Castlewellan and Monaghan. This demonstrates the uniqueness of the region as far as the home rule leadership was concerned and no other part of the country was subjected to the same type of 'invasion'. While it is difficult to state with certainty it would appear the party's dismal showing at the 1874 general election was responsible for this new burst of activity as outside of Cavan the party had failed to make any inroads in the region. However, it was an 'invasion' which quickly ran out of momentum providing no long or medium term gains for the movement in the region.

The lack of local organisation continued to be a major problem for the home rule movement in south-east Ulster. However, during the 1874 general election Louth proved to be the single bright spot. Here the movement had three separate groups to fight the election on its behalf – the Louth Farmers' Club, The Louth Independent Club and the Catholic clergy. Although the Louth Independent Club was only a few months old when the 1874 general election occurred it still endeavoured to mount as effective a campaign as its limited resources allowed. It played its part in bringing about the most important home rule victory in the whole election, the defeat of the Liberal candidate, Chichester Fortescue. The existence of such organisations contrasted with other constituencies where the Catholic clergy were the only group with the organisational capabilities. The availability of only one such group at the selection meetings meant the candidates were only interested in their own particular grievances, the university question for example, to the detriment of others which faced the country. However for the rest of the decade the Louth Independent Club proved to be an ineffective force due to the split which divided the home rule movement in the county.

The root cause of this split was Philip Callan who in 1874 had been elected M.P. for both Dundalk and Louth. Callan was considered the principal asset of the movement in the borderlands region,[30] but his greatest failing was an independent political line which rendered him objectionable to the Liberals in the 1860s, although he had been first elected to represent Dundalk in 1868. Indeed it had created many problems for the home rule movement in the 1870s and the last thing he was prepared to do was assist the movement expand into neighbouring counties like Monaghan, as was expected of him by the national leadership.

Callan regarded himself as the principal power broker in Louth politics after he had been returned for both Dundalk and Louth in 1874. He thus felt he had the right to have a major say in his replacement's selection. At the same time the Louth Independent Club felt justified, having canvassed for Callan's return in both Dundalk and Louth, in deciding which seat Callan would vacate and who would replace him. While the Louth Independent Club won out, it sowed dissension between the two groups which manifested itself during the general elections of 1880 and 1885. It highlighted the problems which the home rule movement encountered in many areas, not alone in Louth, where a strong local candidate was able to dominate the electoral process, especially from his power base in north Louth, with his own machine, while the party had to take second place. Only after the centralisation of the home rule movement in the early 1880s with the succession of Charles Stewart Parnell to the leadership and control of local organisations coming into the hands of the National League branches, did the dominance of local figures like Callan cease.

By far the more important organising group within Ireland were the Catholic clergy. Throughout the late 1860s and 1870s the bishops and priests were the major political power brokers in the country. Their participation in political affairs reached its height in the 1868–1873 period because of their interest in the church disestablishment and Catholic university questions. Within south-east Ulster the clergy's role in the Liberal victory at the 1868 election was as important as in the rest of the country, with Dr Kieran of Armagh and Bishop Leahy of Dromore playing significant roles in Louth and Newry, although the former remained neutral in Dundalk.[31] Perhaps the only constituency where the clergy failed to play a significant role was in Monaghan, a factor which militated against the home rule advancement in the county in the following decade. Considering the importance of the 1868 election with its strong religious content, the decision to disregard the county and to acquiesce in the return of Leslie and Shirley was strange. Monaghan was one of the few northern constituencies along with Cavan in which the Catholic clergy could hope to influence the result.

The prevalence of this attitude among the Monaghan clergy was also evident at the 1871 by-election when they were absent from the nomination meeting.[32] This was in sharp contrast to counties such as Mayo and Longford where the clergy totally dominated the election proceedings. This situation can be attributed to the intervention of the bishop of Clogher, Dr

James Donnelly, who had developed good relations between the clergy and landowners of Monaghan and was unwilling to risk a conflict in the county where the only loser would be the tenants.[33] In the past Monaghan landlords, such as Henry deBurgh, had used their powers as landowners and openly forced the tenants to vote for their candidates.[34]

Overall the role of the Monaghan clergy was important, more so than in most of the rest of the region because of the even balance of Catholic and Protestant voters. The successes of the Liberals at the 1880 general election and Tim Healy at the 1883 by-election was at the behest of the clergy and the bishop. At the same time the uncommitted clerical attitude in 1874 resulted in the Conservatives securing both seats. It was the clergy's failure to lead and give direction which deprived both the home rule and Liberal candidates of the success they needed.

While the Monaghan clergy took up a neutral stance in elections this was not true of their more politically conscious counterparts in Louth, highlighting further the contrasting attitudes within the region. The refusal of the Louth clergy to follow the directives of their bishop, the archbishop of Armagh, Daniel McGettigan, who urged support for the two outgoing Liberal members at the 1874 general election, was the first indication of the refusal of the lower clergy to take up the normal unified political stand during elections in the county. Throughout the 1860s one of the foundation stones of the clergy's electoral invincibility was their unity, with all the priests taking the majority viewpoint which was usually determined by the senior clergy.[35] In this manner the clergy were able to ensure total support for their nominee at election time, and nowhere was this more evident than at the 1868 general election. The events in Louth and Mayo in 1874 highlighted only all too clearly the breakdown of this unified approach amounting to a mutiny by the lower clergy.[36] Clearly such feelings permeated the laity too, as they were prepared to follow the line of the clergy rather than the archbishop. Indeed there were even church walkouts, such as in Knockbridge, after a letter from the archbishop was read out in favour of the outgoing Liberal M.P.s, O'Reilly Dease and Fortescue.[37] Once the clergy had refused to follow McGettigan's directive it was clear that Fortescue's chances of retaining the seat were greatly diminished. In this way it can be seen that the archbishop was out of touch with feelings on the ground, McGettigan maintaining that the opinions of newspapers were misleading the public concerning support for home rule.[38]

The question must be asked why did the clergy oppose the directives of their archbishop regarding support for Fortescue? Since 1873 a more radical nationalist sentiment amongst the lower clergy had been manifesting itself with deaneries throughout the country beginning to express support for the concept of home rule. Much of this expression was fuelled through the clergy's disappointment with the government's university bill of 1873. However, while clergy were expressing this new found independence in most parts of the country including Louth, it was not evident in Monaghan or Down.

In the past the clergy had been the main organisation available to nationalists in seeking electoral success. However, by 1874 nationalist groups, independent of the clergy, sprang up in several areas. The importance of the County Louth Independent Club is that it provided nationalists with a vehicle, independent of the bishops or clergy, which could bring about the return of nationalist representatives. As was evident from the 1874 Louth contest, without such a body the danger existed that the local bishop could exert influence for a local Liberal and ensure there was no opposition. The existence of such clubs, although localised and few in number, helped move popular politics away from the grip of the bishop and made it more representative.

Fortescue's defeat in Louth epitomised the decline of the Liberal party throughout the three southern provinces and the rise of the home rule party as the dominant political force in the country. This decline in 1874 was as much a trouncing as 1868 had been a major victory. It resulted in a major retrenchment for the party, increasing its regional influence, though its minor national significance was unaffected. As L. J. McCaffrey correctly points out, the Liberal party was unable to survive the two extremes towards which the Irish political scene was moving.[39]

The rise of the home rule movement in the 1870s provided Ulster Catholics with the potential to play an important role in politics for the first time, but the party's weaknesses throughout the decade meant it was the 1880s before this potential was realised. Prior to the 1880s Catholics if they participated at all in political affairs did so through an alliance with Presbyterians in the Liberal party. However, such a situation was not advantageous to Catholics as their particular grievances were not readily highlighted in such an alliance. Only at isolated elections did specifically Catholic issues come to dominate the contests, as in the 1868 general election when church disestablishment was an issue. However, such elections polarised the communities with all Protestant voters voting en bloc, as in Newry when 89.1 per cent of all Protestants voted for the Conservative candidate and 96.6 per cent of all Catholics voted Liberal.[40]

Given the volatile state of Irish elections in the 1850s and 1860s it was anticipated that the formation of the home rule movement would further polarise the two communities at the subsequent electoral contests, but in fact this did not occur. The issues which produced electoral violence were land, as at the 1854 election, and church disestablishment in 1868, the latter actually resulting in deaths in Drogheda and Monaghan at election time.[41] 1868 was the last nineteenth-century election in which the army was used nationally at election time, with troops being employed at every polling station in the country. The absence of electoral violence in the 1870s must be ascribed to the secret ballot act of 1872 and the increase in the number of polling stations: from three in each county to ten in Louth, twelve in Monaghan, sixteen in Armagh and twenty-six in Down. In addition to this, violence was curtailed because of the failure of the home rule league to become a significant force in the borderlands region over this period.

By the mid-1870s electoral violence and intimidation was more extensive in south Ulster counties, such as in Armagh in 1874 and 1875, and Down in 1880, than in the rest of the country.[42] The responsibility for this rested with the two-cornered contests between Liberals and Conservatives that continued to exist exclusively in most of the northern constituencies. It was also more likely that violence would erupt between supporters of the same political ideals, as occurred in the home rule party between Philip Callan and A. M. Sullivan at the 1880 general election in Louth. During those contests in which home rule candidates competed as in Monaghan in 1871 and 1874, the elections passed off peacefully, although the authorities had anticipated violence and drafted in additional constabulary from neighbouring counties.

For all concerned the 1874 general election represented a turning point, not alone in that the home rule movement was contesting its first general election on a national scale, but also due to the manner in which the provisions of the secret ballot act were being enforced for the first time. These new provisions brought about a new attitude to electioneering in Ireland, as is evidenced by the directions given out by the home rule candidates in Monaghan and Louth, concerning the use of the vote.[43] People were informed through the newspapers how to mark their ballot paper, putting the appropriate mark beside the names of the home rule candidates. In the earlier electoral contests democratic representation in Ulster had been virtually non-existent as the landlords monopolised the power structure in a manner closely akin to the clergy in other counties. The 1872 ballot act should have provided the nationalists with an equal stake in political events, but this did not occur. While the home rule movement made massive inroads in the south of the country, the same cannot be said of south-Ulster. The Catholic voters tended not to vote as a block, but rather in a fragmented way, unlike their Protestant counterparts who displayed a united approach.

The extent of ignorance of the provisions of the 1872 ballot act and the protection it extended to voters can be seen in the allegations made on the Shirley estate in Monaghan that the voters preference would be known resulting in action being taken against tenants. This was just one of a number of alleged irregularities that occurred in Monaghan in 1874, such as undue interference of voters by bailiffs and treating of voters.[44] Nevertheless, the 1872 secret ballot act opened up Ulster to electoral contests to a degree which had not been witnessed before. At the 1874 election all but two of the twenty-eight Ulster seats were contested. Despite this change the home rule movement gained no advantage as Monaghan and Cavan were the only Ulster counties they contested.

The acts of 1868 and 1872 had completely transformed the electoral process in Ireland with all candidates now having to be cautious regarding the treating of voters and supporters. After 1872 the situation was so finely balanced that it often required legal interpretations to ascertain whether improper treating had occurred, as in the case of Philip Callan's supporters in Louth in 1880. While it was acknowledged that neither Callan nor his supporters abused the treating regulations, the treating of people in Louth occurred to a much greater extent than in most other parts of the country.[45] The publicans were very generous to those voters regarded as Callan's supporters, providing them with large quantities to drink at a much reduced price or free of charge. It proved difficult to end such a system which had been an integral part of the electioneering process for so long and was viewed with open approval by both voters and non-voters. 1880 was the last general election which recorded the widespread treating of voters, as the expansion of the franchise made the treating of voters an unnecessary and expensive luxury. This inevitably worked to the advantage of the home rule movement as it reduced considerably the expenditure at election time.

The eventual home rule breakthrough in south-east Ulster in the 1880s polarised the two communities in a manner that was not evident in the 1870s. Prior to this the nationalists were not regarded as a major threat, but it was now clear that they were the main opposition group to the Conservatives. Being in the main Catholic, unlike the Liberal party, they were a more identifiable opposition. The problem was exacerbated by the massive increase in Catholic voters brought about by the 1884 franchise act and which brought areas of Donegal, Tyrone, Fermanagh and parts of Armagh under the control of the home rule party. This threat became more real when that party won seventeen of the thirty-three Ulster seats at the 1885 general election, and seven of the twelve seats in south-east Ulster. Clearly the home rule movement had broken through the borderlands obstacle and had become a major force in Ulster, something which it had been denied throughout the 1870s.

The failure of the home rule movement to make any impact in south-east Ulster in the 1870s must be attributed to its failure to involve itself in organising and orchestrating the different political power brokers in the region. In other areas of the country early difficulties were overcome with the withdrawal of the Conservatives after 1868 and the Liberals after 1874 leaving the field open to the home rule movement. However, these political opponents remained in south-east Ulster and were not overcome through the electoral process so that the distinctiveness of the region's political life became more apparent than before. The home rule party under Butt in the 1870s failed in the same way that O'Connell's repeal and the tenant right movement of the 1850s had failed when local circumstances in south-east Ulster, and particularly in Monaghan, dictated that national trends were not mirrored in the borderland locality.

Abbreviations

Cal. doc. Ire.,	*Calendar of documents relating to Ireland* (5 vols, London, 1875–86).
Cal. justic. rolls Ire.,	*Calendar of the justiciary rolls, or proceedings in the court of the justiciar of Ireland,* ed. J. Mills (2 vols, Dublin, 1905, 1914).
Cal. S. P. Ire.	*Calendar of the state papers relating to Ireland,* (24 vols, London, 1860–1911).
H.C.	House of commons sessional papers.
I.H.S.	*Irish Historical Studies* (1938–).
J.R.S.A.I.	*Journal of the Royal Society of Antiquaries of Ireland* (1892–).
Louth Arch. Soc. Jnl.	*Journal of the County Louth archaeological society.* (1904–).
N.H.I.	*New History of Ireland* , ed. T. W. Moody, F. X. Martin, F. J. Byrne, (10 vols, Oxford, 1976–).
N.L.I.	National Library of Ireland, Dublin.
P.R.I. rep D.K.	*Report of the Deputy Keeper of the public records in Ireland* (Dublin, 1869–).
P.R.O.	Public Record Office, London.
P.R.O.I.	Public Record Office of Ireland, Dublin.
P.R.O.N.I.	Public Record Office of Northern Ireland, Belfast.
R.I.A. Proc.	*Proceedings of the Royal Irish Academy* (Dublin, 1836–).
S.P.O.	State Paper Office, Dublin.
U.J.A.	*Ulster Journal of Archaeology* (1853–).

Notes and References

CHAPTER 1

1. J. C. Beckett, *A short history of Ireland* (5th edn. London, 1973), p.186. A notable exception to this generalisation is M. W. Heslinga, *The Irish border as a cultural divide* (Assen, 1962), Perceptions across the border after 1920 are dealt with in Clare O'Halloran, *Partition and the limits of Irish nationalism* (Dublin, 1987) and Denis Kennedy, *The widening gulf: northern attitudes to the independent Irish state, 1919–49* (Belfast, 1988).
2. Padriag Ó Riain, 'Boundary association in early Irish society' in *Studia Celtica*, vii (1972), pp 12–29.
3. Printed in Constantia Maxwell (ed.). *Irish history from contemporary sources,* (London, 1923) pp 79–85; Katharine Simms, *From kings to warlords* (Woodbridge, 1987).
4. For example Raymond Gillespie, *Colonial Ulster–the settlement of east Ulster, 1600–1641* (Cork, 1985), pp 17–20; P. J. Duffy, 'The nature of the medieval frontier' in *Studia Hibernica,* xxii–xxiii (1982–3), pp 21–38.
5. Geoffrey Keating, *Foras feasa ar Eirinn,* i, ed, David Comyn (Irish texts Society, London, 1902), pp 105–111.
6. Brendan Jennings (ed), *Wild geese in Spanish Flanders, 1582–1700* (Dublin, 1964), p. 201.
7. George Storey, *A continuation of the impartial history of the wars of Ireland* (London, 1693), pp 270–1.
8. Annie Hutton (ed.), *The embassy in Ireland of Mgr. G. B. Rinuccini* (Dublin, 1873), p. 53.
9. Oliver MacDonagh, *States of mind: a study of Anglo-Irish conflict 1780–1980* (London, 1983), pp 19–20.
10. The usefulness of various units for study is discussed in Raymond Gillespie, Gerard Moran, 'Writing local history' in Raymond Gillespie, Gerard Moran (eds), *'A various country': essays in Mayo history 1500–1900* (Westport, 1987), pp 11–23.
11. L. M. Cullen, *The emergence of modern Ireland, 1600–1900* (London, 1981), pp 109–11.

CHAPTER 2

1. A. T. Q. Stewart, *The Narrow ground – aspects of Ulster 1609–1969* (London, 1977), p. 182.
2. R. H. Buchanan, 'An historic frontier: the Cooley Peninsula', unpublished lecture to the Louth Historical Society, April 1982.
3. See P. MacCon Mídhe, 'Bás na Gaeilge i ndeisceart Cho Árd Mhacha', *Irish Press* 10/11 March 1966; also 'Census na gCainnteóir Dútchais i gCúige Uladh amuigh de Gaedhealtacht Thír Chonaill', *An tUltach*, xx(1943) and data compiled by Dr. K. Devine, Dept of Computer Science, Queen's University, Belfast.
4. D. Seers, B. Schaffer, M. L. Kiljunen (eds), *Underdeveloped Europe – studies in core-periphery relations* (Sussex 1979).
5. Brendan Smith, 'The concept of the march in medieval Ireland – the case of Uriel' in *R.I.A. Procs,* lxxxviii, sect C (1988), pp 257–269.
6. L. M. Cullen, *The emergence of modern Ireland* (London, 1981), pp 109–139.
7. T. Jones Hughes, 'Town and Baile in Irish placenames' in N. Stephens and R. E. Glasscock (eds), *Irish geographical studies in honour of Estyn Evans* (Belfast 1970), pp 244–258.

8. Warwick County Record Office, 'A map and Survey of the West Moiety of the Barony of Farney' by J. H. Clarke surveyed in 1789/90.
9. D. MacIomhair, 'Townlands of County Louth in AD 1301' in *Louth Arch. Soc. Jn,* xvi (1965), pp 42–49.
10. D. MacIomhair, 'History of Fir Rois' in *Louth Arch. Soc. Jn.,* xv (1964), pp 321–348.
11. J. H. Andrews, 'Topographical divisions' in Victor Meeley (ed), *Encyclopedia of Ireland* (Dublin 1968), pp 142–150.
12. William Reeves, 'On the townland distribution of Ireland' in *R.I.A. Procs,* vii (1862), p. 476.
13. See Benignus Millet, 'Dioceses in Ireland up to the fifteenth century' in *Seanchas ArdMhacha,* xii (1986), pp 1–42.
14. Mark Hennessy, 'Parochial organisation in medieval Tipperary' in W. Nolan (ed), *Tipperary – history and society* (Dublin 1985), pp 60–70; P. J. Duffy, 'Territorial organisation of landownership and its transformation in Co. Monaghan 1591–1641' in *Irish Geography,* xiv (1981), pp 304–322. Generalisations at this regional level are safe but assuming a perfect continuity at individual parish level is unsafe in some instances; see G. F. McGleenon, 'The medieval parishes of Ballymore and Mullabrack' in *Seanchas ArdMhacha,* xii (1987), pp 11–54.
15. Quoted in J. H. Andrews, *Plantation acres* (Belfast 1985), pp 11; see also W. Love 'A seventeenth century map of Dromiskin' in *Louth Arch. Soc. Jn,* xv (1964), pp 351–355.
16. See T. McErlean, 'The Irish townland system of landscape organisation in T. Reeves-Smyth and F. Hamond (eds), *Landscape Archaeology in Ireland: BAR British Series, 116* (Oxford 1983), pp 315–339. A surveyor in Co. Fermanagh in 1716 was scathing about notional forms of land assessment . . . "their judgement is made by the summs it grazeth which can be no rule because the thickness of the wood hinders the grass from growing" (quoted in Ordnance Survey Memoirs, Co. Fermanagh, Parish of Drumkeeran, currently being compiled in Institute of Irish Studies from original mss. in R.I.A.)
17. Steven Ellis, *Tudor Ireland* (London 1985), pp 33. See also Harold O'Sullivan's essay below.
18. Quoted in E. P. Shirley, *Some account of the territory or dominion of Farney* (London 1845), p. 97.
19. P. J. Duffy, 'Farney in 1634 – an examination of Thomas Raven's survey of the Essex estate' in *Clogher Record,* xi (1983), pp 245–256.
20. P. J. Duffy, 'The evolution of estate properties in south Ulster 1600–1900' in W. J. Smyth and Kevin Whelan (eds), *Common ground – essays on the historical geography of Ireland* (Cork 1988), pp 84–109.
21. See Katharine Simms, 'The O'Hanlons, the O'Neills and the Anglo-Normans in thirteenth century Armagh' in *Seanchas ArdMhacha,* ix (1978), pp 70–94.
22. W. J. Smyth, 'Society and settlement in seventeenth century Ireland – the evidence of the 1659 census' in Smyth and Whelan, *Common ground,* pp 55–83.
23. See Raymond Gillespie's essay below and Raymond Gillespie, *Colonial Ulster – the settlement of east Ulster 1600–1641* (Cork 1985), pp 84–112.
24. Stein Rokkan and D. W. Urwin, *Economy, territory, identity – politics of west European peripheries* (London 1983), pp 66–117.
25. W. H. Crawford, 'Economy and society in south Ulster in the eighteenth century' in *Clogher Record,* vii (1975), pp 241–258.
26. See T. J. Barron, 'A poitín affray near Ballybay 1787' in *Clogher Record,* viii (1974), pp 182–193.
27. M. McEvoy, 'The Peep of Days Boys and Defenders in the County Armagh' in *Seanchas ArdMhacha,* xii (1986 and 1987), pp 123–163 and 60–127; L. M. Cullen, *Modern Ireland,* p. 109.
28. Warwick Record Office, 'A map of the estate of the Rt. Hon Lord Weymouth . . . by Nathaniel McKinlie (1735)' and Longleat Library, 'Survey of part of the Manor of Farney . . . by Bernard Scalé (1777)'.
29. J. A. Edwards, 'The landless in mid-nineteenth century County Louth' in *Louth. Arch. Soc. Jn,* xvi (1966), pp 103–110.
30. *Second report of the commissioners appointed to enquire into the manner in which railway communications can be most advantageously promoted in Ireland,* H. C. 1837–38 [145] xxxv, pp 471–862.
31. P. J. Duffy, 'Rural household change in south Ulster 1911–1984,' paper read to Institute of British Geographers conference, Leeds, January 1985.

32. Jonathan Bell, 'Hiring fairs in Ulster' in *Ulster Folklife,* xxv (1979), p. 18.
33. Brenda Collins, 'Proto-industrialisation and pre-famine emigration' in *Social History,* vii (1982), pp 127–146.
34. Patrick Kavanagh, *The Great Hunger* (Dublin 1942). See P. J. Duffy, 'Carleton, Kavanagh and the south Ulster landscape c.1800–1950' in *Irish Geography,* xviii (1985), pp 25–37; P. J. Duffy, 'Patrick Kavanagh's landscape' in *Éire-Ireland,* xxi (1986), pp 105–119.

CHAPTER 3

1. Thomas Kinsella, *The Táin* (Oxford, 1986) provides a good translation.
2. W. F. de Vismes Kane, 'The Black Pig's Dyke: the ancient boundary fortification of Uladh' in *R.I.A. Procs.,* xxiii, sect C (1909), pp 301–328.
3. C. J. Lynn 'The Dorsey and other linear earthworks' in *Studies on early Ireland: essays in honour of M. V. Duignan* ed. B. G. Scott (Belfast, 1982), pp 121–8.
4. E. M. Jope (ed.), *An archaeological survey of County Down* (Belfast, 1966), pp 144–6.
5. de Vismes Kane 'The Black Pig's Dyke'.
6. Fionnula Williams, 'The Black Pig and linear earthworks' in *Emania,* iii (1987), pp 12–9.
7. Aidan Walsh, 'Excavating the Black Pig's Dyke' in *Emania,* iii (1987), pp 5–11.
8. Walsh, 'Excavating the Black Pig's Dyke', p. 10.
9. Lynn, 'The Dorsey'.
10. M. G. L. Baillie, 'The dating of the timbers from Navan Fort and the Dorsey, Co. Armagh' in *Emania,* iv (1988), p. 39.
11. I am grateful to Dr M. Baillie for this information.
12. John O'Donovan, *Letters containing information to the antiquities of the Cos. Armagh and Monaghan collected during the process of the Ordnance Survey in 1835,* Typescript, Bray 1927.
13. Wade Tarzia, 'No trespassing. Border defence in the Táin Bó Cuailgna' in *Emania,* iii (1987), pp 28–33.
14. Tom Condit and Victor M. Buckley, 'The Doon of Drumsna – gateways to Connacht' in *Emania,* vi (1989), pp 30–32.
15. Cecile O'Rahille, *Táin Bó Cuailgne, Recension I* (Dublin, 1976), pp 150–1.
16. Brandon Barringer, 'On the track of the Black Pig' in *University Museum Bulletin,* xix (1955), pp 3–16.
17. J. P. Mallory, *Navan Fort, The ancient capital of Ulster* (Belfast, 1986).
18. Baillie, 'The dating of the timbers from Navan Fort', pp 37–40.
19. Mallory, *Navan Fort,* p. 19.
20. Mallory, *Navan Fort,* p. 19.
21. Mallory, *Navan Fort,* p. 19.
22. Frank Mitchell, *Shell guide to reading the Irish landscape* (Dublin, 1986), pp 162–3 Fig 6.4.
23. OS 6" Sheet:– Louth 4:10:6 (45.8 cm from West, 18.8 cm from South) J 0587, 1255.
24. J. Dunn, *The ancient epic tale Táin Bó Cuailnge* (London, 1914), pp 133 sqq.
25. Diarmaid Mac Iomhair, 'Townland survey of County Louth: Faughart Upper' in *Louth Arch. Soc. Jnl,* xvii (1966), pp 111–125.
26. By kind permission of Cambridge University collection of aerial photographs – ALK 22, Dr. JKS St. Joseph (1970).
27. Barry Raftery, 'Freestone Hill: an iron age hillfort and bronze age cairn', in *R.I.A. Procs.,* lxviii, sect C (1969) pp 1–108.
28. Barry Raftery, 'Irish hillforts' in *The Iron Age in the Irish Sea Province: CBA Research Report* ed. Charles Thomas (Cardiff, 1972) pp 37–58.
29. Bernard Wailes, 'Dun Ailinne' in *Current Archaeology,* xxii (September 1970), pp 308–11.
30. Mac Iomhair, 'Townland survey', p. 112.
31. Vincent Hurley, 'The distribution, origins and development of temple as a church name in the south-west of Ireland' in *Journal of the Cork historical and archaeological society* lxxxiv (1979), pp 74–94.
32. I am grateful to Dr Katharine Simms for this information.
33. V. M. Buckley, *Archaeological inventory of County Louth* (Dublin, 1986), p. 74.
34. Mitchell, *Reading the Irish landscape,* pp 153–4.
35. G. F. Mitchell, 'Post-boreal pollen diagrams from Irish raised bogs', in *R.I.A. Procs.,* lvii, sect B (1956), pp 185–251.

36. F. J. Byrne, *Irish kings and high-kings* (London, 1973), p. 108.
37. V. M. Buckley, 'Ulster and Oriel souterrains – an indicator to tribal areas?' in *U. J. A.*, 3rd ser, xlix (1986), pp 108–10.
38. Kathleen Hughes, *Early Christian Ireland: Introduction to the sources* (London, 1972), pp 19–20.
39. Mitchell, *Reading the Irish Landscape,* pp 156–7.
40. G. F. Barrett and B. J. Graham, 'Some considerations concerning the dating and distribution of ringforts in Ireland'. *U. J. A.,* 3rd ser, xxxviii (1975), pp 33–45.
41. G. F. Barrett, 'Aerial photography and the study of early settlement structures in Ireland' in *Aerial Archaeology,* vi (1980), pp 27–38.
42. Buckley, *Archaeological inventory of Co. Louth,* pp 63–68.
43. Buckley, *Archaeological inventory of Co. Louth,* pp 47–58.
44. Dudley Waterman, 'Excavations at White Fort, Drumaroad, Co. Down' in *U. J. A.*, 3rd ser xix (1956), pp 73–86.
45. B. B. Williams, 'Excavations of a rath at Coolcran, Co. Fermanagh' in *U. J. A.*, 3rd ser., xlviii (1985), pp 69–80.
46. Conleth Manning, *Irish Field Monuments* (Dublin, 1985), p. 4.
47. A. T. Lucas, 'Souterrains: the literary evidence' in *Béaloideas,* xxix–xxxi (1971–3), pp 165–91.
48. T. Fagin, *Ordnance Survey memoirs for the parish of Aghadowey* (1838) Section 4, p. 20.
49. T. H. Mullin, *Aghadowey* (Belfast 1972), pp 8–9.
50. V. M. Buckley, A. L. Brindley, 'A breakdown of the monuments in Cos. Louth and Monaghan', in *IAPA Newsletter,* No. 1 (1985), p. 18.
51. Williams, 'Coolcran, Co. Fermanagh'.
52. Buckley, *Archaeological inventory of Co. Louth,* pp 29–45.
53. Thomas Wright, *Louthiana or an introduction to the antiquities of Ireland* (London, 1758) Bk III, pp 16–7, Pl X.
54. Etienne Rynne, 'Souterrain at Donaghmore' in *Louth Arch. Soc. Jnl.*, vix (1959), pp 148–153.
55. Etienne Rynne, 'Souterrain at "Killylagan", Cortial, Co. Louth' in *Louth. Arch. Soc. Jnl.*, xv (1961), pp 5–10.
56. V. M. Buckley, 'A souterrain at Rossdreenagh, Co. Monaghan' in *U. J. A.* 3rd ser, xlix (1986), pp 104–5.
57. *Ancient laws of Ireland* (6 vols, London 1865–1901), v, p. 95.
58. A. T. Lucas, 'Souterrains: the literary evidence', p. 167.
59. *Contributions to a dictionary of the Irish language'* (Royal Irish Academy), S. V. uaimaireacht.
60. Helen Roe, *Monasterboice and its monuments,* (Longford, 1981), pp 76–8.
61. C. J. Lynn, 'The excavation of Rathmullan, a raised rath and motte in Co. Down' in *U. J. A.*, 3rd ser, xliv–xlv (1981–2), pp 65–171.
62. V. M. Buckley, ''Uaimha na Ulaid' – Some researches on the souterrains of Cos. Antrim and Down' (B. A. thesis, Queen's University, Belfast, 1978).
63. Buckley, 'Ulster and Oriel Souterrains', p. 110.
64. Williams, 'Coolcran, Co. Fermanagh' p. 75.
65. Michael Ryan, 'Native pottery in early historic Ireland' in *R.I.A. Procs.*, lxxii, sect C (1973), pp 619–645. Fig 4.
66. Byrne, *'Irish kings and high-kings',* p. 124.

CHAPTER 4

1. Robin Frame, 'War and peace in the medieval lordship of Ireland' in J. F. Lydon (ed.), *The English in medieval Ireland* (Dublin, 1984), pp 126–7; B. Smith, 'The concept of the march in medieval Ireland; the case of Uriel' in *R.I.A. Proc.*, lxxxviii, sect C (1988), pp 257–69.
2. *Close rolls of the reign of Henry III, 1234–7* (London, 1908), p. 364; *Annals of Ulster,* ed. W. M. Hennessy and B. MacCarthy (4 vols. Dublin, 1893), *sub anno.* 1244.
3. *Cal. doc. Ire.,* 1252–84, p. 417.
4. Aubrey Gwynn, 'Armagh and Louth in the twelfth and thirteenth centuries' in *Seanchas Ardmhacha,* i (1954–5), pp 1–11; Katharine Simms, 'The origins of the diocese of Clogher' in *Clogher Record,* x (1980), pp 180–98.

5. T. E. McNeill, *Anglo-Norman Ulster* (Edinburgh, 1980), pp 6–15, *N.H.I. II,* pp 114–6, 134–6.
6. A. J. Otway-Ruthven, 'The partition of the de Verdon lands in 1332' in *R.I.A. Proc.,* lxvi (1967–8) sect. C (1968), pp 403–5; M. Archdall, *Monasticon Hibernicum* (Dublin, 1786), p. 452.
7. *Cal. justic. rolls Irel., 1305–7,* p. 16.
8. *Ibib.*, pp 186–7.
9. *Ibid.*, p. 259.
10. P.R.O.I., R.C. 8/10, p. 240; P.R.O.I., K.B. 2/6, pp 45–6; D. Mac Ivor, 'The Knights Templar in County Louth' in *Seanchas Ardmhacha,* iv (1960–1), pp 72–91.
11. *Cal. justic. rolls Ire., 1308–14,* p 276.
12. Robin Frame, *Colonial Ireland* (Dublin, 1981), pp 27–32.
13. *Annals of Ulster, sub anno* 1297.
14. *Annals of Connacht,* ed. A. Martin Freeman (Dublin, 1944), *sub anno* 1315.
15. *Tracts relating to Ireland* (2 vols, Dublin, Irish Archaeological Society, 1841–43) ii, John Dymmok, A treatise of Ireland, ed. Richard Butler, p. 21.
16. R. Frame, 'English officials and Irish chiefs in the fourteenth century' in *The English Historical Review,* xc (1975), pp 748–77.
17. *Cal. justic. rolls Ire., 1295–1303, 1305–7, 1308–14;* P. Connolly, 'Pleas held before the chief governors of Ireland, 1308–76' in *Irish jurist,* new series xviii (1983), pp 101–31.
18. P.R.O., E.101/230/19; *Cal. doc. Ire., 1285–92,* no. 169; P.R.O., E.352/127.
19. *Annals of Connacht, sub anno* 1252; *Cal. doc. Ire., 1252–84,* no. 1219; *Chartul [aries of] St. Mary's [Abbey] Dublin,* II ed. J. T. Gilbert (2 vols London, 1884), p. 320; A. J. Otway-Ruthven, 'Royal service in Ireland' in *J.R.S.A.I.,* xcviii (1968), p. 43.
20. *Annals of Connacht,* sub anno 1252.
21. *Cal. justic. rolls Ire., 1305–7,* pp 31–2.
22. *Cal. justic. rolls Ire., 1308–14,* pp 237–9.
23. *The Annals of Inisfallen,* ed. Sean Mac Airt (Dublin, 1951), *sub anno* 1315.
24. J. R. S. Phillips, 'The Anglo-Norman nobility' in Lydon (ed.) *The English in medieval Ireland,* pp 94–9.
25. *Cal. doc. Ire., 1302–7,* no. 149.
26. *Cal. justic. rolls Ire., 1308–14,* p. 51.
27. H. G. Richardson and G. O. Sayles, *The administration of Ireland, 1172–1377* (Dublin, 1963), pp 10–1, 36, 80–1; G. J. Hand, *English law in Ireland, 1290–1323* (Cambridge, 1967), pp 41–4; *Cal. justic. rolls Ire.*, 1305–7, p. 179.
28. P.R.O.I., R.C. 7/4, pp 220–1; *Calendar of the patent rolls, 1301–7* (London, 1898), p. 70.
29. *Cal. justic. rolls Ire., 1305–7,* p 355; *Cal. doc. Ire., 1293–1301,* no 48.
30. P.R.O.I., R.C. 7/10, pp 592–3.
31. *Jacobi Grace, Annales Hiberniae,* ed. R. Butler, (Dublin, 1842), p. 61; G. O. Sayles, *Documents on the affairs of Ireland before the king's council* (Dublin, 1979), no. 151; P.R.O.I., R.C. 8/16, pp 27–8.
32. *Cal. justic. rolls Ire., 1305–7,* pp 175–7, 486–7.
33. *Ibid.*, pp 502–3.
34. *Cal. justic. rolls Ire., 1308–14,* p 161.
35. R. R. Davies, 'Kings, lords and liberties in the march of Wales, 1066–1272' in *Transactions of the Royal Historical Society,* 5th series, xxix (1979), p. 46.
36. *Cal. justic. rolls Ire., 1308–14,* pp 170–1.
37. Katharine Simms, 'The Gaelic lordships of Ulster in the later middle ages' (Ph.D. thesis, Trinity College, Dublin, 1976), p. 327.
38. K. W. Nicholls, 'The register of Clogher' in *Clogher Record,* vii (1971–2), pp 413–21.
39. *Calendar of the Ormond deeds, 1172–1350,* ed. Edmund Curtis, (Dublin, 1932), no. 268.
40. P.R.I. rep. D.K. 38, p. 53.
41. P.R.O.I., EX.2/1, pp 89–90.
42. See above pp 42–3.
43. *Cal. justic. rolls Ire., 1305–7,* pp 175–7.
44. P.R.O.I., K.B. 2/7, p. 17.
45. *Hist[oric &] mun[icipal] doc[uments of] Ire[land]. 1170–1320* ed. J. T. Gilbert (London, 1870), p. 385.
46. Otway-Ruthven, 'Partition of the de Verdon lands', p. 406.

47. P.R.O.I., EX.2/1, p. 96.
48. *Cal. justice. rolls Ire., 1305–7,* pp 502–3.
49. K. W. Nicholls, *Gaelic and Gaelicised Ireland in the middle ages* (Dublin, 1972), chapters 2, 3; Katharine Simms, *From kings to warlords* (Woodbridge, 1987).
50. Katharine Simms, 'The O'Hanlons, the O'Neills and the Anglo-Normans in thirteenth century Armagh' in *Seanchas Ardmhacha,* ix (1978), p. 87.
51. Brendan Smith, 'The concept of the march in medieval Ireland', *R.I.A. Proc.,* lxxxviii sect C (1988), pp 257–69.
52. *Sciant presentes et futuri quod nos Donaldus O'Hanlon, Rex de Erthir, dedimus, concessimus et hac presenti carta . . . confirmavimus Waltero Douedale seniori et Galfrido filio Elye omnia terras et tenementa de Drumgaha et Douelerg cum omnibus suis pertinentiis in Erthir . . .* (N.L.I., D. 15, 565 no. 121); *Dowdall deeds,* ed. Charles McNeill and A. J. Otway-Ruthven (Dublin, 1960), pp 52–3.
53. See below p. 50.
54. *P.R.I. rep D.K.* 39, p. 35
55. *Cal. justic. rolls Ire., 1305–7,* pp 502–3.
56. P.R.O.I., EX.2/1, pp 89–90, 96; *Cal. justic. rolls Ire., 1305–7,* pp 280–1.
57. *Ibid.,* pp 175–7.
58. P.R.O.I., K.B. 2/4, p. 598.
59. A. J. Otway-Ruthven, 'The organisation of Anglo-Irish agriculture in the middle ages' in *J.R.S.A.I.,* lxxxi (1951), pp 1–13. See above pp 45–60.
60. See above p. 43.
61. *Annals of the kingdom of Ireland by the Four Masters* ed. John O'Donovan (7 vols., Dublin, 1851), *sub anno* 1321.
62. *Ibid., sub anno* 1331.
63. A. J. Otway-Ruthven, *A history of medieval Ireland* (London, 1968), pp 222–3, 271–2; R. Frame, 'The Bruces in Ireland' in *I.H.S.,* xix (1974), pp 3–37.
64. *Chartul. St. Mary's Dublin,* ii, pp 297, 350.
65. *Calendar of the close rolls, 1313–8* (London, 1893), p. 368.
66. *Hist. & Mun. doc. Ire.,* p. 385.
67. See above p. 49.
68. See above pp 48–9.
69. Katharine Simms, 'The O'Hanlons, the O'Neills and the Anglo-Normans', pp 89–90.
70. See above pp 45–6.
71. *Cal. justic. rolls. Irel., 1308–14,* pp 209–10.
72. P.R.O.I., R.C. 8/1, pp 16, 18.
73. *Cal. justic. rolls Ire., 1305–7,* pp 186–7.
74. *Cal. justic. rolls Ire., 1308–14,* pp 167, 169–70.
75. D. Mac Ivor, 'The estate of Benedict Pipard of Pipardeston, A.D. 1316' in *Louth Arch. Soc. Jnl.,* xiv, no. 3, (1959), p. 166.
76. P.R.O., C.134 Ed. II, 59.
77. Otway-Ruthven, 'Partition of the de Verdon lands in 1332', p. 421.
78. J. R. S. Phillips, 'Documents on the early stages of the Bruce invasion of Ireland' in *R.I.A Proc.,* lxxxix, sect. C. (1979), pp 262–3.
79. Katherine Walsh, *A fourteenth century scholar and primate, Richard Fitz Ralph in Oxford, Avignon* and Armagh (Oxford, 1981), pp 285–8.
80. *Cal. justic. rolls. Ire., 1305–7,* pp 175–7.
81. P.R.O.I., K.B.2/7, pp 7–8.
82. P.R.O.I., R.C. 8/1, p. 15; *Cal. justic. rolls. Ire., 1295–1303,* p. 29.
83. *Cal. justic. rolls Ire., 1305–7,* pp 502–3; *Cal. justic. rolls Ire., 1308–14,* pp 237–9.
84. *Statutes and ordinances and acts of the parliament of Ireland, King John to Henry V.,* ed. H. F. Berry, (Dublin, 1907), pp 211, 267.
85. Simms, 'Gaelic lordships', p. 324.
86. Robin Frame, 'Power and society in the lordship of Ireland, 1272–1377' in *Past and Present,* no. 76 (1977), pp 18–22; J. F. Lydon, 'Lordship and crown: Llwelyn of Wales and O'Connor of Connacht' in R. R. Davies (ed.), *The British Isles, 1100–1500* (Edinburgh, 1988), pp 48, 52, 60.
87. *Calendar of documents relating to Scotland* ed. J. Bain (Edinburgh, 1887), iii, no. 640; P.R.O., SC 8/270/1348.

88. *Cal. justic. rolls Ire., 1295–1303,* p. 221.
89. *Cal. justic. rolls Ire., 1308–14,* 237–9, 280, etc.
90. *Ibid.*, pp 199–200.
91. J. F. Lydon, 'The Braganstown massacre, 1329' in *Louth Arch. Soc. Jnl.*, xix (1977), pp 5–16; Robin Frame, *English lordship in Ireland, 1318–1361* (Oxford, 1982), pp 32–3, 190–1.
92. Lydon, 'Braganstown massacre', p. 9; *Statutes and ordinances,* pp 195–213.
93. *Annals of the Four Masters sub anno* 1328.
94. Lydon, 'Braganstown massacre', pp 9–10.

CHAPTER 5

1. The argument for sixteenth century political nationalism is given in Brendan Bradshaw, *The Irish constitutional revolution of the sixteenth century,* (Cambridge, 1979), pp 258–88.
2. The text of Laudabiliter is printed in Edmund Curtis, R. B. McDowell (eds), *Irish historical documents,* (London, 1943), pp 17–18.
3. S. G. Ellis, 'Henry VII and Ireland, 1491–1496' in J. F. Lydon (ed), *England and Ireland in the later middle ages,* (Dublin, 1981), pp 237–54.
4. For developments in fifteenth century England, J. R. Lander, *Government and community: England 1450–1509,* (London, 1980), pp 175–330.
5. For the gentry in England, Lawrence Stone, *The crisis of the aristocracy,* (Oxford, 1965) and in Wales, Joan Thirsk (ed), *The agrarian history of England and Wales,* iv (Cambridge, 1967), pp 357–81.
6. Glamor Williams, *Recovery, reorientation and reformation: Wales c.1415–1642,* (Oxford, 1987), pp 253–78; B. P. Levack, *The formation of the British state,* (Oxford, 1987), *passim.*
7. Until 1233 Uriel was included in the shire organisation of Ulster but after this date it came under the central administration of the Lordship, with its own sheriff, A. J. Otway-Ruthven, *A history of medieval Ireland,* (London, 1967), p. 174.
8. J. O'Laverty, *Diocese of Down and Connor ancient and modern,* (5 vols, Dublin, 1878–95, i, pp 34–37.
9. Katharine Simms, 'The O'Hanlons, the O'Neills and the Anglo-Normans in thirteenth-century Armagh' in *Seanchas Ardmhacha,* ix (1978–9), pp 70–94.
10. E. P. Shirley, *The history of the County of Monaghan,* (London, 1879), pp 13–14; Phillip Moore 'The MacMahons of Monaghan, 1500–1593' in *Clogher Record,* i (1955), pp 22–38.
11. *The annals of Ulster,* ed, W. M. Hennessy, B. MacCarthy (4 vols, Dublin, 1893–1901), sub anno. 1444.
12. Tomás ÓFiaich, 'The O'Neills of the Fews' in *Seanchas Ardmhacha,* vii (1972–3), pp 1–15.
13. Aubrey Gwynn, 'Armagh and Louth in the twelfth and thirteenth centuries' in *Seanchas Ardmhacha,* i (1954–5), pp 1–11.
14. For a collection of deeds and other documents relating to Dundalk and County Louth from the thirteenth to the seventeenth centuries see *Dowdall deeds,* ed. Charles McNeill and A. J. Otway-Ruthven (Dublin, 1960).
15. *N.H.I.,* ii, ch. 18.; H. G. Tempest, 'Pale ditch at Siddan' in *Louth Arch. Soc. Jnl.*, x (1941–4), pp 50–54; Edmund Curtis, *A history of medieval Ireland,* (London, 1978) p. 353.
16. S. G. Ellis, *Tudor Ireland: crown, community and the conflict of cultures, 1470–1603,* (London, 1987), pp 57–8; Brendan Smith, 'The concept of the march in medieval Ireland: the case of Uriel' in *R.I.A. Procs.,* lxxxviii, sect. C (1988), pp 257–69; Cecile O'Rahilly, *Táin Bó Cuailgna: Recension I,* (Dublin, 1976), p. 154 (Machaire Connailla); in County Monaghan there were several Machaire, Shirley, *County Monaghan,* chs. 10 and 17.
17. Ellis, *Tudor Ireland,* p. 57; S. G. Ellis, 'Parliaments and great councils, 1483–99' in *Analecta Hibernica,* xxix (1980), pp 104–5.
18. Father Colmcille, *The story of Mellifont,* (Dublin, 1958), pp 147–51, see also p. 131 where Collon is described as on the 'frontiers of the march'. The 'taking of coign and livery in the English shires' was one of the charges laid against Gerald earl of Kildare in 1494, Curtis, *Medieval Ireland,* p. 350.
19. *Dowdall deeds,* pp 250–1.
20. P.R.O.I., Bellew Papers 1121/1, 2; for County Louth gentry who entered into recognisances in 1523 in connection with felonies including coign and livery see *State Papers, Henry VIII, 1515–38,* ii, pt. 2, pp 108–11.

21. Farney was the typical 'debateable land', at once 'recognised [by the English] as parcel of the county of Louth [but] claimed' by the Irish as part of MacMahon's country, Shirley, *County Monaghan,* pp 14, 15–20.
22. John P. Clarke, 'Notes on the devolution of title to the manors of Louth, Castlering, and Ash, County Louth', in *Louth Arch. Soc. Jnl.,* xxi (1985-8), pp 257–73. In 1562 the wardship and marriage of Christopher, son and heir of William Darcy of Platten, was granted to Henry Draycott of Mornington, including the manor of Staunton [Stonetown] in County Louth, *Fiants Elizabeth,* no. 454.
23. Shirley, *County Monaghan,* pp 91–2.
24. A. J. Otway-Ruthven, 'The partition of the de Verdon lands in Ireland in 1332' in *R.I.A. Procs.,* lxvi, sect. C (1968), pp 401–55.
25. *Dowdall deeds,* pp x–xi, 96; *Statute rolls of the parliament of Ireland:. . . reign of Edward IV,* ed. H. F. Berry and J. F. Morrissey (2 vols, Dublin 1914–39), i, pp 837–42.
26. *Statute rolls of the parliament of Ireland: reign of Henry VI,* ed. H. F. Berry (Dublin, 1910), p. 177.
27. *Stat. Ire., 1–12 Edw. IV,* pp 63, 743; see also *Stat. Ire., Hen. VI,* pp 561–5.
28. *Stat. Ire., 12–22 Edw. IV,* p. 861. This must have been a spurious claim since Dungooley was part of the De Verdon lands since the conquest, Otway-Ruthven 'de Verdon lands', p. 409; lands held by the earl of Kildare when attained in 1537 included the 'manor and lands in Downgoill', *Cal. Carew Mss, 1515–74,* pp 131–2; they still formed part of the earl of Kildare's estate in the late seventeenth century, see P.R.O.I., Quit Rent Office, Books of Survey and Distribution, Co. Louth.
29. *Cal Carew Mss 1515–74,* p 131, Harold O'Sullivan, 'A 1575 rent-roll with contemporaneous maps of the Bagenal estates in the Carlingford district' in *Louth Arch. Soc. Jnl.,* xxi (1984–8), pp 46–7.
30. Ciaran Brady, 'Conservative subversives: the community of the Pale and the Dublin administration, 1556–86' in P. J. Corish (ed.), *Radicals, rebels and establishments: Historical Studies XV,* (Belfast, 1985), pp 11–32; *Cal. Carew Mss, 1575–1588,* p. 197; *Cal. Carew Mss, 1589–1600,* p. 355.
31. All of these families are found as proprietors of land along the border with County Monaghan in 1641, P.R.O.I. Quit Rent Office, Books of Survey and Distribution, Co. Louth.
32. For the Moores of Mellifont see John Lodge, *The peerage of Ireland* (Revised by Mervyn Archdall, 7 vols, Dublin, 1789) ii, pp 83–115; for the Bagenals, P. H. Bagenal, *Vicissitudes of an Anglo-Irish family,* 1530–1800 (London, 1925); O'Sullivan, 'Rent roll of the Bagenal Estates'; for the Plunketts see *Burke's peerage, baronetage and knightage* (London, 1956), pp 1, 371–73.
33. *Annals of the kingdom of Ireland by the Four Masters,* ed. John O'Donovan (7 vols, Dublin, 1851), *sub anno* 1504.
34. *Ibid, sub anno* 1495–8.
35. Ó Fiaich, 'The O'Neills of the Fews'. pp 15–16.
36. *Ibid.,* pp 25–64.
37. *Ibid.,* pp 13–15.
38. *Ibid.,* pp 13–15.
39. Shirley, *County Monaghan,* pp 31–2.
40. *Ibid.,* pp 31–2.
41. Ó Fiaich, 'The O'Neills of the Fews'. pp 15–16.
42. Laurence McCorristine, *The revolt of Silken Thomas* (Dublin, 1987), pp 61, 67, 86, 91, 116; *S. P. Henry VIII,* ii, pt. 3, pp 247–9.
43. *S. P. Henry VIII,* ii, pt. 2, p. 259.
44. For this campaign see *N.H.I.* iii, pp 43–48.
45. Shirley, *County Monaghan,* pp 32–8.
46. *Annals of the Four Masters, sub anno* 1539.
47. Harold O'Sullivan, 'The Franciscans in Dundalk' in *Seanchas Ardmhacha,* iv (1960–1), p. 36.
48. Bradshaw, *Constitutional revolution,* pp 87–186.
49. For Primate Dowdall see James Stuart, *Historical memoirs of the city of Armagh,* ed. Ambrose Coleman (Dublin, 1900), pp 143–56; Aubrey Gwynn, *The medieval province of Armagh, 1470–1545* (Dundalk, 1946, pp 249–75.

50. Bradshaw, *Constitutional revolution,* p. 212.
51. *Cal. Carew Mss, 1515–74,* pp 175–6.
52. Bradshaw, *Constitutional revolution,* pp 196–200.
53. Shirley, *County Monaghan,* pp 38–9.
54. Richard Bagwell, *Ireland under the Tudors,* (3 vols, reprint London, 1963) i, pp 262–5.
55. *Ibid.;* Constantia Maxwell (ed), *Irish history from contemporary sources, 1509–1610,* (London, 1923), pp 111–12.
56. For freeholding in Monaghan see Shirley, *County Monaghan,* ch. 5 and tables in subsequent chapters; Peadar Livingstone, *The Monaghan story* (Enniskillen, 1980) ch. 7; For the Magennis lordship, Harold O'Sullivan, The Trevors of Rosetrevor, a British colonial family in seventeenth century Ireland (M. Litt. thesis, Trinity College Dublin, 1985) ch. 2; for the O'Neills of the Fews see Ó Fiaich, 'The O'Neills of the Fews', pp 25–65; the O'Hanlons were least fortunate in Orior since Sir Oghie's son, Oghie Oge, participated in the O'Dogherty revolt of 1608 thus compromising his father whose estate was forfeited and granted to Sir Oliver St John, George Hill, *An historical account of the plantation of Ulster at the commencement of the seventeenth century, 1608–1620* (Belfast, 1877), pp 64, 309–14.
57. *Cal. Carew Mss, 1515–74,* pp 188–93.
58. Curtis and McDowell, *Irish historical documents,* pp 107–9; Maxwell, *Contemporary sources,* pp 108–10; for Shane O'Neill see *N.H.I.* iii, pp 80–86.
59. P.R.O., SP 63/63/3; Harold O'Sullivan, 'Rothe's castle, Dundalk, and Hugh O'Neill', in *Louth Arch. Soc. Jnl.,* xv (1961–4), pp 290–1.
60. *S. P. Henry VIII, 1538–46,* pp 439–40.
61. Bagenal, *Vicissitudes of an Anglo-Irish family,* pp 27–9; O'Sullivan, 'Rent roll of the Bagenal estates', passim.
62. O'Sullivan, 'Rent role of the Bagenal estates', p. 36.
63. 11 Eliz., c. 1; *N.H.I.,* iii, p. 93; Shirley, *County Monaghan,* pp 60–6.
64. Shirley, *County Monaghan,* p. 72; Moore, 'The MacMahons of Monaghan', pp 30–1; for the O'Hanlons see *Cal Carew Mss: The Book of Howth,* p. 213.
65. Quoted in O'Laverty, *Diocese of Down and Connor,* i, p. 84.
66. Bagwell, *Tudors,* ii, pp 304–5.
67. O'Sullivan, 'Rothe's castle'; *Fitzwilliam accounts 1560–65* (Annesley collection) ed. A. K. Longfield (Dublin, 1960), pp 87–106.
68. *Cal. S. P. Ire., 1509–73,* p. 312.
69. The only full length biography of Hugh O'Neill is Sean O'Faolain, *The great O'Neill* (London, 1942).
70. For the succession struggles following Shane's death see N. P. Canny 'Hugh O'Neill, earl of Tyrone and the changing face of Gaelic Ulster' in *Studia Hibernica,* x (1970), pp 20–3.
71. Bagwell, *Tudors,* ii, pp 239–95.
72. *Ibid.,* pp 269–70.
73. *Cal. S. P. Ire., 1586–88,* pp 332–7.
74. Bagenal, *Vicissitudes of an Anglo-Irish family,* ch. vii.
75. Bagwell, *Tudors,* iii, pp 223–5.
76. Peadar Mac Duinnshleibhe, 'The legal murder of Aodh Rua Mac Mahon, 1590' in *Clogher Record,* i (1955), pp 39–52.
77. For the partition of Monaghan, P. J. Duffy, 'Patterns of landownership in Gaelic Monaghan in the late sixteenth century' in *Clogher Record,* x (1979–81), pp 304–22.
78. Ballymascanlon is shown on Robert Lythe's map of 1568 as 'E[a]]r[l of] Ty[r]o[ne]' O'Sullivan, 'Rent roll of the Bagenal estates' p. 43.
79. For the battle of Clontibret, An tAthair Lorcan O'Mearin, 'The battle of Clontibret' in *Clogher Record,* i (1956), pp 1–28; Ó Fiaich, 'The O'Neills of the Fews', p. 30.
80. *Cal. S. P. Ire., 1592–6,* p. 457.
81. Bagwell, *Tudors,* iii, pp 234–5.
82. *Ibid,* p. 239.

CHAPTER 6

1. Walter Harris, *The antient and present state of the County of Down* (Dublin 1744), p. 92.
2. *Cal. S. P. Ire., 1608–10,* p. 553; *Cal. S. P Ire., 1574–85,* p 436; Bagenal and Essex's activities are discussed above pp 67–70.

3. Paul Walsh (ed.) *Beatha Aodh Ruadh ÓDomhnaill* (2 vols Irish texts Society, London, 1948–57) i, p. 29.
4. Tomás Ó Fiaich, 'The O'Neill's of the Fews' in *Seanchas Ardmhacha* vii (1973–4), pp 34–49.
5. *Annals of kingdom of Ireland*, ed. John O'Donovan (7 vols, Dublin, 1851), *sub anno* 1596.
6. P.R.O., SP 63/178/53, v.
7. For example *Cal. S.P. Ire., 1606–8,* pp 169–71; Nicholas Canny, 'Hugh O'Neill and the changing face of Gaelic Ulster', in *Studia Hibernica*, x (1980), pp 25–29.
8. Raymond Gillespie, *Colonial Ulster – the settlement of east Ulster, 1600–1641* (Cork, 1985), pp 24–5; W. H. Crawford, 'The evolution of Ulster towns, 1750–1850' in Peter Roebuck (ed.), *Plantation to partition* (Belfast, 1981), pp 145–6. For example of trading and landholding contacts see P.R.O.I., Chancery pleadings A 228, E 73, E 87, I 41, I 154, I 278, all calendared in K. W. Nicholls, 'A calendar of the salved chancery pleadings relating to County Louth' in *Louth Arch. Soc. Jn.*, xvii (1969–72), pp 250–60; xviii (1973–6), pp 112–20.
9. J. T. Gilbert (ed), *A contemporary history of affairs in Ireland* (3 vols, Dublin, 1879) i, p. 673.
10. John Hanly (ed), *The letters of Saint Oliver Plunkett, 1625–81* (Dublin, 1979), p. 313.
11. For developments in Ulster see Raymond Gillespie, 'Continuity and change: Ulster in the seventeenth century' in Ciaran Brady, Mary O'Dowd, Brian Walker (eds), *An illustrated history of Ulster* (London, forthcoming).
12. *A history of congregations in the Presbyterian church in Ireland, 1610–1982* (Belfast, 1982), pp 267, 450–1.
13. J. S. Reid, *History of the Presbyterian church in Ireland* (3 vols, Belfast, 1867) iii, pp 3–6; J. C. Beckett, *Protestant dissent in Ireland* (London, 1948), pp 55–7.
14. Sir William Brereton, *Travels in Holland and the United Provinces, England, Scotland and Ireland*, ed. E. Hawkins (Chetam Society, London, 1844) pp 132–3; see below pp 98–9.
15. Hanly, *Letters,* p. 73.
16. Trinity College, Dublin, MS 883/2, f. 270; British Library, Harley MS 2138, f. 169v.
17. Brereton, *Travels,* p. 133.
18. Hanly, *Letters,* p. 73.
19. Seamus Pender (ed), *A census of Ireland circa 1659* (Dublin, 1939). The context is explained in W. J. Smyth, 'Society and settlement in seventeenth century Ireland; the evidence of the "1659 census"' in W. J. Smyth, Kevin Whelan (eds), *Common ground; essays on the historical geography of Ireland* (Cork, 1988), pp 55–83.
20. The evidence is conveniently gathered in L. P. Murray, *The parish of Creggan in the seventeenth and eighteenth centuries* (Dundalk, 1940), pp 4, 20, 36; Philip Robinson, *The plantation of Ulster* (Dublin, 1984), pp 97–103, 165–7.
21. *N.H.I.*, iii, p. 475.
22. Hanly, *Letters,* p. 75; R. C. Simington, *The civil survey 1645–56* (10 vols, Dublin, 1961), pp 69–70.
23. The north Armagh situation is described in Raymond Gillespie, *Settlement and survival on an Ulster estate; the Brownlow leasebook, 1667–1711* (Belfast, 1988).
24. Ó Fiaich, 'O'Neills of the Fews', p. 62; R. J. Hunter, 'The Ulster plantation in the counties of Armagh and Cavan' (M. Litt, thesis, Trinity College, Dublin, 1969) pp 606–10.
25. P.R.O.I., Quit Rent Office, Books of Survey and distribution Co. Louth.
26. *Report to the lord lieutenant of the commissioners appointed to enquire into the state of the fairs and markets in Ireland,* H.C. 1852–3 (1674) xli, appendix. There may also have been other fairs such as that at Mullaghcrew on 15 August mentioned in a poem by Niall Mac Cana, Enrí Ó Muireasa (ed), *Céad de cheolta Uladh* (Newry, 1983), p. 53.
27. Raymond Gillespie, 'The small towns of Ulster, 1600–1700', in *Ulster Folklife* (forthcoming).
28. *Cal. S. P. Ire., 1669–70,* pp 591–2; Hanly, *Letters*, p. 160.
29. T. W. Moody, 'Redmond O'Hanlon', in *Proceedings of the Belfast Natural History and Philosophical Society*, 2nd ser, i (1937), pp 7–33.
30. Edmund Hogan (ed), *A description of Ireland, c. 1598* (Dublin, 1878), pp 3, 21.
31. *Cal. S. P. Ire., 1608–10,* p. 195.
32. *Cal. S. P. Ire., 1625–32,* p. 216.
33. *Cal. S. P. Ire., 1625–32,* p. 216; Raymond Gillespie, *Conspiracy: Ulster plots and plotters in 1615* (Belfast, 1987), pp 35–7.
34. Bodleian Library, Oxford, Carte Ms 45, f. 309.

35. Gillespie, *Colonial Ulster,* passim; Raymond Gillespie, 'Landed society and the Interregnum in Scotland and Ireland' in Rosalind Mitchison, Peter Roebuck (eds), *Economy and society in Scotland and Ireland, 1500–1939* (Edinburgh, 1988), pp 38–47.
36. Bodleian Library, Oxford, Carte Ms 45, f. 309. For some important comments on the functions of a borderland in the development of banditry P. Moss, 'Bandits and boundaries in Sardinia' in *Man,* xiv (1979), pp 447–96.
37. David Rothe, *Analecta sacra,* ed. P. F. Moran (Dublin, 1884), p. 100.
38. Plunkett's relations with the tories are dealt with in Donnchadha Mac Phóil, 'Blessed Oliver Plunkett and the tories' in *Seanchas Ardmhacha* iii (1958–9), pp 251–60.
39. Bodleian Library, Oxford, Carte Ms 45, f. 309.
40. J. P. Prendergast, *Ireland from the Restoration to the Revolution* (London, 1887), p. 106.
41. Breandán Ó Buachalla (ed.), *Cathal Buí: amhrain* (Dublin, 1975), pp 84–5.
42. Plunkett's ideal cleric, a secular priest educated on the continent and with considerable learning, is set out in the career of Edward Drumgoole whom he praised highly, Donnchadha Mac Phóil, 'The clergy of Oliver Plunkett' in *Seanchas Ardmhacha,* xi (1984–5), pp 49–52.
43. Hanly, *Letters,* pp 87, 114, 134, 277–8.
44. Brendan Jennings, 'An appeal of the Ulster Franciscans against Blessed Oliver Plunkett' in *Seanchas Ardmhacha,* ii (1956–7), pp 114–6; Hanly, *Leters,* p. 328.
45. The text of the decrees is printed in P. F. Moran, *Memoir of the Venerable Oliver Plunkett* (Dublin, 1895), pp 150–3.
46. Seosamh Ó Dufaigh, Brian Rainey (eds), *Comhairle Mhic Clamha Ó Achadh na Muilleann* (Lille, 1981); *A list of the names of the popish parish priests . . . in the kingdom of Ireland* (Dublin, 1705).
47. Tomás Ó Fiaich, 'The fall and return of John McMoyer' in *Seanchas Ardmhacha* ii (1958–9), pp 51–86; L. P. Murray, 'The life and times of Father Edmond Murphy' in *Louth Arch. Soc. Jnl,* vii (1929–32), pp 335–47.
48. R. M. Young (ed), 'An account of the barony of O'Neilland' in *U. J. A.* 2nd ser iv (1898), p. 241.
49. Cainneach ÓMaonaigh, *Seanmónta chúige Uladh* (Dublin, 1965); Bodleian Library, Oxford, Rawlinson Ms D1208, f. 117.
50. A Selection of these poems is printed in Seosamh Mag Uidhir (ed.), *Pádraig Mac A Liondáin; dánta* (Dublin, 1977) and Sean Ó Gallchóir (ed), *Seamas Dall Mac Cuarta; dánta* (Dublin, 1971). A guide to the locations of other poems is given in these volumes.
51. For example, Mag Uidhir, *Mac A Liondáin,* poem 3, poem 6; Ó Gallchoir, *Mac Cuarta,* poem 12, 16; see also p. 12.
52. For the social context of the poetry see Tomás Ó Fiaich, 'The political and social background of the Ulster poets, in *Léachtaí Cholm Chille,* i (1970) pp 23–33; Ó Fiaich 'Filíocht Uladh mar fhoinse don stair shóisialta san 18ú aois in *Studia Hibernica,* xi (1971), pp 80–129; Seosamh Watson, 'Coibhlint an dá chultúir: Gaeil agus Gaill í bhfilíocht Chuige Uladh san ochtú hAois déag', in *Eighteenth-century Ireland,* iii (1988) pp 85–104.

CHAPTER 7

1. H. G. Tempest, 'The Moyry pass' in *Louth Arch. Soc. Jn.,* xiv (1957), pp 82–90; G. A. Hayes-McCoy (ed.), *Ulster and other Irish maps c.1600* (Dublin, 1964), p. 2.
2. The dates for all the fairs and markets mentioned in this paper have been taken from *Report to the lord lieutenant of the commissioners appointed to inquire into the state of the fairs and markets in Ireland,* H. C. 1852–3, (1674) xli, appendix.
3. Thomas Molyneaux, 'Journey to the North, August 7th, 1708' in R. M. Young (ed.), *Historical notices of old Belfast and its vicinity* (Belfast, 1896), p. 153.
4. T. G. F. Paterson, 'The Black Bank and Fews Barracks' in *U. J. A.,* 3rd series, i (1938), pp 108–11.
5. Richard Barton, *A dialogue concerning some things of importance to Ireland, particularly to the county of Ardmagh* [sic] (Dublin, 1751), p. 17.
6. *The distressed state of Ireland considered, more particularly with respect to the North, in a letter to a friend* (1740), p. 3.
7. Armagh Public Library, Lodge MSS, 'Monaghan'.

8. John Donaldson, *A historical and statistical account of the barony of Upper Fews in the county of Armagh 1838* (Dundalk, 1923), pp 10–16.
9. W. A. McCutcheon, *The industrial archaeology of Northern Ireland* (Belfast, 1980), pp 247–52, 288–93; H. D. Gribbon, *The history of water power in Ulster* (Newton Abbot, 1969), pp 81–109.
10. P.R.O.N.I., Massereene – Foster MSS, D.562/1270, 'Scheme of Robert Stevenson 1795'.
11. W. S. Mason (ed.), *A statistical account, or parochial survey of Ireland* (3 vols, Dublin, 1814–6), ii, 85.
12. *The reports and observations of Robert Stephenson made to the trustees of the linen manufacture for the years 1760 and 1761* (Dublin, 1762), p. 98.
13. Amy Monaghan, 'An eighteenth century family linen business: the Faulkners of Wellbrook, Cookstown, Co. Tyrone' in *Ulster Folklife,* ix (1963), pp 38, 41–3.
14. *Reports of Robert Stephenson,* p. 85.
15. Mason, *Statistical account,* i, no. xi; ii, nos iv and xii.
16. John Rocque's map of County Armagh 1760 as corrected for Charles Coote, *Statistical survey of the county of Armagh* (Dublin, 1804); G. Taylor and A. Skinner, *The post roads of Ireland* (Dublin, 1776); W. H. Crawford, 'Economy and society in eighteenth century Ulster' (Ph.D. thesis, Queen's University Belfast, 1982), ch.5.
17. W. H. Crawford, 'The evolution of the linen trade in Ulster before industrialisation', in *Irish Economic and Social History,* xv (1988) pp 32–53.
18. L. M. Cullen, *An economic history of Ireland since 1660* (London, 1972), p. 100.
19. Harold O'Sullivan, 'A history of Dundalk' in *Tempest's Annual* 1967, pp 57–67.
20. J. B. Leslie, 'Some notes on Dundalk' in *Louth Arch. Soc. Jn.,* iv (1916), pp 165–6.
21. C. D. Purdon, note 'On the establishment of the linen trade in Dundalk' in *Journal of the Historical and Archaeological Association of Ireland,* 3rd series, i (1868), pp 17–20; G. T. Stokes (ed.), *Pococke's tour in Ireland in 1752* (Dublin, 1891), pp 4–6.
22. Purdon note, pp 19–20.
23. *An inquiry into the state and progress of the linen manufacture of Ireland* (Dublin, 1757), pp 163–4.
24. *The reports and observations of Robert Stephenson made to the trustees of the linen manufacture for the years of 1764 and 1765* (Dublin, 1766), pp 57, 134.
25. D. J. Dickson, 'Manuscripts of Irish domestic interest in repositories in Philadelphia' in *Analecta Hibernica,* xxxiii (1986), p. 209.
26. A. W. Hutton (ed.), *Arthur Young's tour in Ireland (1776–1779)* (2 vols, London, 1892), i, 115.
27. *Journals of the house of commons of the kingdom of Ireland* 1777, Appendix, dlxviii–dlxx, dxc–dxci.
28. *Commons' jn. Ire.* 1800, appendix, dccclxix – dccclxxii.
29. W. H. Crawford, 'Change in Ulster in the late eighteenth century' in T. Bartlett and D. W. Hayton (eds.), *Penal era and golden age* (Belfast, 1979), pp 193–4; W. A. McCutcheon, *The canals of the north of Ireland* (London, 1965), pp 22, 24–5.
30. Coote, *Statistical survey of Armagh,* pp 380–2; M. S. D. Westropp, *Irish glass* (London, 1970), pp 130–3; W. H. Crawford and B. Trainor (eds), *Aspects of Irish social history 1750–1800* (Belfast, 1969), pp 83.
31. Stokes, *Pococke's tour,* p. 7.
32. W. Harris, *The antient (sic) and present state of the county of Down* (Dublin, 1744), pp 88, 141; S. Lewis, *A topographical dictionary of Ireland* (2 vols, second edition, Dublin, 1847), i, 627–8.
33. Coote, *Statistical survey of Armagh,* pp 360–1.
34. Ibid., pp 334, 380.
35. Quoted in Cullen, *Economic history,* p. 80.
36. P.R.O.N.I., T.1490, Agent's reports to Lord Paget on the condition of his estates in County Down and County Louth, 1783.
37. *Evidence taken before her majesty's commissioners of inquiry into the state of the law and practice in respect to the occupation of land in Ireland* pt. i, H.C. 1845, xix, 362.

CHAPTER 8

1. T. W. Freeman, *Pre-famine Ireland: A study in historical geography* (Manchester, 1957), p. 173.
2. J. A. Edward, 'The landless in mid-nineteenth century County Louth', in *Louth Arch. Soc. Jnl.* xvi (1966), p. 106.

3. L. M. Cullen, *The emergence of modern Ireland 1600–1900* (London, 1981), p. 166.
4. L. A. Clarkson and E. Margaret Crawford, 'Dietary directions: A topographical survey of Irish diet, 1836', in Rosalind Mitchison and Peter Roebuck (eds.), *Economy and society in Scotland and Ireland 1500–1939* (Edinburgh, 1988), p. 178.
5. *Report of Commissioners for Inquiring into the conditions of the poorer classes in Ireland (Poor Inquiry (Ireland)),* PP 1836 (36) xxxi, Appendix D.
6. George O'Brien, *The economic history of Ireland from the union to the famine* (London, 1921), p. 175.
7. *Poor Inquiry (Ireland),* Appendix D, Question 8 (3).
8. Clarkson and Crawford, 'Dietary Directions', pp 171–3.
9. Joel Mokyr, *Why Ireland starved: A quantitative and analytical history of the Irish economy 1800–1850* (London, 1983), p. 18.
10. See Constantia Maxwell, *The stranger in Ireland* (Dublin, 1979), p. 235, in which extracts from Sir John Carr's tour of Ireland in 1805 are reprinted.
11. Michael Scott (ed.), *Hall's tour of Ireland,* i (2 vols. London, 1984), p. 36.
12. *Poor Inquiry (Ireland),* Appendix E, PP 1836(37) xxxii, p. 33.
13. *Poor Inquiry (Ireland),* Appendix D, p. 370.
14. *Ibid.*, p. 104.
15. Clarkson and Crawford, 'Dietary directions'. pp 173–8.
16. *Poor Inquiry* (*Ireland*), Appendix D, p. 347.
17. *Ibid.*, p. 341. The meaning of the work 'kitchen' in this context is anything eaten as a relish with the main staple food such as bacon, fish or an egg.
18. *Poor Inquiry (Ireland),* Appendix D, p. 93.
19. *Ibid.,* p. 96.
20. *Ibid.,* p. 111.
21. *Ibid.,* p. 107.
22. *Ibid.,* p. 291.
23. Charles Coote, *Statistical survey of the County of Armagh* (Dublin, 1804), p. 251.
24. See Clarkson and Crawford, 'Dietary directions', p. 178.
25. *Poor Law Inquiry* (*Scotland*), H.C. 1844[597] xxiii, part iv, appendix, Q. 19.
26. *Poor Inquiry (Ireland*), appendix D, question 9(4).
27. *Ibid.*, Question 11(6).
28. *Ibid.*, Question 24(11).
29. Conacre land is rented on a seasonal basis only, usually for the potato season, by Irish landless labourers. The terms of the tenureship were variable see Samuel Clark, *Social origins of the Irish land war* (Princeton, 1979).
30. Mokyr, *Why Ireland Starved,* p. 23.
31. *Poor Inquiry (Ireland*), appendix D, p. 301.
32. *Ibid.*, p. 279.
33. *Ibid.*, p. 284.
34. See *Ibid.*, p. 93 and John Fitzgerald, 'The organization of the Drogheda economy 1780–1820, (M. A. thesis, University College, Dublin 1972), pp 127 & 129.
35. *Reports From assistant handloom weavers' commissioners on . . . Ireland* H.C. 1840[43–I] xxiii, p. 596.
36. *Poor Inquiry (Ireland*), H.C. 1836[38] xxxiii, appendix F.
37. Mokyr, *Why Ireland Starved* p. 64; Cormac O'Grada *Ireland Before and After the Famine* (Manchester University Press, 1988), pp 23–4.
38. *Poor Inquiry (Ireland)*, appendix F p. 257.
39. Edwards, 'The landless in mid-nineteenth century Louth'. p. 105.
40. *Poor Inquiry (Ireland),* Appendix E p. 15.
41. *Second report of the commissioners appointed to inquire into the manner in which railway communications can be most advantageously promoted in Ireland* Railway Commission, H. C. 1837–8[145] xxxv, appendix B, No 9.
42. Freeman, *Pre-famine Ireland,* p. 174.
43. Railway Commission, Appendix B, No. 4.
44. H. D. Inglis, *A journey throughout Ireland during . . . 1834,* ii (London, 1835), pp 327–8).
45. *Poor Inquiry (Ireland*), Appendix E.
46. *Ibid.,* p. 15.
47. *Ibid.,* pp 16, 18, 20, 32, 33 & 36.

48. W. O. Atwater & C. D. Woods, 'Dietary studies in New York City in 1895 and 1896' extracts in B. S. Rowntree, *Poverty: A study of town life* (London, 1913), p. 122.
49. See E. Margaret Crawford, 'Aspects of Irish diet 1839–1904' Ph.D. thesis, University of London, 1985, pp 221–3.
50. *Ibid.*, pp 336–7; E. Margaret Crawford, 'Dietary diversion and deadly diseases', unpublished paper presented to the Annual Conference of the Economic and Social History Society of Ireland, Limerick, 1984.
51. J. Brown, 'Medical report of the Dundalk "Destitute Sick Society" together with a sketch of the Medical topography and statistics of the town and parish' *Dublin Journal of Medical Science,* 15 (1839), pp 410–23.
52. N. S. Scrimshaw, C. E. Taylor, J. E. Gordon, *Interactions of nutrition and infection,* WHO Monograph series, No 57 (1968), chapter 2.

CHAPTER 9

1. See Brendan MacGiolla Choille. 'Fenians, Rice and ribbonmen in County Monaghan. 1864–67' in *Clogher Record,* vi (1967), pp 221–52.
2. See Police records, S. P. O., Fenian papers F. files, 1867–71, (5129R), dated 1 Dec. 1869: (7479R), dated 27 June, 1871.
3. *Freeman's Journal,* 10 Oct, 1969; N.L.I. Larcom Papers, MS 7704.
4. *Dublin Daily Express,* 11 & 13 Oct. 1869; N.L.I., Larcom Papers, MS 7704. Madden went so far as to try and have the great amnesty demonstration at Cabra in October 1869 banned on the grounds that it was contrary to the party processions act.
5. Oliver McDonagh, *States of mind: A study of Anglo-Irish conflict, 1870–1980* (London, 1983), pp 18–20.
6. N.L.I., *Larcom Papers,* MS 7735: M. R. Beames, 'The ribbon societies: lower-class nationalism in pre-Famine Ireland' in C.H.E. Philpin (ed). *Nationalism and popular protest in Ireland* (Cambridge, 1987). pp 245–263: Ambrose Macaulay, *Patrick Dorrian, bishop of Down and Connor, 1865–85* (Dublin, 1987), pp 74–5.
7. Police reports in S.P.O., Fenian papers, F. files 1867–71. (4739R), dated 13 Oct. 1869.
8. For an account of the 1872 by-Galway election see M. Ryan *Fenian Memories* (Dublin, 1945), pp 41–4; For Mayo election see G. Moran, 'The changing course of Mayo politics, 1867–1874' in R. Gillespie and G. Moran (eds), *'A various country': essays in Mayo history, 1500–1900* (Westport, 1987), pp 146–153.
9. Pedar Livingstone, *The Monaghan story* (Enniskillen, 1980), pp 334–5; Joseph H. Murnane, nane, 'Dr James Donnelly, bishop of Clogher, (1865–93) and the ascendancy in Monaghan' in *Clogher Record,* xii (1987), p. 279.
10. Circular dated 27 Dec. 1873 in N.L.I., Isaac Butt Papers, MS 830.
11. See meeting at Carrickmacross, *Nation,* 13 June, 1873 p. 6.
12. John Madden to Butt, 6 Mar. 1874, N.L.I. Isaac Butt Papers, MS 8696 (5); L. J. McCaffrey, Home rule and the general election of 1874' in *IHS* (ix 1954–5), pp 96–8.
13. J. Magee, 'The Monaghan election of 1883 and the invasion of Ulster' in *Clogher Record,* v (1974), p. 148.
14. N.L.I. Larcom Papers, MS 7763; *Freeman's Journal,* 11 July 1871, Flanagan had demonstrated forcefully in 1868 against church disestablishment and church disendowment, stressing that the loyalty of Orangemen was conditional, See A. McClelland. 'Orangeism in County Monaghan' in *Clogher Record,* ix (1978), pp 394–5.
15. T. W. Healy, *Letters and leaders of my day,* (2 vols London, 1928), i, p. 190.
16. See F. Thompson, 'The Armagh elections of 1885–6' in *Seanchas Ardmhacha* viii (1977), p. 362.
17. Butt to Callan, 26 Jan. 1874, N.L.I., Butt Papers MS 831.
18. *Irishman,* 10 Sept. 1874, p. 80: A similar situation existed in Clare at the 1880 election when Capt William O'Shea secured a seat for himself by financing the whole campaign for himself and his running mate, The O'Gorman Mahon see Healy, *Letters,* i, p. 154; Katherine O'Shea. *Charles Stewart Parnell; His love story and political life* (London, 1914), pp 132–3.
19. B. M. Walker, 'The land question and elections in Ulster, 1868–86' in S. Clark & J. S. Donnelly (eds), *Irish peasants: Violence and political unrest. 1790–1914,* (Manchester, 1983), pp 235–242.

20. *Shorthand writer's notes of the evidence and judgement of the Louth county election petition: and the bill of particulars lodged with the master of common pleas, Ireland* (hereafter *Louth election petition)*, H.C. 1880 (300), lviii, 403; p. 101, q. 48822.
21. B. M. Walker, 'Party organisation in Ulster. 1865–1892: Registration agents and their activities' in Peter Roebuck (ed), *Plantation to partition: essays in Ulster history in honour of J. L. McCracken* (Belfast, 1981), pp 197–9.
22. *Nation*, 18 Oct. 1879.
23. *Louth election petition*, pp 100–1 qs. 4876–7.
24. B. M. Walker, 'The Irish electorate, 1868–1915' in *IHS*, xviii, (1972–3). p. 360.
25. For an account of the organisation and registration of voters during the Parnellite period, see C. C. O'Brien. *Parnell and his Party, 1880–1890* (Oxford, 1957), pp 126–133.
26. Walker, 'Irish electorate', pp 364, 367–8.
27. *Ibid.* pp 372–385.
28. N.L.I., Butt Papers, MS 8693(6), Galbraith to Butt, 28 Sept, 1871; *Freeman's Journal*, 2 Sept. 1873.
29. *Nation*, 16 June, 1877, p. 11.
30. *Louth election petition*, p. 107.
31. David Thornley, *Isaac Butt and home rule* (London, 1964), pp 42, 44; *Nation*, 12 Sept. 1868, p. 56.
32. N.L.I., Larcom papers, MS 7763; *Daily Express*, 18 July, 1871.
33. Murnane, 'James Donnelly', pp 269–70.
34. J. H. Whyte, *The Independent Irish party, 1850–59* (Oxford, 1958), pp 65–6; There was also the problem that individual landowners, such as Lord Rossmore, controlled large numbers of the total county electorate on their estates, K. T. Hoppen, 'Landlords, society and electoral politics in nineteenth century Ireland', in C. H. E. Philpin (ed), *Nationalism and popular protest*, pp 299–300.
35. E. Larkin, *The consolidation of the Roman Catholic church in Ireland, 1860–70* (Dublin and Chapel Hill, 1987), pp 346–7; G. Moran, 'Politics and electioneering in County Longford, 1868–1880', in R. Gillespie and G. Moran (eds), *Longford: essays in county history* (Dublin, forthcoming), ch 8.
36. For Mayo see Moran, 'Mayo politics', pp 146–153.
37. *Freeman's Journal*, 9 Feb, 1874, p. 3.
38. McGettigan to Cullen, 30 Jan, 1874, Dublin Diocesan Archives, Cullen Papers, 1874, (Bishops).
39. McCaffrey, 'Home rule', pp 210–211.
40. K. T. Hoppen, *Elections, politics and society in Ireland, 1832–1885* (New York, 1984), p. 267; S. A. Royle, 'The Lisburn by-election of 1863' in *IHS*, xxv (1986–7) p. 280.
41. See Gerard Rice, 'The Drogheda election of 1868' in *Journal of the old Drogheda society*, iii (1978–9), pp 3–14: McClelland, 'Orangeism in County Monaghan' p. 396; Hoppen, *Elections, politics and society*, p. 395.
42. See *Irishman*, 14 Feb, 1874, p. 519: McGettigan to Cullen, 31 Dec. 1875. Dublin Diocesan Archives, Cullen Papers, (Bishops), 1975: *Shorthand writer's notes of the judgement and evidence and trial of the Down county election petition*, H.C. 1880, (260) lvii, 567.
43. *Freeman's Journal*, 11 Feb, 1874, p. 3.
44. *Ibid.*, 11 Mar. 1874, p. 7: Thomas Sherry to Butt, 14 Feb. 1874, N.L.I., Butt Papers, MS 8696(4).
45. *Louth Election Petition*, p. 117.

Index